DEVOTIONS®

JANUARY

"In your unfailing love you will lead the people you have redeemed. . . . The LORD will reign for ever and ever."

—*Exodus 15:13, 18*

Gary Allen, Editor | **Margaret K. Williams,** Project Editor | Photo © Liquid Library

DEVOTIONS® is published quarterly by Standard Publishing, Cincinnati, Ohio, www.standardpub.com. © 2010 by Standard Publishing. All rights reserved. Topics based on the Home Daily Bible Readings, International Sunday School Lessons. © 2007 by the Committee on the Uniform Series. Printed in the U.S.A. All Scripture quotations, unless otherwise indicated, are taken from the HOLY BIBLE, NEW INTERNATIONAL VERSION®. NIV®. Copyright © 1973, 1978, 1984 by Biblica, Inc.™ Used by permission of Zondervan. All rights reserved. Where noted, Scripture quotations are from the following, used with permission of the copyright holders, all rights reserved: *The Revised Standard Version of the Bible (RSV)*, copyrighted 1946, 1952, © 1971, 1973.

Alpha and Omega

This is what the LORD says—Israel's King and Redeemer, the LORD Almighty: I am the first and I am the last; apart from me there is no God (Isaiah 44:6).

Scripture: Isaiah 44:6-8
Song: "How Great Thou Art"

"I am the first and I am the last." That says it all. Even Aristotle described God as the First Cause. In other words, everything comes from somewhere. My parents caused—created—me, and their parents created them. My great-grandparents created my grandparents, and on and on back . . . until we come to the first human beings that ever existed. God created Adam and Eve. Before that, there was no humanity. In fact, there was never a point where there was *nothing*. "Before God" . . . never existed. There was always God, and there will always be God.

God is my Creator, but He is also my designer and my assembly line worker. God is my everything. He gave me life, and then He gave His Son to give me new life *again*. He is my creator, redeemer, and protector. He is my hope and my joy and my peace.

I love my wife like crazy. Without her, I would hope to be positive enough to say, "I'm miserable." But without God, I am nothing. There can't even be such a thing as "without God."

O God, creator of Heaven and earth, thank You for being at the center of everything, creating and sustaining all that exists. But most of all, thank You for the incredible sacrifice of Your Son Jesus Christ on my behalf. In His name I pray. Amen.

January 1, 2. **John H. Boys** has been many things, including a tree-trimmer in Colorado and tour-guide in Montana. Now, he and his wife, Janet, and their two children live in Cassville, Missouri.

Creator of All

This is what the LORD says—your Redeemer, who formed you in the womb: I am the LORD, who has made all things, who alone stretched out the heavens, who spread out the earth by myself (Isaiah 44:24).

Scripture: Isaiah 44:21-28
Song: "Omnipotent Lord, My Savior and King"

God knows all. That's why I don't exactly surprise Him when I come up short. He already knows where I'll succeed and where I won't, but He continues to call me to a deeper commitment.

Long ago, my wife's grandmother and her great-grandmother pieced together three quilts. My wife and each of her sisters received one for Christmas last year.

Janet's quilt means a great deal to her. She and I shopped around, but we couldn't find a quilt rack that was exactly what we wanted. So I made one myself.

I selected the wood carefully and tested the stain color. I sanded and drilled holes for knobs and put everything together. (The hardest part always seems to be finding the studs in the wall.) Eventually everything worked out, and now the quilt is hanging beautifully.

This project reminded me once again that God created everything. He designed wood and planted the first tree. He invented color and made the eye to see. He produced sound and built the voice to sing. In fact, He even thought the "first" thought.

Almighty Father, thank You for this day and for Your glorious creation. When I am tempted to worry or fret about my circumstances, remind me of Your awesome power—and that You remain in control of all things. In Jesus' name, I pray. Amen.

No Ordinary God

Who among the gods is like you, O LORD? Who is like you—majestic in holiness, awesome in glory, working wonders? (Exodus 15:11).

Scripture: Exodus 15:11-18
Song: "Awesome God"

As a teacher, I hear the word *awesome* a lot. Young people use it to describe anything from a new pair of shoes to a good grade on a math quiz. Like the word *love*, the term is used much too casually, in my opinion. Webster's dictionary defines *awe* as "a mixed feeling of reverence, fear, and wonder, caused by something majestic, sublime, sacred, etc."

What a beautiful word! Only our God—and the things of His creation—can match this description. I always feel deep, reverent awe when I go outside and peer up at the sky on a starry night. I am so small, and God is so big

I especially remember the surge of wonder I felt one summer when I went snorkeling around San Salvador Island. I marveled at the brilliant world of creatures living beneath the sea. This vivid handprint of God took my breath away.

My glorious God made the sea, the ground that I walk on, and the air that I breathe. He is truly magnificent, awesome in glory . . . and I love Him.

Awesome Father, help me to reverence You today. May I see the wonders of Your works with brand new eyes. Change the way I think about You and how I speak about You. You are awesome and infinite in love. In Jesus' name, amen.

January 3–9. **Barbara Tuttle** is an educator and author living in Lansing, Michigan. At the end of the day, she and her husband like to ask each other, "Did you see God today?"

Get Off the Fence

How long will you waver between two opinions? If the LORD is God, follow him; but if Baal is God, follow him (1 Kings 18:21).

Scripture: 1 Kings 18:17-29
Song: "People Need the Lord"

I am acquainted with many people who are "on the fence" about God. They seem to agree to the idea that God must exist, and yet there's little passion in their lives to follow Him. Perhaps they attend church on Christmas and Easter and give a nod to His blessings before the Thanksgiving turkey. If they were asked who Jesus is, most would likely say: "The Son of God."

But if God is truly who He says He is, then He's worthy of my utmost devotion. He is the one I always turn to when I come to the end of myself. My heavenly Father alone has the power to intervene in my life's circumstances.

Yes, I do depend on His compassion to see me through when life gets hard. For example, His loving hands were the ones that held me up when my eldest son died. When my whole world fell apart, God did not fail me. He carried me through my deepest valley.

God, only God, really understood how my heart was breaking. Only He could hold me together and give me strength to put one foot in front of another, to keep on walking. Where else would I turn?

Heavenly Father, thank You for always being there for me. My deepest need is for You, so help me to turn to You first and to trust in Your strength always. And I have loved ones and friends who face disappointment; show me how to point them to You as well. In the holy name of Jesus, my Lord and Savior, I pray. Amen.

Big Time Renewal

"Answer me, O LORD, answer me, so these people will know that you, O LORD, are God, and that you are turning their hearts back again." Then the fire of the LORD fell and burned up the sacrifice, the wood, the stones and the soil, and also licked up the water in the trench (1 Kings 18:37, 38).

Scripture: 1 Kings 18:30-38
Song: "Revive Us Again"

I know that I can't live out my Christian life on a mountaintop, or I would never experience the growth that comes through struggles. But God knows that I need to go to the mountaintop sometimes for a breath of holy revival air.

Recently I began to take my Christian walk for granted. I lost the enthusiasm that I had at the beginning when I always expected great things from God. I was just going through the motions.

But God knew how to jolt me out of my complacency. I witnessed a wonderful answer to prayer. A young man at church was told by his doctors that nothing more could be done for him. His kidneys were completely shutting down. James was waiting at death's door, but our Sunday school class prayed earnestly for him. Months later, he returned to our church, glowing with good health. God had worked in James's life, and He also worked powerfully in my own heart. Yes, God's power gave me goose bumps and stirred my faith.

Great and mighty God, thank You for reviving my faith when You see it languishing. Help me to keep my faith active and alive. I praise You for the mountaintop experiences in my life. Help me to take the exciting vision I receive there into the valley, that it might give me renewed hope. In Christ's name, amen.

When You Pray

The prayer offered in faith will make the sick person well; the Lord will raise him up. If he has sinned, he will be forgiven. Therefore confess your sins to each other and pray for each other so that you may be healed (James 5:15, 16).

Scripture: James 5:13-18
Song: "Did You Think to Pray?"

Every once in a while a sermon really hits home with me. One such sermon was preached by a beloved minister many years ago. This message radically changed the way I pray.

Our minister shared that he'd listened to thousands of prayer requests, and many of them echoed similar themes. Often these petitions were for major and minor health concerns. Other requests poured in for help with finances, relationships, and "traveling mercies." He affirmed these requests, reminding us that God is concerned with every detail of our lives. He truly wants us to pray at all times, to lay our burdens at His feet.

But then the preacher suggested that God also delights to hear us pray for one another's "inner life." He encouraged us to develop a greater awareness of the condition of our own hearts, and the spiritual growth of those we care about.

So now when I pray about my friend's surgery or my neighbor's financial struggle, I remember to pray for their spiritual development, the process of sanctification that Christ is working in them. Our sin has left us broken, and God wants to heal us. Let us pray!

Lord, thank You for coming to heal me. Teach me to be more like You and to have a greater awareness of the spiritual needs of others. In the name of the Father, the Son, and the Holy Spirit, I pray. Amen.

God's Time Out

The LORD, the God of their fathers, sent word to them through his messengers again and again, because he had pity on his people and on his dwelling place. But they mocked God's messengers, despised his words and scoffed at his prophets (2 Chronicles 36:15, 16).

Scripture: 2 Chronicles 36:15-23
Song: "Have Thine Own Way, Lord"

God saw His people slipping away, and it broke His heart. He sent messengers to warn them of their unfaithfulness. But His warnings fell on deaf ears—the people laughed. Finally, God had to act, because the people's hearts were growing cold towards Him. God handed them over to the Babylonian king. And how great was the fall of Jerusalem!

When I was raising my children, they acted the same way sometimes. When they misbehaved, I gave them a warning (or two). If they continued to misbehave, I disciplined them. Often they were sent to their rooms for a time-out.

But I didn't leave them in their rooms forever. After the time-out period was up, I went into their rooms and we had a talk. I reminded them of why they had been disciplined, and these moments often brought us closer together. The purpose of my discipline was to bring restoration, to break the bonds of stubbornness in my children's hearts, and to draw us closer together. And isn't that how God works with us too?

Merciful God, I want to respond to You with an open heart when You're trying to get my attention. Thank You for warning me when my heart begins to stray, and may I never take Your grace for granted. In the name of Your Son, my blessed Savior, I pray. Amen.

Got Any Mountains?

I will go before you and will level the mountains; I will break down gates of bronze and cut through bars of iron. I will give you the treasures of darkness, riches stored in secret places, so that you may know that I am the LORD (Isaiah 45:2, 3).

Scripture: Isaiah 45:1-8
Song: "Show Your Power"

Do you have any significant problems or obstacles in your life these days? Well, they are just a little pile of beans to God. He has the power to move things out of your way with a sweep of His majestic hand.

Just ask the Israelites. He dried up their Jordan River and parted the Red Sea. He once even stopped the earth's turning, apparently just to set back the clock (see Joshua 10).

My husband and I have a "little problem" right now. We just put our house on the market; we need to sell it, and soon. But the economy is in a slump, and the housing market in our area has taken a significant downturn. The heavy snow outside doesn't exactly beckon house hunters either.

Our neighbors shake their heads at the sign on our lawn. "Good luck with that," they say. But God has led us to move forward and put this house on the market anyway. We believe He's active in our lives. If we are seeking to move in His will, then we can surely trust Him to take care of any "little problems" that stand in our way.

Almighty God, sometimes the problems that I face seem overwhelming—too big for me to handle. And they are! So help me to make it a habit to turn these problems over to You. In the name of Jesus I pray. Amen.

Where Is My Attention?

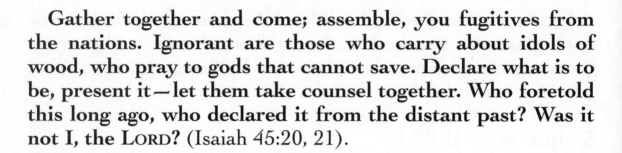

Gather together and come; assemble, you fugitives from the nations. Ignorant are those who carry about idols of wood, who pray to gods that cannot save. Declare what is to be, present it—let them take counsel together. Who foretold this long ago, who declared it from the distant past? Was it not I, the LORD? (Isaiah 45:20, 21).

Scripture: Isaiah 45:14-25
Song: " I Give You My Heart"

I carried around a pink fuzzy rabbit's foot when I was a child. It was a fad at my school. The rabbit's foot was supposed to be a good luck charm.

I might as well have been carrying around a wooden idol, because I trusted in that thing to grant me blessings. Ha! It had no more power to do so than the "man in the moon."

I no longer carry around a good luck charm of any kind. I have learned, however, that anything that demands too much of my attention can become an idol for me, taking God's place of priority. For instance, I have developed an uneasy conviction about spending excessive time surfing the Internet and staring at pointless television shows.

Technology is amazing. In a sense, I have the whole world at my fingertips. But this technology has no more power than a rabbit's foot to meet my deepest needs. It has no power to awaken my inner life, fix my brokenness, forgive my sins, or save my soul.

Heavenly Father, guard my heart and mind from anything that demands my excessive attention. Help me to set limits on "screen time," so that I will not be too influenced by the values of the world. In Jesus' name, amen.

Peering Behind the Mask

Then hear from heaven, your dwelling place. Forgive and act; deal with each man according to all he does, since you know his heart (for you alone know the hearts of all men) (1 Kings 8:39).

Scripture: I Kings 8:33-40
Song: "Who Am I?"

When I was a youngster, my sister and I attended masquerade parties. We disguised ourselves by painting our faces. Later plastic masks replaced the makeup. Once, because of the positioning of the nose vents, vapor collected inside my mask, and the heat fogged my glasses, forcing my face to drip with perspiration. It was worth the discomfort, though, because people never did discover my identity.

Even though I am an adult, donning a mask is still part of my occasional routine. When people ask, "How's it going?" I smile, and my mask replies that I am fine, perfectly fine. My mask protects me from exposing my disappointments, hurts, frustrations, guilts, and sins. It conceals emotional places I don't want others to explore. My mask insulates me and prohibits others from perceiving any transparency that might encourage deeper fellowship.

Yet my mask neither deters nor daunts the Lord. The creator of the universe sees through my well-intended mask. Nothing prevents Him from peering beneath it and examining my heart. Before Him, I stand maskless and fear no rejection.

Lord God of Heaven, I'm glad You see beneath my layers of camouflage. Thank You for forgiving my sin and for loving me unconditionally. In Jesus' name, amen.

January 10–16. **Vicki Hodges** and her family live in the Rocky Mountains of Hotchkiss, Colorado. She teaches high school Spanish and loves to travel.

Splitting the Darkness

As he neared Damascus on his journey, suddenly a light from heaven flashed around him. He fell to the ground and heard a voice say to him, "Saul, Saul, why do you persecute me?" (Acts 9:3, 4).

Scripture: Acts 9:3-6, 10-18
Song: "Open My Eyes, That I May See"

Our daughter Aimee recently moved to New York City to serve with a Christian organization. She mentors young college women and does administrative work for the organization. For a country girl who grew up in the Rocky Mountains, it's a culture shock. We've tried to help her with homesickness by keeping in touch via e-mail.

As I watched the sunset last night, I wanted to describe for Aimee its incredible colors, the reds, oranges, purples, and blues—and how every minute these colors changed. The old day sky gave way to the new night sky.

Then suddenly I saw the first star shining, which I realized had been shining all the time, but I couldn't see it until the sky darkened. I was wishing that, with all of today's technology, I could e-mail Aimee what my eyes were seeing.

What did Saul feel the moment he observed the brightness of the Lord's presence? What did he sense when he realized that Jesus had been shining all the time, but he couldn't see Him until sin's darkness was removed?

Lord, remove the obstacles in my life that prevent me from seeing You. Help me see Your beauty with fresh eyes today. In Jesus' name I pray, amen.

Fossils Speak

Therefore this is what the LORD says: "If you repent, I will restore you that you may serve me; if you utter worthy, not worthless, words, you will be my spokesman. Let this people turn to you, but you must not turn to them" (Jeremiah 15:19).

Scripture: Jeremiah 15:19-21
Song: "Protector of My Soul"

Our son recently participated in a debate between secular humanists and creationists on his college campus. The topic was, "What is the biological and fossil record evidence for a common ancestor between ape and man?" Each debater presented points for eight minutes, and then offered a four-minute rebuttal, finishing with concluding remarks. The debate lasted two hours, followed by an open forum.

Before the debate, our son and the other debaters were nervous. So was I! I was afraid the humanist-trained science people would shred the creationists. Then I realized my son is also a science major but has the added advantage of a strong biblical foundation.

After the debate, my son and a friend drove to a restaurant for a late dinner. Members from the humanist society that had attended the debate filled half of the restaurant. When they saw Mark, they waved him to their table and invited him to join them for nachos.

Mark willingly acted as a spokesperson for God. He prepared as much as possible, and then trusted the Lord to use him to speak truths about our great creator.

Lord, grant me the courage to speak up for You with worthy words. Draw people to yourself and be glorified. In Jesus' name, amen.

Moose on the Loose

Listen to this, O house of Jacob, you who are called by the name of Israel and come from the line of Judah, you who take oaths in the name of the LORD and invoke the God of Israel—but not in truth or righteousness (Isaiah 48:1).

Scripture: Isaiah 48:1-5
Song: "The Heart of Worship"

Some people have dogs and squirrels in their backyards. We have moose! A few years ago, officials reintroduced moose into our mountain range. This winter, a cow moose left the mountains and wandered into our small town. Nightly, she made the rounds from one yard to the next, munching on accessible shrubs and plants.

Recently the local newspaper published the account of her death. A necropsy revealed that she had died as the result of consuming a substantial amount of Japanese Yew. It's a popular ornamental plant, often chosen by landscapers and homeowners because it is an evergreen and bears scarlet fruits resembling berries. The problem is that most parts of the plant are highly toxic, containing Taxine, an alkaloid that inhibits cardiac function. So, the moose died from cardiac arrest. While the plant appeared appetizing, it was noxious and deadly.

The Israelites looked good on the outside. They called themselves people of God and offered prayers to Him. Yet they practiced idolatry. Their sinful, misdirected worship carried a high level of toxicity to sincere faith in the Lord.

Father, show me any idols in my life—and help me get rid of them! My desire is to worship You in truth and in righteousness. I pray this prayer in the name of Jesus, my merciful Savior and Lord. Amen.

Detecting the Hidden

You have heard these things; look at them all. Will you not admit them? "From now on I will tell you of new things, of hidden things unknown to you" (Isaiah 48:6).

Scripture: Isaiah 48:6-8
Song: "Hide Me in Your Holiness"

"See the action! Verify the species! Watch 'em strike!" A popular outdoor gear catalog that my husband received in the mail featured this alluring ad. The gadget is definitely suited for the serious fisherman.

In our area, ice fishing is a popular winter sport. Many ice fishermen have begun using sonar underwater viewing systems to monitor the hidden depths of the water below the ice. These waterproof video cameras can even expose fish hidden beneath clutter and all sorts of cover.

Even though my husband thinks these newfangled ice fishing devices sound like fun, he prefers to remember the look of the lake before it froze. He likes to recall the inlets where he watched fish feed. He remembers the shoreline full of willows that snagged his hook as he prepared to snap his line into the water. He particularly likes to dredge up memories of watching the top of the water where most of the fish liked to feed in the fall.

I mention this to encourage each of us to ask today: What new, hidden things will God delight in showing us through the clutter and stress of our lives?

Heavenly Father, many things are hidden from me now. Help me be patient as I wait for You to reveal new things to me. I want to hold on for the ride and prepare for action, Lord! In the name of Your Son, my Savior, I pray. Amen.

No Tracking Chips Required

Listen to me, O Jacob, Israel, whom I have called: I am he; I am the first and I am the last. My own hand laid the foundations of the earth, and my right hand spread out the heavens; when I summon them, they all stand up together (Isaiah 48:12, 13).

Scripture: Isaiah 48:9-13
Song: "He Owns the Cattle on a Thousand Hills"

Last week I talked to a computer tech. He told me he manages 110 servers and 700 computers at a nearby community hospital. I learned the hospital would soon put computer chips in all patient wristbands and on all pieces of mobile equipment for tracking.

With this new system, hospital employees can easily locate a patient who may be in another room for a scan or may even be several blocks away. And it's important to know where every piece of equipment is at all times too. It must be quickly found and transferred wherever and whenever it is needed. A portable pump, for instance, will now easily be located with the use of these chips.

Without the aid of any such tracking system, the Lord knows the position of everything in the cosmos. He knows the whereabouts of each person, never having to wonder where we are or what we're doing. Since He is the Creator, He sustains all of His creation. Nothing takes Him by surprise.

Father, sometimes it seems I am alone, and my situation is unknown to You. Yet when I look down, I realize You have settled a firm foundation of the earth under me. And when I look up, I see a canvas painted with galaxies. Thank You for displaying handiwork that reminds me of Your constant presence. In Jesus' name, amen.

Every Drop

This is what the LORD says—your Redeemer, the Holy One of Israel: "I am the LORD your God, who teaches you what is best for you, who directs you in the way you should go" (Isaiah 48:17).

Scripture: Isaiah 48:14-22
Song: "There Is a Redeemer"

"Here is a land where life is written in the water." Colorado's Poet Laureate, Thomas Hornsby Ferril, wrote these opening words of a poem that appears in the rotunda of our state capitol. He understood that in our dry climate, water is essential for survival and income.

The mountains near our home contain many man-made reservoirs. These collect snowmelt and store water for irrigation purposes. Hundreds of ranchers and farmers depend on this water from spring through fall.

The elected officials of the water companies supervise the collection and distribution of this water. Reservoirs can only store a certain amount of water, and the officials must monitor the water content in the snow pack throughout the winter months. So before winter snowmelt is complete, officials calculate the amount of water to disperse. This avoids damage to the dams, excessive depletion, and oversupplying recipients. These men have a lot of responsibility for being good caretakers.

My point? It is a relief to know the Lord is the supreme caretaker of my life. He always has my best in mind.

Almighty and everlasting God, I'm glad You are the living water that nourishes. Your loving care astounds me, and I'm grateful. In the name of Jesus, who lives and reigns with You and the Holy Spirit, one God, now and forever, amen.

Here They Come

See, they will come from afar — some from the north, some from the west, some from the region of Aswan (Isaiah 49:12)

Scripture: Isaiah 49:8-13
Song: "In Christ There Is No East or West"

For almost an hour we had listened to the words of Paul VI as he spoke to the crowd. We stood in the courtyard heat of his summer residence south of Rome. Our bodies soaked and our throats parched, we welcomed the benediction, because now we could trudge through massive doors with hundreds of others seeking relief from the stifling temperature.

Just down a slope in the middle of a square was a large fountain that scores of us spied simultaneously. Several arrived before we did and were dipping their hands in the fountain, trying to get enough water to satisfy their thirst. That's when I remembered a collapsible cup I'd stowed in my day bag. Pulling it out, I offered it to a German man on my left who, in turn, gave it to a woman by his side who came from somewhere in South America. And on it went, first to one and then another, all the way around the fountain.

Nothing draws people together like the fountain of living water. In Christ we are one.

Lord Jesus, I see You standing in the center of the world, inviting your children to yourself. I come and bring others with me. I stand with them where You are. I extend to them my concern and give them my care. I love them in Your name. All glory to You, who reigns with the Father and the Spirit forever. Amen.

January 17–23. **Phillip H. Barnhart** retired after 45 years serving churches in three states. Since retirement, he has served as interim minister and written books. He lives on Perdido Bay in Florida.

Surprise, Surprise

It will be good for that servant whose master finds him doing [good] when he returns. . . . The master of that servant will come on a day when he does not expect him and at an hour he is not aware of (Matthew 24:50).

Scripture: Matthew 24:45-51
Song: "My Lord, What a Morning"

When I was 15, I worked in a men's clothing store for a fair but demanding employer. One time he was going out of town on a Tuesday to return Saturday. Before he left, he told me to put 30 boxes of Florsheims on shelves in the shoe department.

The next day, after school, I was ready to do that when Jim and Ralph came in to see why I'd missed basketball practice. My explanation took a while, it was closing time, and I left the store. On Thursday, I stayed after school for a club meeting and, finally getting to the store, had so much to do I forgot about the shoes.

But the boss wasn't coming back until Saturday, right? There was still Friday to get the job done. However, my employer had a change of plans and returned early. He was in the store a couple of hours on Friday before I arrived. Need I say more?

The Bible speaks with confidence, over a thousand times, of the return of Jesus Christ.

He is coming again. Let us be found doing good.

Lord Jesus, I do not know when you are coming again, but I do know there is much I can do to ready myself for Your return. I can seek Your purpose in my life, follow the light when I know it comes from You, and obey you in small things. I pray this prayer in Your precious name. Amen.

Word and Life

But do not do what they do, for they do not practice what they preach (Matthew 23:3).

Scripture: Matthew 23:2-12
Song: "More Like the Master"

I am a doctor of ministry, and my brother is a doctor of medicine. (A friend quipped that the Barnhart family has "a pair of docs.") I preach the gospel, and my brother practices the healing arts. Together, we preach and practice.

God calls each Christian to both preach and practice. We are to exhibit a congruence of word and life, be who we say we are, do with life what our words indicate we stand for and live out the Word convincingly on a daily basis.

We keep faith alive in us and make it strong coming from us, by practicing what we preach. Ortho*doxy* becomes ortho*praxy* (*praxis* is the biblical Greek word for "practice" or "act"—as in the book of Acts). In other words, ideally, our right belief should lead to good behavior, our orthodox doctrines should lead to ethical deeds. Without that correlation, the salt loses its flavor, and the light flickers. It is told of the twentieth-century Christian martyr Dietrich Bonhoeffer that he never said anything he did not also attempt to put into practice.

So if people want to see God, let them look to those who belong to Him. We can teach by what we know—but we can only reproduce by how we live.

Father in Heaven, Your Son Jesus went about doing good. Forgive me when I just "go about." Help me follow up my words with deeds that bring You pleasure and honor. May I be who I say I am, and may I pray until my prayer becomes my work. O Lord, make my life a sermon today! In Jesus' name, amen.

He Is Good News

To the weak I became weak, that I might win the weak. I have become all things to all men, that I might by all means save some. I do it all for the sake of the gospel, that I may share in its blessings (1 Corinthians 9:22, 23, *Revised Standard Version*).

Scripture: 1 Corinthians 9:19-23
Song: "I Will Sing the Wondrous Story"

I listened to a renowned teacher of preachers, Henry Mitchell, lecture on sermon construction at a conference in Nashville years ago when he introduced his favorite emphasis: celebration. "Every sermon must end in celebration," he said several times. Dr. Mitchell's wife, an applauded theologian herself, sat on the front row of the lecture hall and, after hearing her husband repeatedly tout the necessity of celebration, said, "Well Henry, it *is* good news."

It is the good news of God the Father who creates each of us one of a kind. It is the good news of God the Son who assesses us worth dying for. It is the good news of God the Holy Spirit who keeps us company on a daily basis so we never have to go anywhere alone.

Yes, the gospel is the good news of love, invitation, acceptance, forgiveness, call, and adoption. No news is good news but good news is better news, and that is the news we have: the good news of Jesus Christ. The good news *is* Jesus Christ.

Lord Jesus, thank You for the good news You are to me. It is shouting news in my heart and blessing news on my life. It is the good news of Your love that comes to me when I seek it most—and even comes at me when I turn away. In Your name, amen.

God Provides

When they arrest you, do not worry about what to say or how to say it. At that time you will be given what to say, for it will not be you speaking, but the Spirit of your Father speaking through you (Matthew 10:19, 20).

Scripture: Matthew 10:16-24
Song: "Speak for Jesus"

"I have been given so much," she said after accepting my suggestion to inventory her blessings. She had put pencil to paper, listing and numbering the gifts from God to her life. It looked as if she'd run out of paper, and her pencil would wear down to a tiny nub. After awhile, she seemed almost embarrassed by her blessings.

Have you ever watched a nest of baby birds being fed by their mother? They speak to her in high-pitched chirps and open their tiny mouths as wide as possible, straining their thin necks to reach towards her. The mother bird then drops the food into their opened mouths and satisfies their hunger. That is a picture of God's provision for us. He says to us, "Open wide your mouth and I will fill it" (Psalm 81:10).

We live in the promised land of benefits and blessings. We drink out of our saucers because our cups have overflowed. We sit at God's table and have just finished one piece of blessing when God says, "Here, have another." And Matthew tells us this is true, even in times of severe persecution. We need not fear as to how we will defend ourselves. God will provide.

God, I've heard I am to count my blessings and name them, one by one. But I don't think I can count that high. You have indeed opened the windows of Heaven and poured out blessing after blessing on me. Thank You, in Jesus' name. Amen.

Hope Gets Up

A bruised reed he will not break, and a smoldering wick he will not snuff out, till he leads justice to victory. In his name the nations will put their hope (Matthew 12:21).

Scripture: Matthew 12:15-21
Song: "Jesus, My Only Hope"

Hope is irrepressible. You can kick it around, knock it down, stomp on it, but it always gets up. Sometimes people tell us not to get our hopes up, but that's exactly what hope is for and precisely what hope does. Hope gets up.

An Ethiopian legend tells about a shepherd boy named Alemayu. One night he was stranded on an icy mountain, clothed in the thinnest of wraps. When he got back safely to the village, they asked him how he had survived under such life-threatening circumstances.

He explained that the sky was dark, the night biting cold, and he thought he would die. But then he saw a shepherd's fire far off on another mountain. He kept his eyes on the red glow of the fire and hoped of being warm.

Our lives have a strong gravitational pull in the direction of hope. Hope makes today possible and tomorrow desired. Hope keeps the door open to the future. We go forward because of hope.

Almighty and most merciful Father, thank You for the gift of hope. It is a deep reservoir from which I draw, a full fountain from which I drink. Help me to live within that hope, to embrace it close up and never regard it from afar. May hope always light my way. In the name of Jesus, who lives and reigns with You and the Holy Spirit, one God, now and forever, amen.

God Knows You

Listen to me, you islands; hear this, you distant nations: Before I was born the LORD called me; from my birth he has made mention of my name (Isaiah 49:1).

Scripture: Isaiah 49:1-7
Song: "O God Who Shaped Creation"

God, who counts sparrows and numbers hairs, knows who you are. You are not anonymous in His eyes. As you approach Him for any reason, you need no introduction. God has no vagueness toward you, no ambiguity about you. He knows exactly who you are.

You are known in such a way because you were handcrafted, not mass produced. God didn't crank you out on an assembly line where each looks like all. You are unique. You are individualized. When God made you, He stamped "one of a kind" on what He made. You are not a copy. You are an original. There are no cookie-cutters in Heaven.

God made you and God knows you. Furthermore, God has *always* known you. Way back then in forever before anyone else gave a thought to you, God knew you prior to the creative act that gave you existence, God loved you, made plans for you, and gave purpose to you. You were always in God's heart. You were always on God's mind.

Now, do you wish to come to Him in prayer today with a burden on your heart? Do you think He could understand "where you're coming from"?

Dear God, You knew me before the stars were put in place or the oceans formed. You held me in the heart of Your plan. Thank You for putting Your eternal fingerprints all over me and keeping me forever on Your mind. In Jesus' name, amen.

A Reconciled Account

God was reconciling the world to himself in Christ, not counting men's sins against them. And he has committed to us the message of reconciliation (2 Corinthians 5:19).

Scripture: 2 Corinthians 5:16-21
Song: "Redeemed, How I Love to Proclaim It!"

I loathe balancing the checkbook. I'm happy to pay bills and to dutifully record credits and debits into our ledger. I'm familiar with our online banking account. I'm smart and quite responsible. But when it comes time to reconcile our checkbook ledger with the online bank statement, I become impatient.

It seems as if there's always some small discrepancy that I just can't resolve. And that is when (I'm embarrassed to admit) I am relieved to hand the task to my husband. But after all, I could spend hours pouring over my checkbook and not get the balance right.

Worse, I could spend a lifetime trying to be in harmony with my heavenly Father and not get it right. I can't do it alone. I need the help of a third party—I need Jesus. God's perfection and my imperfection are fully at odds. Only the gift of Christ's blood can bring agreement between us. And the relief this reconciliation brings should make us want to tell all the world about the one who makes it possible.

My Lord Jesus Christ, I am so grateful to You for making peace between me and the Father. Give me the courage and grace to share this profound message with others in kind and meaningful ways. In the name of the Father, the Son, and the Holy Spirit, I pray. Amen.

January 24–30. **Stacie Roth Miller**, of Fort Wayne, Indiana, spends most of her time caring for her daughter and twin sons. She also helps with her husband's chiropractic business.

Infinitely Clean

Day after day every priest stands and performs his religious duties; again and again he offers the same sacrifices, which can never take away sins (Hebrews 10:11).

Scripture: Hebrews 10:10-18
Song: "Lamb of God, I Look to Thee"

"I can't keep up with them," I said under my breath. "I should just give up altogether."

My three preschool children were destroying the house more quickly than I could clean it. I was tired and overwhelmed. Sweeping the kitchen floor seemed pointless, as it would only be covered in food and dirt again in a matter of hours. No matter how many loads of laundry I washed, there were always more to be done. And if I bothered to clean a bathroom, that's undoubtedly when someone would "help" by smearing soap all over the mirror.

Likewise, religious life must have been tiring for the Jewish people of Bible times. Again and again they offered sacrifices that would make them clean, but only for a moment. They soon would have to repeat the process, not unlike a chore.

Jesus changed all that with His supreme sacrifice, giving himself to us as the perfect and eternal substitute lamb. Today, He offers a cleansing that not only completely purifies us, but also repels our future stains. There may not be a one-time treatment that will keep my home sparkly clean. But I'm thankful there's an eternally effective treatment for my heart.

Father in Heaven, I am wearied by my own sin. Your Son is the only one able to clean my heart, and I gladly hand that burden to Him. Thank You for Your amazing and unconditional love. In the name of Christ my Savior I pray. Amen.

A Flattering Imitation

Be imitators of God, therefore, as dearly loved children and live a life of love, just as Christ loved us and gave himself up for us as a fragrant offering and sacrifice to God (Ephesians 5:1, 2).

Scripture: Ephesians 4:25–5:2
Song: "More Like Jesus Would I Be"

Imitation is *not* always the sincerest form of flattery. Children often re-enact what they see every day in their parents. I find that sometimes this is a brutally honest image of myself that I'd rather not see.

Let me explain: I love to watch my preschool daughter pretending to cook on her kitchen set or lovingly reading a book to her baby doll. But there are moments when she raises her voice in anger at her baby brothers, *using the words from my own mouth!* Then I am not flattered by what I see and hear of myself in her. I am deeply ashamed.

Paul instructs us, as Christ's followers, to imitate our heavenly Father. It is not an easy challenge to mimic one we've not seen, heard, or felt in a tangible way. But we can see the perfect example of Jesus in Scripture, and we are able to communicate with Him through prayer. Like children, we will mirror what we see daily. So we need to be intimately familiar with Christ's ways if we are to become more like Him. We won't be perfect until we see Him, face to face. But our sincere efforts will bring Him pleasure.

Almighty and gracious Father, thank You for Your word, and for Your perfect example. As I draw nearer to You, may my life be a better reflection of Your character, and may You be pleased. In the name of Jesus, amen.

Triumphant Failure

For if, by the trespass of the one man, death reigned through that one man, how much more will those who receive God's abundant provision of grace and of the gift of righteousness reign in life through the one man, Jesus Christ (Romans 5:17).

Scripture: Romans 5:12-17
Song: "The Gift of Love"

It seems to happen to me at least once a week. I begin cooking dinner for my family, only to find that I am missing one or more ingredients for a full meal. In a frenzy I scrounge through my pantry for a substitute, often only to create a dish that is decidedly subpar. And yet, there have been times when such improvisations have turned a dull meal into remarkable fare, a better version of my original plan.

In the same way, God not only salvaged us humans from our own failures, but He gave us an even brighter hope. At creation, God proclaimed everything He had made to be "good." But with one selfish choice, we ruined our relationship with Him.

Or so it seemed. Unlike my lucky accidents in the kitchen, God knew just what to add in order to remedy the man-made disaster: His Son, Jesus, as a sacrifice for our sin. Because of Christ we have a secure hope, no matter what our past or future failures may be. We may have made a mess out of God's genesis, but He "fixed" our mistakes with a triumphant revelation.

O God, creator of Heaven and earth, I am so grateful that You are willing and able to take on my mistakes and failures. You've given me hope and a bright future in return. Thanks be to You! I pray this prayer in the name of Jesus, my merciful Savior and Lord. Amen.

Childlike Faith

"Do you understand what you are reading?" Philip asked. **"How can I,"** he said, **"unless someone explains it to me?"** So he invited Philip to come up and sit with him (Acts 8:30, 31).

Scripture: Acts 8:30-35
Song: "Bringing in the Sheaves"

My friend Paula was the child in school who constantly exasperated her teachers with endless questions. As an adult, she challenges me to think more deeply about my faith, if only because she knows how to ask the difficult questions. She asserts that while childlike faith is simplistic trust, it can also be thought of as a thirst for truth. "Having a childlike faith is all about asking questions," she recently said to me. "Children want to know everything!"

In Acts 8, the eunuch is like a child eager for knowledge. He welcomes Philip's help, and rather than berating him for his lack of understanding, Philip responds positively to the eunuch's desire to learn.

You see, God blesses simple faith (see John 20:29) and rewards those who earnestly seek Him (see Hebrews 11:6). The important thing is not whether or not we have questions, but where we look for the answers. Truth comes only from pursuing God and His wisdom. We never know how or when understanding will come to us, but God promises that those who seek will find.

Father in Heaven, thank You that You are greater than my understanding. Guard my heart and my mind as I seek Your truth today. And through the search draw me into a closer relationship with You. In the name of Jesus, amen.

Leading Man

He was despised and rejected by men, a man of sorrows, and familiar with suffering. Like one from whom men hide their faces he was despised, and we esteemed him not (Isaiah 53:3).

Scripture: Isaiah 52:13–53:3
Song: "Hallelujah! What a Savior!"

"Can't sing. Can't act. Slightly bald. Can dance a little." These words are rumored to have been written about a man who would become one of the most famous celebrities of all time. Unimpressed by the young would-be star's screen test, RKO studios nearly passed up a once-in-a-lifetime opportunity. They had in mind a different kind of leading man, and so they very nearly missed out on the great Fred Astaire.

Many Jews in biblical times also had in mind a certain type of leading man to be their Savior. Their hero would be upper-class and strong, someone who would appear with fanfare to rescue them from their enemies. Born into a low social status and plain in appearance, Jesus wasn't their idea of a Messiah. The religious leaders of the day rejected Him, looking for someone they thought would be greater.

Of course, they are not alone in this. Often I too am guilty of ignoring God's plan when it doesn't match my flawed expectations. In truth, His design is bigger and better than I could ever imagine. And I don't want to miss out on that.

Dear Father in Heaven, You are thoroughly trustworthy. Yet I am often full of fear, lacking faith in Your goodness and power. Forgive me my fears and selfish desires, and may Your will be done in and through me today, by the power of Your Holy Spirit. In Christ's name I pray. Amen.

The Whipping Boy

He was pierced for our transgressions, he was crushed for our iniquities; the punishment that brought us peace was upon him, and by his wounds we are healed (Isaiah 53:5).

Scripture: Isaiah 53:4-12
Song: "Beneath the Cross of Jesus"

To be beaten for someone else's misdeeds seems absurd. Yet in the fifteenth and sixteenth centuries in England, use of a "whipping boy" was the royal practice. Young princes were not to be disciplined by anyone other than the king himself. The tutors, therefore, were driven to creative means of correcting poor conduct. At the prince's birth, caretakers would choose a well-born boy to be a friend and scapegoat for him. This punishment became more effective as bonds formed between the lads.

This method would seem even more bizarre if a prince were to take on suffering for one of his subjects—and by choice! It's stranger still if this person were not his friend, but clearly his enemy.

And yet, that is exactly what Jesus has done for all of us. He took punishment in our stead, so that we would not get what we truly deserve. But like the prince and his whipping boy, this exchange is only useful when there is a relationship. Then the love of such a friend can break our hearts, and we can be truly grateful.

Jesus, You bore the pain that I deserved. Such love and grace are unfathomable! I owe You my life, the greatest thanks-offering I have. Help me this day to live with joy and gratitude in my heart. Help me to remember who I am in You and to recall what value You have placed on my life. You paid for my life with Your precious blood, something I can never repay. All glory to You! And in Your name I pray. Amen.

Take Note and Take Heart!

"The days are coming," declares the LORD, "when I will fulfill the gracious promise I made to the house of Israel and to the house of Judah" (Jeremiah 33:14)

Scripture: Jeremiah 33:14-18
Song: "Precious Promise"

In Billy Graham's book *Peace with God*, there's a chapter titled "The Devil" in which Dr. Graham quotes a poem by Alfred J. Hough. It has these lines: "Men don't believe in the devil now, as their fathers used to do."

As a nation and as individuals, have we tended to forget the source of evil? Perhaps this is just another symptom of society's now generally "post-Christian" perspective. But it is a mistaken approach with serious consequences.

Let's be encouraged, however, and remember that God's promises do not fail. There's a way for the righteous to take, the way of growing toward God. Recovery for a nation and for an individual comes along as we continually acknowledge Him and trust His promises to prevail, finally, against all opposition.

As we're told in Hebrews 10:23, "He [God] who promised is faithful." Even as God made unbreakable promises to Jeremiah, so His promises to us are sure and steadfast. Yes, His Word is full of promises. We just need to take note and take them to heart.

Loving God, help me to be encouraged by Your Word and to rely on Your promises daily. In the precious name of Jesus I pray. Amen.

January 31. **David R. Nicholas** is a minister and writer who lives with his wife, Judith, in New South Wales, Australia. His interests are history, stamp-collecting, and photography.

DEVOTIONS®

FEBRUARY

"I tell you the truth, no servant is greater than his master."

—*John 13:16*

Gary Allen, Editor   **Margaret K. Williams,** Project Editor   Photo © Liquid Library

Instant Everything

John answered them all, "I baptize you with water. But one more powerful than I will come, the thongs of whose sandals I am not worthy to untie. He will baptize you with the Holy Spirit and with fire" (Luke 3:16).

Scripture: Luke 3:7-18
Song: "Come, Holy Spirit"

I came across this little quip recently: "When you don't know what to do, don't do anything." Do you agree?

I believe that we can apply the principle to our relationship with God and our desire to do His will. God has promised us power, but we may forget that His power is given in His perfect timing. Sadly, "Fools rush in where angels fear to tread" is true when it comes to living for Christ. To our detriment we often try to force God's hand.

We've become impatient, haven't we? We live with fast foods and seem to expect "instant everything," from coffee to computer searches—just "Google it"—*now!* Yet God repeatedly calls us to wait on Him.

John told the people to wait for the mighty prophet coming after him. To know the fullest power of God, the people needed to be patient. Jesus came not only to save from sin but to endow us with power for living. Speed may be the name of the game these days. But we do well to wait on the Lord.

Dear Lord, thank You for Your promised power. Your blessings are more than can be counted. Thank You in Jesus' almighty name. Amen.

February 1–6. **David R. Nicholas** is a minister and writer who lives with his wife, Judith, in New South Wales, Australia. His interests are history, stamp-collecting, and photography.

Only a Stable

After Jesus was born in Bethlehem in Judea, during the time of King Herod, Magi from the east came to Jerusalem and asked, "Where is the one who has been born king of the Jews? We saw his star in the east and have come to worship him" (Matthew 2:1, 2).

Scripture: Matthew 2:1-6
Song: "Joy to the World"

An early Christian father of the church was, Justin Martyr (born about 100 AD), who lived near Bethlehem, said that Jesus was born in a cave-like stable under an inn.

How uncomplicated was the birth of God's son! In a stable? I suspect the wise men were surprised to learn that he had been born in such humble circumstances.

Since the time of Jesus, His birth site has been cluttered with religious symbols. Apparently, countless numbers of people have sought to actually complicate the site, presuming to make it more holy.

The truth is that wise people recognize a child was born—and that child was God's Son who came to save us from our sins. We are wise when, like the Magi of old, we accept this fact and invite Jesus to rule as king of our lives. Why? Because as writer Brennan Manning puts it: "The greatest single cause of atheism in the world today is Christians who acknowledge Jesus with their lips and walk out the door and deny him with their life style." May it not be so of us.

Father, thank You for sending Jesus to pay the price of all my sin. May I continuously thank You. In the holy name of my Lord and Savior, I pray. Amen.

Twisted by Knaves

They all asked, "Are you then the Son of God?" He replied, "You are right in saying I am." Then they said, "Why do we need any more testimony? We have heard it from his own lips" (Luke 22:70).

Scripture: Luke 22:66-70
Song: "Only Believe"

When I was coming to believe in Christ, some words by Rudyard Kipling helped me greatly to grow in courage. The words are from his poem "If—"

"If you can bear to hear the truth you've spoken twisted by knaves to make a trap for fools . . ."

I found much wisdom in the poem regarding what it takes to be a man of integrity. But there was no integrity in the questioning of Jesus in our Scripture today. Instead, there was trickery underway as Jesus stood before the religious council. He must have thought as He stood there, "If only they would believe."

It's so easy to ask questions, isn't it? Getting the right answer is a different matter. Years ago a friend asked me a question about his marriage. I knew what he wanted me to say, but he asked the wrong question. He should have asked, "How can I *save* my marriage?"

When it comes to belief in God, so much time is wasted with questions and answers. This ignores the wisdom we find in Hebrews 11:6, which tells us that without faith we cannot please God. We must first believe He exists.

Loving Father, all praise to You for Jesus. Help me to daily grow stronger in faith and share that faith with others. In Jesus' name. Amen.

Need Help Remembering?

True worshipers will worship the Father in spirit and truth, for they are the kind of worshipers the Father seeks. God is spirit, and his worshipers must worship in spirit and in truth (John 4:23, 24).

Scripture: John 4:16-26
Song: "In the Garden"

In the days of the Communist revolution in Russia, a group of peasants met secretly to worship. Police broke into the room and wrote down the names of all present. They finished with 30 names.

As they were leaving, an elderly worshiper said, "One name is missing."

"All right, then tell me who is the one missing?" asked the officer in charge.

The answer came, "Jesus Christ."

"But that's a different matter," the policeman responded.

We Christians know it's not a different matter. For whenever we gather in His name—He is present. Every time Christians meet there's an unseen presence.

Years ago I would often see a wall plaque when I entered the home of Christians that said: "Christ is the head of this house, the unseen guest at every meal, the silent listener to every conversation." Sadly, though, we can forget that God is the unseen presence. Staying in a spirit of prayer throughout each day can help us remember.

Dear Lord, I thank You today for Your unseen presence in my life and church. Please help me never to forget the comfort and guidance You offer each moment of my life. In Jesus' name I pray. Amen.

A Long, Lingering Look

The next day John was there again with two of his disciples. When he saw Jesus passing by, he said, "Look, the Lamb of God!" When the two disciples heard him say this, they followed Jesus (John 1:35-37).

Scripture: John 1:35-42
Song: "Behold the Glories of the Lamb"

The other day I had some photographs developed. I showed the results to a friend and could hardly believe my eyes as he flicked through the bunch of photos at great speed. I almost wondered if he thought it was a pack of cards.

The quick look. The short glance. What an instant world we live in! How rushed and speedy our actions have become.

When John the Baptist said, "Look, the Lamb of God," he had something different in mind. In fact, the words of the Bible's original language give the idea of *taking a long look,* not just a quick glance.

So, the solution? Let's take enough time to fully consider Jesus. To look thoroughly at His character as it comes through in the Gospels—and then seek to emulate Him as the Holy Spirit gives us the grace to do so.

The old song put it this way, "Turn your eyes upon Jesus. Look full in His wonderful face."

A full look, not just a glance.

Almighty and most merciful God, please forgive me for the times I turn my eyes away from You. Help me to begin anew today with a fuller study of Your Son's magnificent character and actions. Do continue working in me to complete the maturity that You desire in my Christian growth. In the name of Jesus, the beautiful Lamb of God I pray. Amen.

The Pointing Finger

What good is it for a man to gain the whole world, yet forfeit his soul? Or what can a man give in exchange for his soul? (Mark 8:36, 37).

Scripture: Mark 8:27–9:1
Song: "Give of Your Best to the Master"

Charlemagne, the French king, had occupied his massive tomb for 300 years. Yet Emperor Frederick Barbarosa doubted the stories of the burial, and he decided that he must reopen the tomb.

There was a rush of air.

Tapestries and curtains dissolved to dust.

On a throne sat Charlemagne. Garments intact. His scepter still grasped.

Around Charlemagne's neck was a gold chain. Across his knees his sword named *Joyeuse*. On his lap was an open Bible, with an index finger pointing to a particular text. Can you guess what it was? *What good is it for a man to gain the whole world, yet forfeit his soul?* I've often wondered about the monk who, at the last moment before the tomb was sealed, gently laid the great king's finger in place.

The great truth of our wealth is this: We can't take it with us. As Paul reminds us in 2 Cpromtjoams 4:18, we are to fix our eyes not on the seen, which is temporary, but on the unseen, which is eternal. All of which encourages me to make the things of God my life's priority.

Father in Heaven, thank You for Your Word and for the many reminders that this world is not my home. May I seek first Your kingdom today in all my desires and goals. In the name of Jesus, my Savior, I pray. Amen.

Hot Spots

Surely the day is coming; it will burn like a furnace (Malachi 4:1).

Scripture: Malachi 4:1-6
Song: "Burn in Me"

My husband and his fellow firefighters were cleaning up after a house fire they had extinguished. One of the guys casually put out his hand to lean against a wall.

"Ow!"

He jerked his hand off the wall—quick. He'd found a "hot spot"—a hidden, smoldering internal fire that could rekindle the blaze. They tore into the wall and found it. Those smoldering embers would have brought them back in a few hours to another inferno.

Firefighters are well acquainted with hot spots. That's why crews spend additional time at sites long after the big fire is out.

When God brings cleansing to the earth, He will do it with fire. No hot spots will be left after His purging on "that day that is coming" (v. 1). Those who have remained faithful to Him and revered His name will run freely on the renewed earth.

"Surely the day is coming," the Word says. We want to look up and experience the healing of "the sun of righteousness" (vv. 1, 2). Are you ready for the Lord's fiery day?

Lord, Your Word teaches that You are a cleansing fire. Burn out any hot spots of sin in me. I want to be like refined gold—free of impurities. In Jesus' name, amen.

February 7–13. **Kathy Douglas** lives in northwest Ohio. She is the happy grandmother of triplet grandsons who—unfortunately for her—live in southern California.

Look, Ma! I'm Flying!

You yourselves have seen what I did to Egypt, and how I carried you on eagles' wings and brought you to myself (Exodus 19:4).

Scripture: Exodus 19:1-6
Song: "On Eagles' Wings"

Mark built his own airplane from the wheels up, and his flight instructor offered to take "Harriet Mable" on her maiden flight. When he landed her some time later, this experienced pilot's words weren't encouraging.

"You'll never get her up," he told the inexperienced pilot and builder. "I didn't think I'd ever get her off the ground! Not enough power in that engine."

Mark did "get her up" on his own. But he did it after he had purchased and mounted a bigger, more powerful engine.

After 400 years of captivity, the Lord had no problem bringing His people out of Egypt. It was like perching them on eight-foot wingspans of eagles. At the Red Sea they thought they had been stopped. The pursuing Egyptian army did too. But the God of Israel brought His people to himself.

God can do on the individual level what He did for the nation of Israel. He can deliver us from bondage to old habits. He can free us from the imprisonment of previous failures. He can give us wings to fly.

O God, creator of Heaven and earth, thank You that I don't have to be a prisoner of my past failures. I praise You that You free me to worship You and honor You with my life starting fresh each day. Please help me to stay free of temptation and to commit my ways to Your guidance. In the name of the Jesus, I pray. Amen.

Going It Alone?

Yet I reserve seven thousand in Israel—all whose knees have not bowed down to Baal and all whose mouths have not kissed him (1 Kings 19:18).

Scripture: 1 Kings 19:11-18
Song: "Onward Christian Soldiers"

Japan has a long history of resistance to the gospel of Jesus Christ. In 1637, Japanese soldiers murdered over 30,000 Christians. Their intent? Eradicate Christianity from the small island country.

The church was decimated, but not destroyed. It went underground. Missionaries continued to arrive on the island, and by the year 2000 Japan boasted an estimated 1.7 million believers.

In 2006, Jen began her new job in a US city after her cross-country move. When she went to work, she took a Christian book she had been reading. On her break, she read between bites of her sandwich. One of her coworkers approached her.

"Are you a Christian too?" A new friendship was forged as the two women found more in common than their professions.

We may reside in a country where the message of Christ is banned. We might relocate to a city where we think no one follows Jesus. Yet the Lord has His people everywhere. Elijah found them in idolatrous Israel. Missionaries of the mid-1600s found them in Japan. Jen found them at her place of employment. Look to find—or provide—some Christian fellowship today.

My dear Heavenly Father, sometimes I too feel isolated. I ask you to show me another Christian with whom I can share in the good things of God. Or help me to be the seeker. Lead me to another believer who needs my Christian fellowship. In the name of Jesus, Lord and Savior of all, I pray. Amen.

Plumb and True

I saw a man whose appearance was like bronze; he was standing in the gateway with a linen cord and a measuring rod in his hand (Ezekiel 40:3).

Scripture: Ezekiel 40:1-4
Song: "Finally Home"

Plumb line. Plumb bob. Water level. Builder's level. Transit. Spirit level. Laser.

When they constructed our first house, the carpenters used taut plumb lines and chalk to build straight walls. For our second home, the chalk and cord were left in the toolbox. A laser projected the needed plumb lines to follow.

Throughout human history, builders have used an assortment of measuring devices to erect structures that are straight. For centuries the plumb line guided the builders. Today, lasers keep building construction plumb and level.

Of course, if the laser battery goes dead, those older tools still suffice. The carpenter brings out the time-tested standards.

When an angel took Ezekiel to view the future Jerusalem, the prophet saw that the new city is fashioned to perfection. Each courtyard, gate, and room meets a standard of unparalleled faultlessness. Those who have been remade perfect in the image of Christ will feel comfortably at home in this place. Why? Neither the redeemed nor the new Jerusalem have been made by human hands. What God fits for eternity is plumb and true.

Gracious Father, You are the maker of all things. I praise You that one day I'll stand faultless before Your throne. I'm humbled to know that in that place where all is perfection, I'll fit in. I'll feel—and truly be—at home. In the name of Jesus, I pray. Amen.

Courtroom Drama

He will judge between the nations and will settle disputes for many peoples (Isaiah 2:4).

Scripture: Isaiah 2:1-4
Song: "What a Day That Will Be"

Courtroom dramas have been popular in both books and on television. Perry Mason, the attorney featured on a television show by the same name from 1957 to 1966, enjoyed legal success weekly. With even-tempered aplomb, he won every case. (It helped that every one of his clients was innocent.) The pompous district attorney—amazingly enough—retained his job, in spite of defeat after defeat.

Usually both sides going into a courtroom think they have the winning case. Be they individuals, corporations, or even countries, both sides present their arguments to the presiding judge. Whether it's on television or in real life, the judge's decision stands, often to the dissatisfaction of one of the parties involved.

How unlike the final courtroom! When God the judge hands down His rulings, both sides will have justice. No brokenhearted family members will need to have the last word in court to vent their frustrations. No nation will "train for war anymore" (v. 4). God's decree will stand outside the court as well as inside. No cries of "unfair" will echo. A glorious day of peace and justice lies ahead.

Sometimes life isn't fair, **Father,** but I know that You're in control. Help me wait patiently for the time when life will be just and fair and free of conflicts. And in the meantime, give me the courage to treat others with mercy and grace, for Your glory. In Jesus' name I pray. Amen.

Growing Up in Church

Within your temple, O God, we meditate on your unfailing love. Like your name, O God, your praise reaches to the ends of the earth (Psalm 48:9, 10).

Scripture: Psalm 48:9-14
Song: "Better Is One Day"

Gordon grew up as a PK—a "preacher's kid." As a boy he felt as if he were seldom allowed to leave the church building. He was there for every service, every event. Along with his family, he had to be there for extended times before and after those numerous services too.

Sometimes he was there for meetings. His attendance wasn't required, but a young boy couldn't be left home unsupervised. Some days, even on Sundays, he longed for escape.

The one picture we have from Jesus' growing up years tells us that He loved being at the temple in Jerusalem. Long after everyone else had departed, He remained. Listening and learning, He had already begun to astound the temple leaders with His questions and understanding (see Luke 2:41-50).

Are we eager to spend time in worship at church? Or do we anticipate getting church over and done with?

The psalmist formed his life's perspective from within the temple walls. There he grabbed hold of the love, righteousness, and fair judgments of God. Let's do the same when we go to church.

Lord God, the king of glory, help me to focus on You when I go to church. I want to learn more of You and to encourage others to do the same. During this day, may everything I do and say be a form of praise. I pray this prayer in the name of Jesus, my loving Savior and Lord. Amen.

Metamorphosis

After six days Jesus took Peter, James and John with him and led them up a high mountain, where they were all alone. There he was transfigured before them (Mark 9:2).

Scripture: Mark 9:2-13
Song: "Let the Beauty of Jesus"

In a television sci-fi series years ago, one of the characters was a "shape-shifter." He could assume any form. He could look and talk like someone else, or he could look like a table. He could be as obvious or as inconspicuous as he desired. The downside? If he didn't shift back into his actual identity within a specified time frame, he'd become a puddle of goo—a most humiliating experience.

From today's reading we can assume that, with this one point-in-time exception, the Lord Jesus looked like any other man during His incarnation. No shape-shifting tricks and no halo around His head hinted at His uniqueness among men. Isaiah went so far as to say that the Messiah "had no beauty or majesty to attract us to him, nothing in his appearance that we should desire him" (Isaiah 53:2).

We don't have to be shape-shifters to undergo a tremendous inner transformation—becoming like Jesus himself. We're "being transformed into his likeness with ever-increasing glory" (2 Corinthians 3:18). God is changing us from the inside out. Someday our transfiguration will be complete and everlasting.

Lord God in Heaven, sometimes my transformation into Your likeness seems like a frustratingly slow process. Help me patiently to wait on You and live in obedience to Your words. Thank You that You've promised to finish what You've begun in me. In Christ's holy name I pray. Amen.

Celebrate!

We had to celebrate this happy day. For your brother was dead and has come back to life! He was lost, but now he is found! (Luke 15:32, *New Living Translation*).

Scripture: Luke 15:25-32
Song: "Happiness Is the Lord"

A group of recovered drug addicts came to a church and gave testimony of their amazingly "wild" lives before coming to Christ. One young man in the congregation made this observation, "These kids get attention because they were so *bad*. What about we who have stayed faithful to God all this time? Nobody pats us on the back."

Wasn't this the attitude of the elder brother in Jesus' parable of the prodigal son? It seems he couldn't be happy for his brother when the prodigal finally returned to the father. The older brother represents the person who has a form of religion, and self-righteously keeps all the commandments, but is as far from His heavenly Father as the younger brother was from his dad.

No matter where, when, or how a person comes to Christ—whether the convert is young or old, wealthy or homeless—there is reason for us to be joyful when people respond to Christ's salvation. A life-changing decision has been made. An eternal destiny has changed. The Father and all the angels rejoice, and so should we.

Lord, thanks for Your marvelous invitation—to every person—to enter into fellowship with You. May I be a joyful witness to that good news today. In Jesus' name, amen.

February 14–20. **Jewell Johnson,** a retired registered nurse, lives in Arizona with husband LeRoy. They're parents to six children, grandparents to nine. Jewell enjoys reading, walking, and quilting.

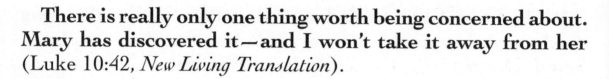

The Most Important Thing

There is really only one thing worth being concerned about. Mary has discovered it—and I won't take it away from her (Luke 10:42, *New Living Translation*).

Scripture: Luke 10:38-42
Song: "Fairest Lord Jesus"

The potatoes need mashing, the gravy has to be stirred, the table needs setting . . . and the bread—who will cut it and get it in the oven? When I'm in the middle of preparing a big dinner for a houseful of guests, I could easily scream, "Can't someone please help me?"

In the story of Martha and Mary, I obviously side with Martha. How about you?

Yet I understand that their story is about much more than just getting food on the table; it's about worship. What is most important to me?

Yes, food is necessary, and it requires preparation. But I must not forget: Jesus is here. Right now—in a church service, in my private devotions—may I listen to Him, express my love for Him, let Him convey His love and care. Later, I can serve all I want.

What happens when we take time to be with Jesus? Our priorities take shape (likely a new shape). We turn from not-so-important things, like the menu, to what is really important: our special guest. The rest of our day will take on a new glow when we take time to listen to Jesus.

Almighty Father, my priorities need adjusting every day. Help me spend my time in the best possible way—in pursuits that honor Your name and advance Your kingdom. I pray. Amen.

A Kingdom Principle

Normally the master sits at the table and is served by his servants. But not here! For I am your servant (Luke 22:27, *New Living Translation*).

Scripture: Luke 22:24-30
Song: "So Send I You"

One fall, in an effort to acquaint new students with faculty members, the college president asked the professors to help freshmen students move into their dormitories.

It was interesting. The teachers, dressed in jeans and T-shirts, carried boxes and suitcases up long flights of stairs to the students' rooms. Rather than lecturing or giving out assignments, these academic leaders now looked to their students to give them directions.

Clearly, the professors' actions reflected an important kingdom principle. However, Jesus' disciples had missed it. Instead, they argued about which of them was the greatest. Thankfully, Jesus used the argument to teach them a rule of His kingdom: His disciples aren't organized like a corporate business, with managers of departments and company directors. Each believer is on the same level; they are all servants.

If we can grasp and apply this truth, our homes, churches, and schools will function more smoothly. Is the sink full of dirty dishes? Put a load in the dishwasher. Does a Sunday school class need a teacher? Offer to help. No job is beneath a Christian. Jesus served, and He is our example.

O Eternal Lord God, deliver me from laziness and any thoughts of how I can promote myself and my interests above Your priorities for me. In other words, please grant me a true servant heart. In the name of Jesus I pray. Amen.

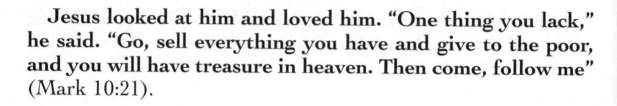

Unconditional Commitment

**Jesus looked at him and loved him. "One thing you lack,"
he said. "Go, sell everything you have and give to the poor,
and you will have treasure in heaven. Then come, follow me"**
(Mark 10:21).

Scripture: Mark 10:17-22
Song: "Nothing Between"

For a long time, I longed to become a Christian. But as Jesus
dealt with my teenage heart, one thing stood in my way: I felt God
wanted me to break up with my boyfriend, who was not a believer.

After weeks of tears and struggle, I surrendered the last shred
of resistance. I decided to follow Jesus and obey His prompt-
ings about something in my life that needed to change.

The young man in the Scripture was not so inclined. When
he heard the requirements for discipleship—sell all and give his
wealth to the poor—he wasn't willing to do it. Because money
was apparently the love of his life, he walked away from the
path of discipleship.

When we contemplate making commitments to Christ, road-
blocks will always pop up to deter us. This is only a test, however. Jesus offers so much more than money or friends. When
we surrender all to follow Him, He promises us treasures in
Heaven. And when God sees a yielded heart, He may even return to us what we had initially let go into His hands.

Father in Heaven, I long to walk in close communion with You. Show me the things
I need to lay aside in order to sense Your very heartbeat. I know that only by walking
close to You will I have the joy and peace I seek. In the holy name of Jesus, my Lord
and Savior, I pray. Amen.

From One Wrinkled Seed

I tell you the truth, unless a kernel of wheat falls to the ground and dies, it remains only a single seed. But if it dies, it produces many seeds (John 12:24).

Scripture: John 12:20-26
Song: "Lead Me to Calvary"

When Lettie Cowman, author of *Streams in the Desert*, became a Christian, she felt led to get rid of several secular books in her library. She was also an excellent pianist and had stacks of music from operas and popular tunes. Again, the Holy Spirit seemed to say, "Does all this glorify your Lord?" The music also went into the fire as Lettie separated herself from lesser things in order to pursue God's higher purposes.

Of course, there is nothing wrong with good books and good music. Forms of art can convey a heavenly beauty and transcendence. It's just that Lettie wanted one, clear-cut focus.

As Jesus prepared for the cross, He spent time with His close friends. During their conversations, He highlighted a basic principle of nature: new life can spring from apparent death. Though Jesus' disciples didn't want to hear of their master's death, the cross was necessary for the salvation of the world.

We too must experience loss if we're to know God's best for our lives. Loss of pride, loss of possession, loss of our own ability to engineer circumstances—these are a few things that may need to fall to the ground and die. Then Christ can produce a harvest through us.

God and Father of all, many voices cry out for my attention and distract me from being Your servant. Bring these idols to my attention, and help me to lay them at Your feet so I can fully behold Your glory. In the name of my Savior, Jesus Christ, amen.

Real Christianity

I have given you an example to follow. Do as I have done to you (John 13:15, *New Living Translation*).

Scripture: John 13:3-16
Song: "Footsteps of Jesus"

Hannah Whitall Smith, author of *The Christian's Secret of a Happy Life*, was quite lonely when she moved from Philadelphia to Millville, New Jersey. Her minister encouraged her to befriend the poor people in her neighborhood. But when Hannah's dressmaker invited her to a meeting of local Christians, she thought, *What can these people teach me? After all, I have preached and taught the Bible for years.*

At the meeting, a lady with a shawl on her head confessed, "My whole horizon used to be filled with this big 'me,' but when I got sight of my humble Savior, this great big 'me' melted to nothing." The words touched Hannah, and she was convinced that "this is real Christianity, the kind I long for."

"Real Christianity" involves doing lowly tasks with love. This principle had escaped Jesus' disciples. They were possessed with a passion . . . to occupy places of honor. At the last supper, Jesus took the place of the lowliest slave and washed His followers' dirty feet. Through this act, He showed them—and us—how we are to serve in God's kingdom.

No job is beneath us. Servants serve.

Almighty and everlasting God, I pray that my old nature—and the world's attitudes—will fall away as I strive to imitate Your Son, Jesus, servant of all servants. Bless me with a truly humble heart, Lord. I know it will take a lot of letting go, but You can give me the will and the courage to do it. In the holy name of Jesus, my Lord and Savior, I pray. Amen.

The Ransom Is Paid

The Son of Man did not come to be served, but to serve, and to give his life as a ransom for many (Mark 10:45).

Scripture: Mark 10:35-45
Song: "At the Cross"

Amos Fortune was freed from slavery in 1769, and with freedom came a desire for others of his race also to escape the slave system.

Working as a tanner, he saved his money, lived frugally, and bought freedom for Lily, a sickly woman. Although she lived only one year after being purchased, Lily died free. Next, Amos paid the price so Lydia, a crippled slave, could be freed. At his death in 1801, Amos had paid the ransom for five slaves to receive their freedom.

Jesus' disciples, James and John, had been with Him for three years when they requested places of honor in His kingdom. Clearly, their priorities were misplaced; they had missed the purpose of Jesus' coming to earth.

Jesus' mission was to pay the ransom required to rescue mankind from sin's slavery. Our redemption involves two important elements—a redeemer and a ransom. God's justice demanded a price be paid for sin. We could not pay the ransom price, but Jesus could. On the cross, with His own blood, He paid in full the price, so we may now live free of sin's power. That is why He is our praiseworthy Redeemer.

Lord God of All, I am grateful for freedom from guilt, condemnation, sin, and its power through my Redeemer, Jesus. Thanks for the powerful, redeeming blood of the Lamb. Thanks for the humility of the Son, who left the realms of glory to enter the realm of my need here on earth. All praise to Him in whose name I pray! Amen.

Pride's Reckoning

The eyes of the arrogant man will be humbled and the pride of men brought low; the LORD alone will be exalted in that day (Isaiah 2:11).

Scripture: Isaiah 2:5-12
Song: "All for Jesus!"

Being the mother of three strong-willed boys, I've spent much of the past decade playing referee. Each child wants absolute domination over the others. Need some examples? Once I walked to our driveway, only to find my oldest stuffing his 5-year-old brother headfirst into the floorboard of our car! Another time, I caught the youngest secretly hiding his older brother's favorite hat. The examples are endless but the goal universal: control. With a motherly tone I warn: "Watch yourself. What *goes* around *comes* around."

As adults, we do something similar, though perhaps in less obvious ways. We want supremacy, to feel in control. So we strong-arm relationships or manipulate circumstances. But Isaiah warns against personal pride: "The LORD Almighty has a day in store for all the proud and lofty" (v. 12).

There is only room on top for one: The Lord God Almighty himself. Ultimately, every knee will bow. Every last one. Better to bend it, willingly and in humility, than to find yourself stuffed in a place you don't want to be.

Dear God, I acknowledge Your absolute authority over my life. I confess there are times when my pride runs unchecked, and for that I'm sorry. In Jesus' name, amen.

February 21–27. **Michele Cushatt,** of Highlands Ranch, Colorado, is a writer and speaker whose passion is to help today's generation discover the authentic God.

The Christian's Classroom

Always learning but never able to acknowledge the truth (2 Timothy 3:7).

Scripture: 2 Timothy 3:1-9
Song: "Changed into His Likeness"

Nobody dreams of being a 43-year-old sitting in the back of an 11th-grade chemistry classroom. High school is for teenagers, not grown-ups, right? Though a few may struggle to pass in four years, eventually everyone moves on. Why? Because we all want to grow up, to graduate from childhood into the adult life that awaits us.

As Christians, however, we sometimes stay stuck in the same classroom for years. We sit in the same classes, read the same Book, study the same subjects, and yet never graduate to real-life application. We remain adults in a child's classroom, always learning, but never allowing the things we've learned to change the way we live.

Paul addresses this dangerous game in his letter to Timothy. There were some in the Ephesian congregation who appeared to be righteous: knowledgeable of Scripture, involved in serving the church. Upon a closer look, however, selfishness, pride, unforgiveness, and lack of self-control belied the deeper truth.

There's nothing wrong with being a life-long learner. The trick is to make sure the learning translates into living. It's in the living that the learning makes all the difference.

God of wisdom and grace, I confess there are times I learn but don't allow the learning to change my heart. I need your transforming power in my life, that I may be a person who daily acknowledges the truth in the way I live. In the holy name of Jesus, my Lord and Savior, I pray. Amen.

Tired of the Waiting Room?

The Lord is not slow in keeping his promise, as some understand slowness. He is patient with you, not wanting anyone to perish, but everyone to come to repentance (2 Peter 3:9).

Scripture: 2 Peter 3:3-10
Song: "So You Would Come"

Nothing frustrates me like rushing to a doctor's appointment, only to find myself stuck in the waiting room far past my "scheduled" time. I try to be prompt and expect others to do the same. It's the respectful thing to do.

On occasion, however, I get myself all worked up, only to discover my doctor is detained due to a serious medical emergency. A child struggles to breathe in the throes of an asthma attack. A pregnant woman goes into pre-term labor, putting both herself and her child at risk. When I realize a life is at stake, my impatience abates. I can afford to wait when someone's life needs saving.

My heart aches for Christ to return. The more I see the pain and injustice around me, the more I long to enter His presence. There tears will cease, loved ones will be reunited, and rejoicing will trump all fear and uncertainty. And there are times, quite honestly, when I'm just tired of sitting in the waiting room of life—until I'm reminded, by Peter's poignant pen, that God's delay means humanity's life.

Heavenly Father, the love You hold for me is unfathomable, and I am so thankful. Thank You, again and again, for Your great patience with me—and for Your heart for redemption. Help me, likewise, to develop a heart that is concerned for the redemption of the world, beginning in my own neighborhood. In Jesus' name, amen.

Heading Home

In keeping with his promise we are looking forward to a new heaven and a new earth, the home of righteousness (2 Peter 3:13).

Scripture: 2 Peter 3:11-18
Song: "Lord, I'm Coming Home"

Nothing compares to the feeling of coming home after a long time away. Whether returning from an extended vacation or a full day of tackling errands and responsibilities, coming home soothes my soul. As I pull into the driveway and remove my coat and shoes at the front door, the day's weariness falls to the floor. *I'm home.*

A few months ago we moved into a new house, leaving our long-time family home behind. Ever since then I've felt out of place, unsettled. It's as if this new dwelling is a temporary detour, and someday I'll return to the familiar place where my children were raised and all kinds of great memories were made. Although this house is wonderful in so many ways, it is not yet home to me.

As believers in Christ, we recognize that our earthly dwellings are temporary. There are times when our soul aches, unsettled and anxious to rest. But as Peter reminds us, we've been promised something more. Another home. Our true home. Someday our feet will cross the beautiful threshold of this mansion in glory. And when they do, the weariness will fall to the floor, and our spirits will soar.

How anxious I am for Your return, **Jesus!** Every day I wait for You to come and take me home. Thank you for the beautiful promise of eternal rest with You. In Your precious name I pray. Amen.

King of the Mountain

All men will hate you because of me, but he who stands firm to the end will be saved (Mark 13:13).

Scripture: Mark 13:1-13
Song: "Stand, Soldier of the Cross"

I was 12 years old when Dad took me to the dirt pile in our backyard. Though his intentions were unclear, his face appeared serious. I knew I needed to pay attention.

I didn't realize how big the pile was until I stood close enough to touch it. As I looked up toward the peak, my father told me to climb on top. I did as he asked, then turned to face him. He reached out his hand and said, "OK, pull me up there with you."

Though he didn't resist, he didn't help either. And I struggled against his weight.

Moving him to high ground proved more difficult than I anticipated. After a minute he went on: "This time, I'm going to try to pull you down from the top." With little effort on his part, I found myself removed from my peak.

The arrow hit its mark, as he went on to explain his little object lesson. Standing firmly planted on the truth of Christ will not be easy. There are many in society today who would like nothing more than to pull us down. However, "he who stands firm to the end will be saved."

Almighty and everlasting God, make me strong, firm, and steadfast when opposition comes because of my commitment to Your kingdom. I know that I can expect this, even to the extent of significant persecution. As I face those trials, may I keep my eyes always on Your Son, the one who overcame every obstacle to do Your will. In His glorious name I pray. Amen.

The Red Carpet

Keep watch because you do not know when the owner of the house will come back—whether in the evening, or at midnight, or when the rooster crows, or at dawn. If he comes suddenly, do not let him find you sleeping (Mark 13:35, 36).

Scripture: Mark 13:28-37
Song: "Majesty"

Hollywood award shows require incredible production. For weeks, the media builds anticipation, discussing actors and actresses, and highlighting the best of the best when it comes to the people and plots of movies. From designer-label jewelry to exquisite attire and pricey hairstyles, no expense is spared in preparation. Even moviegoers and television watchers catch the hype. Food is purchased, parties planned, and everyone gathers to watch glamour make its way down the red carpet.

Seldom, however, does the eternal plot evoke such a dramatic response. With a yawn and half-hearted efforts, our attempts to keep an eye on eternity are often feeble at best. We move through life in a walking slumber, aware of this moment but disconnected from eternity.

Here's a reality check: God's eternal realm exists. The only unknown remains the date and time when Jesus will return to our earthly realm. So I ask myself: Am I ready? Have I fed my soul and dressed myself to meet Him? I want to do what it takes to roll out the red carpet for my Savior.

O God, the king of glory, what a joy it is to know Your Son is coming back! Help me keep my eyes on the horizon, and my heart set on eternity, as I wait and make myself ready for You. In the name of Jesus, who lives and reigns with You and the Holy Spirit, one God, now and forever, amen.

Hanging on Every Word

Heaven and earth will pass away, but my words will never pass away (Mark 13:31).

Scripture: Mark 13:14-27, 31
Song: "The Word of God Shall Stand"

Last week one of the oldest and most beloved metropolitan newspapers printed its final edition. After thousands of plastic-bundled papers were delivered to driveways all over town, the presses stopped, and the doors closed for good. A historic 150-year era came to an end, forced out of existence by a struggling economy.

The remaining city newspaper continues its daily run, the headlines carrying further ominous warnings of the times: bad news about lives overturned, fearful predictions about the chaos of our economic future.

There are moments when bad news seems to be everywhere I turn. And I get overwhelmed.

Jesus understands insecure times. And rather than address each headline, He reminds us of one simple fact: Today's bad news is nothing compared to the good news of the gospel. A day will eventually come when all the world's presses will stop, and the only words left hanging in the air will be the eternal words of salvation and redemption in Jesus Christ. And we will "dwell in the house of the LORD forever" (Psalm 23:6).

Now those are some words worth hanging on to.

Everlasting Father, my heart rejoices in every word that comes from Your lips. Thank You that the good news will always be the salvation that comes through Your Son, Jesus. May I be ready for that day when every tongue will confess His name and every knee will bow to His rule. In His name I pray. Amen.

What a Fine Minister!

The ministry Jesus has received is as superior to theirs as the covenant of which he is mediator is superior to the old one, and it is founded on better promises (Hebrews 8:6).

Scripture: Hebrews 8:6-12
Song: "What a Wonderful Savior"

Do you like your minister at church? Why? Is he a good preacher? an able administrator? a compassionate hospital visitor? These are some of the qualities people look for in their minister. Sadly, we might focus purely on personality or formal education to the downplaying of more biblical standards: the amount of prayer, the dedication to biblical studies, or the ability to make disciples as Jesus commanded.

Now consider the ultimate minister according to the writer of Hebrews. It is none other than Jesus. Why is His ministry so superior to all others? There are many reasons, of course. But here's what comes through in Hebrews: Jesus is superior because He exercises His ministry in a heavenly sanctuary. He has a better covenenat than the old one (of ancient Judaism) to proclaim, one based on grace rather than sacrifice. And He proclaims a better promise than what the Law could offer—not just that today's sins will be forgiven. No, if one trusts in this high priest, all of his or her sins will be forgiven, past, present, and future. What an excellent minister this is!

Father, thank You for the ministry of Your Son, who mediates from His heavenly sanctuary between me and You. Praise You for Your great love! In Jesus' name, amen.

February 28. **Gary Wilde** has been writing and editing Christian publications since 1985. He lives with his wife, Carol, in Moultrie, Georgia. They have twin sons who work as industrial engineers.

My Prayer Notes

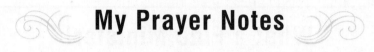

My Prayer Notes

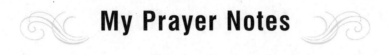

My Prayer Notes

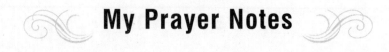

_____

_____

_____

_____

_____

_____

_____

_____

_____

_____

_____

_____

_____

_____

_____

_____

_____

_____

_____

_____

DEVOTIONS®

MARCH

"I will put my laws in their minds and write them on their hearts. I will be their God, and they will be my people."

—Hebrews 8:10

Gary Allen, Editor   **Margaret Williams,** Project Editor   Photo © iStockphoto

Out of Sight—Out of Mind

In his hand are the depths of the earth, and the mountain peaks belong to him (Psalm 95:4).

Scripture: Psalm 95:1-7
Song: "King of Glory, King of Peace"

On a recent trip to Switzerland, I reveled in the majesty of the snow-capped mountains that surrounded the little town where I stayed. Sitting on a third-floor balcony, I enjoyed the view, unobstructed by daily traffic and surroundings. The effort it took to climb the stairs was well worth it.

That mountain view carried great value. In fact, according to a city ordinance, contractors intending to construct a new building must first put up a platform of the same dimensions so people can see how the proposed building will affect their view of the mountains. The structure must remain for 30 days to give residents time to file legal opposition to the plan.

The Bible tells us to get rid of anything in our lives that might lead us into sin or hinder our spiritual growth. As we strive to walk in the path God has placed before us, let us be constantly aware of the "obstructions" of life. Many seemingly good things can rise up to prevent us from keeping our eyes on Jesus. Let's make the effort to come up higher as we revel in the majesty of the King of kings.

As I wonder at the beauty of Your creation, **O Lord,** I stand in awe that You would love me enough to lay down Your life for me. I pray in the name of the Father, the Son, and the Holy Spirit. Amen.

March 1–6. **Barb Haley** has worked as a schoolteacher, Bible quiz coach, and private piano instructor. She and her husband have three grown children and live near San Antonio, Texas.

Prison Opportunity

Pray also for me, that whenever I open my mouth, words may be given me so that I will fearlessly make known the mystery of the gospel, for which I am an ambassador in chains (Ephesians 6:19, 20).

Scripture: Ephesians 6:18-24
Song: "God Will Make a Way"

The story is told of a farmer in Maine who was working in his fields when a stranger stopped by. "How much is your prize Jersey cow worth?" the stranger asked. Thinking for a minute, the farmer answered with a question of his own. "Tell me first, are you a tax assessor, or has my cow been killed by your car?"

In the Scripture passage for today, the apostle Paul had been bound and held for sharing the gospel. No one would have blamed him had he become discouraged or tempted to give up. Here he was, zealously doing what Jesus called him to do, only to end up in jail. But this man of God looked at things differently, considering himself an ambassador in chains. That is, he chose to view his bondage as an opportunity for service.

Life, indeed, is not always fair. We may never understand the ways of God in a particular situation. Thankfully, we know His heart and His promise to work all things for good in the lives of those who love Him.

There is great peace in surrendering our understanding and trusting God. He will never let us down.

Dear Father, life can be so tough to understand. Show me the opportunity in my trials as I focus on Your love. Craddle me in Your arms and remind me that You will never let me be tempted beyond what I can bear. Through Christ, amen.

Through the Eyes of a Child

For in this hope we were saved. But hope that is seen is no hope at all. Who hopes for what he already has? (Romans 8:24).

Scripture: Romans 8:22-27
Song: "My Faith Looks Up to Thee"

Quite some time ago, my family moved across country. Planning to buy our first house, we listed the options we wanted in our new home. My son wanted a tree to climb. My daughter a place to keep a pony. We all had our say, so there were many desires listed on the paper we prayed over for about a month before we moved.

Once we arrived at our new location, we searched for a house, busily forgetting all about the list. A few weeks later, I found the list and read it over with the family. "Wow!" my husband exclaimed. "The house has everything on the list except a place for the pony. I guess that must not be God's will for right now."

"No," my 9-year-old daughter said, matter-of-factly. "That just means God hasn't shown us how He's going to do it yet."

What a great example of hope in what is not yet seen! Webster defines *hope* as "desire plus expectancy." How wonderful to know that our hope of eternity with Jesus is not just something we desire. It's a free gift of grace that we can expect and look forward to.

Lord God of All, You have promised to grant the desires of my heart as I delight in You. Teach me how to delight in You and to put You first in my life. Thank You for the hope of salvation that I have through Your Son's death on the cross. In the name of Jesus my Lord I pray. Amen.

Our Daily Bread

Give us each day our daily bread (Luke 11:3).

Scripture: Luke 11:1-13
Song: "'Tis So Sweet to Trust in Jesus"

Spending a month in Europe, I soon learned many differences in how we live in America and how the Europeans live. Consider, for instance, the bread we ate at mealtimes. In America, we shop for the softest loaf on the shelf, often reaching to the rear for those loaves most recently stocked. In Europe, however, soft bread is hard to find and expensive to buy. The bread we ate was delicious, but crusty and tough.

The difference? American bread is loaded with preservatives that keep it soft. But these same preservatives are known to be less than beneficial to our bodies.

Think about God's provision of manna for the Israelites in the wilderness. The Lord knew what His people needed for that day, and He knows our needs for *this* day, as well. When we worry and fret about tomorrow, we lose sight of God's promise to provide exactly what we need, at exactly the right time.

So, here is what He tells us to pray: "Give us each day our daily bread." May we allow God to pour His grace and strength into us, one day at a time. Only in this way can we accomplish the things He has set before us to do. May we trust Him with our tomorrows too, knowing that He is all we need for the moment, and all we need for the next moment.

Teach me, **O Lord,** to wait on You for all my needs. Help me not to waste time worrying about the future, but to trust You with all my cares as I strive to live for You, one day at a time. Through Christ I pray. Amen.

Power in the Name

Paul, an apostle of Christ Jesus by the command of God our Savior and of Christ Jesus our hope (1 Timothy 1:1).

Scripture: 1 Timothy 1:1-7
Song: "In the Name of Jesus"

"Mom!" I cringed as I heard little footsteps coming my way. "Sissy won't turn her music down so I can read."

With hands on my hips, head cocked, and eyes wide, I quietly replied, "You tell Sissy that I said to turn the music off." Moments later, the house was quiet and still.

The reason? Authority. What my youngest couldn't accomplish on his own, he was able to do in my name.

How often do our eyes skip over biblical salutations? Maybe they've become too familiar, or maybe we're anxious to get to the meat of the passage. But as we pause to meditate on *all* of the Scripture's words, the Holy Spirit reveals fresh insight.

The apostle Paul, commanding Timothy to rebuke false teachers, established the authority by which he spoke. Not just a peer, Paul was an apostle appointed by God. This carried the weight needed to convince new converts to turn away from myths and endless genealogies. Standing fast required conviction and grit—and knowing the source of the truth.

False teachings abound in our world today. As we strive to walk in the truth, let us weigh everything we hear against the authority of God's Word.

Dear Father in Heaven, I pray that You might open my eyes to see the false teachings that bombard me every day through television, radio, and other media. Give me discernment, grace, and strength to live true to Your Word. In Jesus' name, amen.

Bittersweet Exchange

For there is one God and one mediator between God and men, the man Christ Jesus, who gave himself as a ransom for all men—the testimony given in its proper time (1 Timothy 2:5, 6).

Scripture: 1 Timothy 2:1-7
Song: "The Old Rugged Cross"

In April of 2009, 19 American sailors escaped to safety when their ship was hijacked at sea. Pirates used hooks and ropes to sneak aboard, firing guns into the air as they climbed up the stern. "Hurry! Lock yourselves into a cabin," the captain ordered. As the crew obeyed, the captain stepped forward to offer his own life in exchange for the freedom of his men.

How difficult it must have been for the crew to obey, allowing their captain to sacrifice his very life. Surely adrenaline flowed and tempers flared. Surely many of the crew wanted to fight back rather than accept the gift of freedom their captain was providing. And how bittersweet once the crew made it to shore, knowing the suffering their captain was undoubtedly experiencing, knowing they might never see him alive again.

Many years ago, Christ came from Heaven to sacrifice His life for us. As we read the story of His crucifixion, we cringe, not wanting even to imagine the pain He endured for our freedom. How bittersweet to receive the gift of salvation in exchange for His agony. How precious to know He paid our debt in full.

Dear Heavenly Father, thank You for the costly sacrifice You made for my life, giving Your Son as a ransom. Thank You for His atoning work—and for His rising again to proclaim my freedom and salvation. In His precious name, amen.

What an Example!

[Be] eager to serve; not lording it over those entrusted to you, but being examples to the flock (1 Peter 5:2b, 3).

Scripture: 1 Peter 5:1-5
Song: "All Glory, Laud and Honor"

In 1937, 27-year-old British journalist George Hogg slipped through enemy lines to expose Japanese occupation in China. He photographed countless villagers who'd been slaughtered. But before George got the truth out, he was captured and sentenced to death—only to be rescued by resistance leaders and sent to a mountain orphanage far from enemy lines.

Against all odds, George poured himself into mentoring 70 starving war-orphaned boys. Starting with no food, medicines, or writing materials, he and the boys created a compound with classrooms, vegetable gardens, and even basketball courts.

In 1940, Japanese soldiers tried to force the older boys to fight and threatened to take over the compound. George then undertook an impossible journey during the coldest winter in 20 years. He moved 60 boys 700 miles over the mountains, through snow and sand storms, to a town near the Gobi Desert.

Most of the boys survived. When interviewed as elderly men, they said, "George was kind and firm; he became a friend. We just followed him."

Heavenly Father, help me to be an example to follow for someone younger in the faith. I know I can only do it as You give me Your wisdom that I might share it with others. In Jesus' name, amen.

March 7–13. **SanDee Hardwig** is a retired English teacher who lives and writes in Brown Deer, Wisconsin, with her two perky cats, Odie and Milo.

Rescued!

Those who guide this people mislead them, and those who are guided are led astray (Isaiah 9:16).

Scripture: Isaiah 9:13-17
Song: "Hosanna"

It was a dry season; most small bodies of water had dried up. In the midst of Highway 43's heaviest traffic, a mother duck led seven ducklings up the meridian. Where had she laid her eggs? Vehicles zoomed past as the ducks waddled straight ahead.

The determined mother and trusting babies stuck in my heart. I drove back, hoping they'd made it to a patch of grass. All I found was smeared blood and feathers.

A few days later, a neighbor and I rescued nine other misguided ducklings following their mother across busy streets. We put them in a box, and the mother came willingly. She seemed to know that we were helping. We released them at the edge of Milwaukee River. What joy in seeing them swim away! Like us, they would not have made it without a helping hand, someone to guide them.

We are all both guides and followers throughout our lives. Whether one misleads others unintentionally, like the mother ducks, or deliberately leads others astray, as in Isaiah (v. 16), those who are misled can be hurt or injured. God promises never to lead us astray. "For this God is our God, for ever and ever; he will be our guide, even to the end" (Psalm 48:14).

Merciful God, forgive me for being a poor example to others. Thank You for Your tender mercy, for sending Jesus, whose sacrifice makes it possible for us to become more like Him. In Jesus' name, amen.

Selfless Service?

[An elder] must hold firmly to the trustworthy message as it has been taught, so that he can encourage others by sound doctrine and refute those who oppose it (Titus 1:9).

Scripture: Titus 1:5-9
Song: "Hallelujah to the Lamb"

The senior minister dismissed several trusted elders, refusing any ideas except his own. After much prayer, 75 per cent of the members left the church as "walking wounded." I myself visited other churches, still finding it difficult to trust again. But when I found my new church, I felt safe.

What a blessing to find a church where so many serve one another and serve in missions throughout the city! What a blessing to find a growing church where the teachings are biblically based and Christ-centered. Where elders and members work together and worship together in harmony, emphasizing the necessity of prayer and the enabling of God's Spirit.

Leadership in the church is a solemn and sacred responsibility, not to be taken lightly. The apostle Paul gave Titus an important task: to find faithful men whom he could appoint as elders in towns across Crete. He would need to find men who were "self-controlled, upright, holy and disciplined" (v. 8). And, as I found even in our own day, it helps if such ministers have learned to put their own pride aside, making selfless service their ultimate goal.

Lord God, I pray for all elders, deacons, and other church leaders. Help them find daily encouragement in the Scriptures, in the abiding presence of Your Spirit, and in kind words from those whom they serve. In Jesus' name, amen.

Lending a Hand

Do not forget to entertain strangers, for by so doing some people have entertained angels without knowing it (Hebrews 13:2).

Scripture: Hebrews 13:1-7
Song: "Friends in High Places"

Heavy rain poured down. Lightning flashed across the sky. Windshield wipers were inadequate that night, but something caught my attention as I turned into my condo complex. A mother huddled over her small son, shielding him from the storm, so I stopped and asked why they were there.

They were running from an abusive father. Terrified to go home, ashamed to ask for help, the mother sobbed, "He has my baby!" I took the frightened pair to my place to dry off —and to call the police.

After the police forced the father's apartment door open, subdued him, and loaded him into a patrol car, an officer placed the wailing infant in his mother's arms. He was hungry and scared, but unharmed. I never saw them again.

"Weren't you afraid to get involved?" a neighbor asked me.

"Yes, I was afraid," I said, " but they were hurting. I couldn't leave them in the rain."

Do you ever wonder whether you should get involved with a stranger in need? Use wisdom and common sense in making your decision. But also remember the words of Hebrews 13:2.

Dear Lord, thanks for seeing my need, rescuing me, and never leaving nor forsaking me. Give me the courage to go beyond my comfort zone in helping others in need around me. In the name of Jesus, my Savior, I pray. Amen.

High Expectations

Obey your leaders and submit to their authority. They keep watch over you as men who must give an account. Obey them so that their work will be a joy, not a burden, for that would be of no advantage to you (Hebrews 13:17).

Scripture: Hebrews 13:17-25
Song: "Follow On"

Andrew S. Douglas was a fine man and a great school principal. I was blessed to land my first teaching job under his leadership. He ran with integrity the inner-city schools he headed. And I've never known anyone as full of energy and purpose. He was the first and last person in the school building each day.

He was tough when he had to be, but he had a heart of gold. He personally signed birthday cards for each student and teacher. He had high expectations of both teachers and students. Those whose hearts were not into teaching found him a hard taskmaster, but those who taught from their hearts truly respected and trusted him. In fact, I used to joke, "If Andrew Douglas assured us it would help our students, we would run through a brick wall."

It's wonderful to have leaders that inspire and help us. But the writer of Hebrews tells us that we also have a responsibility to our leaders. We can choose whether to make their job easier or more difficult. It all depends on whether we take up the attitude of Jesus himself—the attitude of servanthood.

Lord, You call me to obey those in authority over me. I desire to live honorably according to Your will. Give me the wisdom and discernment to recognize godly leaders. And remind me to pray wholeheartedly for them. Through Christ I pray. Amen.

Heartfelt Pledges

If I am delayed, you will know how people ought to conduct themselves in God's household, which is the church of the living God, the pillar and foundation of the truth (1 Timothy 3:15).

Scripture: 1 Timothy 3:14-16
Song: "Stand Up for Jesus"

When I began teaching, each day began with pledging allegiance to the American flag. Some students paid no attention during the pledge: some ignored it, others talked, threw paper, and fooled around. I determined my students would take it seriously. After some retraining and explaining, when the bell rang, my students pledged the flag daily.

One morning, the principal stopped me on the way to homeroom. While he was talking, the bell rang. I turned and ran to my classroom. Thinking something must be wrong, he ran after me. When we got there, all my students were standing and pledging the flag. I was thrilled, so proud of them. (Later, the principal asked, "How did you get them to do that?")

The apostle Paul poured his heart into the people he led to Christ. He taught and helped set up churches. When Paul was unable to be with them, he sent instructions so people would know how to conduct themselves in God's household, whether he was with them or not (vv. 14-16). Scriptural guidance helps us live godly lives and be examples to others.

Dear God, without You, I can do nothing right. For I continue sinning even when I am determined not to sin. Forgive me for my selfishness and mess-ups. Teach me to be more like You. Help me to help others get to know You. In Jesus' name, amen.

What Kind of Leader?

If anyone sets his heart on being an overseer, he desires a noble task. Now the overseer must be above reproach (1 Timothy 3:1, 2).

Scripture: 1 Timothy 3:1-13
Song: "O to Be Like Thee"

Susan managed a well-known retail store, and her employees loved working with her. Why? Because Susan created great working teams with her employees, teaching, encouraging, and supporting them. In return, her employees worked together, encouraging and supporting one another. Susan was named "Manager of the Year," receiving a plaque and a promotion. Now she trains managers for the company.

The new manager was a harsh overseer, however, who never encouraged and always seemed to downgrade her employees. She stood around giving orders, frequently threatening to fire people. One day she angrily mentioned her divorce and called her children "a pain in the neck." Within a few short weeks, most of the employees had quit.

Today's Scripture calls church leaders to be much more like Susan than the angry, self-centered manager. And they must begin in their own homes, showing themselves to be wise and even-tempered there, long before they may qualify for sacred responsibility in the household of God.

O Lord, thank You for loving me, forgiving my sins, and being the perfect overseer of my life. Whenever you place me in positions of leadership, remind me of the wisdom that flows from Your Word. May I depend on that written Word—and the Living Word, Jesus—as I attempt to influence others for You. In Christ's name, amen.

Loving the Word

You whom I love and long for, my joy and crown, . . . stand firm in the Lord, dear friends! (Philippians 4:1).

Scripture: Philippians 3:17–4:1
Song: "I Stand Amazed"

Sometimes Ms. Judy wondered if her hours of preparation generated significant "takeaway" for her kindergarten Sunday schoolers. Five energetic, near-perfect attenders comprised Ms. Judy's class, and they brought vivid imaginations to their acted-out Scripture stories. Small in number but mighty in excitement, each delighted in choosing a character. At Christmas time, Ms. Judy herself portrayed Mary when the only little girl—Taylor, dressed in dark green velvet—fell to the floor and became the lowly manger donkey.

In the spring, though, the humble little actress auditioned for an unscripted role. In an encounter between Jesus and a certain tax collector, Taylor again assumed her spot beneath the crayon table. "If Zacchaeus had a donkey, I'm it!" she blurted as Carson stood atop the sycamore tree that resembled a chair and Lance, stroking an imaginary beard, spoke a love-filled imperative: "Zacchaeus, come down!" The veteran teacher, not recalling a donkey in Luke's account, nevertheless appreciated the children's desire to stand firm amidst the wonders of God's Word.

Heavenly Father, I bow my heart so as never to outgrow the wonder of Your having made room in Scripture just for me. Do keep me childlike in faith and obedience! In the name of Christ I pray. Amen.

March 14–20. **Kay King** writes from Texas' Sky King Ranch, where she and her husband, Ben, enjoy church, grandkids, cattle roundups, and travel.

Will You Help in His Name?

When he returned, having received the kingly power, he commanded these servants, to whom he had given the money, to be called to him, that he might know what they had gained by trading (Luke 19:15, *Revised Standard Version*).

Scripture: Luke 19:12-23
Song: "In the Service of the King"

Laurie Beth Jones, in her book *Jesus in Blue Jeans,* describes a World War II Italian statue of Christ. Noting hands and feet broken off, a tourist scrawled his resolve on a nearby sign: "*We will be His hands and feet.*"

When Jesus ascended back to Heaven, He left His disciples much work to do before His return. Akin to those servants in this parable, we too are expected to invest our gifts wisely, wherever we may be, until Christ comes back for us.

These days, when I think of who has been the "hands and feet of Jesus" for me, I recall my childhood, my sister, and our daily walks with Mary, our aunt's housekeeper. Thin and gracefully clad in a long print dress, she first straightened her blue bandana and then firmly held restless hands as trains rumbled through the village. All the while, our serene mentor smiled warmly, a strange peace emanating down upon two open-hearted kids. Since then, I have received—through the Holy Spirit—a precious treasure this lady invested. Could my salvation have come through her prayers?

Lord, please make me aware of those around me who need intercessory prayer today. And, if I find someone in any other need, let me be your hands and feet to help. In the name of Jesus, my Savior, I pray. Amen.

Empty-handed Faith

David said to all the assembly, "Now bless the LORD your God." So all the assembly blessed the LORD God of their fathers, and bowed their heads and prostrated themselves before the LORD and the king (1 Chronicles 29:20, *New King James Version*).

Scripture: 1 Chronicles 29:18-25
Song: "Blessed Lord, in Thee Is Refuge"

For several years after I had graduated from Baylor University, a strange recurring dream stole my sleep. In the dream, a math professor handed me a final exam—in spite of the fact that I hadn't attended a single class!

Preparation for testing is never just optional, and neither is preparation for victorious praying. Even though my belief had long been rooted and grounded in God's promises, often I failed to receive answers to my prayers. One day the Lord reminded me of that persistent dream, and I began to recognize the barrier between believing and receiving. Hadn't I ignored some essential preparation time?

In her steadfast walk with the Savior, Corrie ten Boom admonished Christians to hold everything up to Him with an open hand—not only earthly possessions but also burdens and worries. As I purposed to release—throw away—my own doubts and fears, I gained renewed faith. I was able to bless the Lord again with heartfelt praise.

Father, help me to set aside time every day simply to come into Your presence, to speak and to listen. I glorify You right now with empty-handed faith. In the holy name of Jesus, my Lord and Savior, I pray. Amen.

Stay Safe in His Care

Take heed to yourselves, lest your heart be deceived, and you turn aside and serve other gods and worship them (Deuteronomy 11:16, *New King James Version*).

Scripture: Deuteronomy 11:13-21
Song: "A Safe Stronghold Our God Is Still"

Tag Head Description Comments Buyer CD Weight Price Amount. Each heading on the cattle auction sales sheet seemed routine except one. Under "Comments," a terse term named a serious problem in our business operation: "Bucking." The buyer had apparently never known a renegade like the one we'd named "Little Crazy." She strayed, refused range cubes, and bucked wildly. Yet never had she displayed more unruly stamina than the morning we loaded for her auction.

As my husband, Ben, bolted the metal latch on her stall, she vaulted out through a small opening in the trailer top, her hooves missing Ben's head by mere inches. After thanking God, we phoned Jesse, a cowboy welder who forged bars to confine our crazy little calf.

As sinners, we too can "turn aside" and jump out of God's will. Then we get a little crazy, perhaps making one poor decision after another. But the Scripture calls us to take heed to ourselves, to watch out for things that may distract us. In other words, why not stay safe in the shelter of our Lord's love?

Gracious God, I am glad You first loved me enough to invite me to salvation through the redeeming blood of Your Son, Jesus. The longer I serve You, the more I cherish Your provision in every part of my day. May I never wish to bolt away from Your care! In the name of my Savior, Jesus Christ, amen.

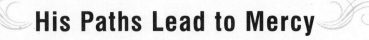

His Paths Lead to Mercy

All the paths of the LORD are mercy and truth, to such as keep His covenant and His testimonies (Psalm 25:10, *New King James Version*).

Scripture: Psalm 25:1-10
Song: "A Perfect Path of Purest Grace"

Visiting a country church potluck dinner, I savored good barbeque and asked who led the congregation. A man in his early 40s, wearing camouflage, replied, "God calls me Butch." Soon I would understand how closely this truck-driver minister traveled with his Lord.

When he was diagnosed with stage-four cancer, Butch underwent radical surgery and chemotherapy. Yet he preached at his dad's funeral, and continued to feed his flock.

Butch drew deeply from divine wells of strength. Facing sleeplessness he spent long nights worshiping Jesus, one moment after another. He let Heaven's love press through hopelessness, persuaded that God somehow would receive the glory.

Months of arduous treatment ensued, but Butch saw his path as a "path of the Lord"—one that led to real life. In fact, one day he looked to June, his radiant wife, and whispered a quotation from Watchman Nee: "Only resurrection life can pass through the Cross and survive."

Almighty and most merciful God, thank You for the blessed assurance that Christ has already walked this path before me. I have received Him as my champion, and now I choose to walk in Him, one step at a time. Lord, You lead, and I will follow. In the name of Jesus, who lives and reigns with You and the Holy Spirit, one God, now and forever, amen.

My Hero

Love is patient, love is kind. It does not envy, it does not boast, it is not proud (1 Corinthians 13:4).

Scripture: 1 Corinthians 13:1–14:1.
Song: "Give of Your Best to the Master"

Only the pronunciation of "hero" has changed since our son Kyle called his minister "Brudder Hinton." Though the boys smuggled GI Joe toys into church, they took home unforgettable values from Jimmy Hinton's sermons. For instance, he stated that the value of no family Christmas gift ever exceeded their offering to help the needy. It was a principle this man lived, both in good times and even in tragic ones.

On Valentine's Day 2003, en route to a concert, the church's chartered bus lost control and overturned during a violent thunderstorm. Our minister's first conscious realization confirmed that his beloved wife of more than 50 years had died upon impact. While I cannot imagine how he must have committed his companion to God, he proceeded to do what heroes always do—help others unselfishly. In spite of personal injuries, this man went about the dreadful scene doing good, until he was himself hospitalized.

At Dolores's memorial service, Brother Hinton turned a tear-stained face upward and affirmed, with a deliberate nod, the soloist's lyrics—"The Anchor Holds." Perhaps it was Jimmy and Dolores's final "amen" to a love that would never let them go.

Thank You, **Precious Lord,** for placing such a special reflection of Your kindness in my church family. Give me the patience and kindness to support and encourage all who suffer. In Jesus' name I pray. Amen.

God-Room Trust

We trust in the living God, who is the Savior of all men, especially of those who believe (1 Timothy 4:10, *New King James Version*).

Scripture: 1 Timothy 4:6-16
Song: "It Took a Miracle"

When Mary and Loretta left Ohio to attend a women's faith conference at Duquesne University, neither suspected it would be a "God-room" adventure. (In *Rebel With a Cause*, Franklin Graham explains this term as an impossible undertaking made possible only by God.)

The women had to park several blocks from the arena but were rewarded by wonderful inspirational faith messages. But after the final session, they returned to Mary's car to make a shocking discovery. The entire back panel of the silver Riviera had been heavily damaged. Disappointed, they began their journey home. But the distance proved exactly what they needed for a single prayer: "Lord, please make this car like new."

Hours later, inside Mary's garage, the two opened car doors to see, in their words, "just how bad the hit-and-run wreck really was." But even before doubt could weaken trust, God must have smiled and found room to perform a miracle. Indeed, the car was like new—undented, unscratched, and undoubtedly the recipient of a daring prayer of faith.

O God, Creator of Heaven and earth, I know faith comes by hearing, and hearing by the Word of God. I rededicate my trust in You, the only one who overrules the impossible by powerful mercy—and apparently by divine delight. In the name of my Savior, Jesus Christ, amen.

How Will You Be Remembered?

They chose Stephen, a man full of faith and of the Holy Spirit; also Philip, Procorus, Nicanor, Timon, Parmenas, and Nicolas from Antioch, a convert to Judaism (Acts 6:5).

Scripture: Acts 6:1-6
Song: "The Love of God"

In an old cemetery in Los Angeles, there is a tombstone with these simple words, "That's All Folks!" The tombstone is for Mel Blanc, the voice of cartoon character Bugs Bunny. Those words made Blanc famous and are what he is most remembered for today. Even though he's been dead for over two decades, his life and words are still remembered.

Most people, particularly those who consider themselves young and vibrant, don't spend much time considering how they will be remembered. But advancing age (and mortality) play an important role in helping us consider the seriousness of everyday actions. One day the only thing people will have of us is a memory, and today we control what that memory will be.

No matter how well we live our lives, one day all of us will need a tombstone. What that tombstone says about us will depend on how we live today. Wouldn't it be great to have a tombstone that reads, "Full of faith and of the Holy Spirit"?

God, You know my actions and my motivations. There is nothing in the world that is hidden from Your eyes. Empower me with Your Holy Spirit to live a life that causes people to remember You when they remember me. In Jesus' name, amen.

March 21–27. **Aaron Sharp** is a graduate of Dallas Theological Seminary and lives in Little Elm, Texas, with his wife Elaina and their puppy Ruthie Jo.

Ready for the Unexpected?

But understand this: If the owner of the house had known at what hour the thief was coming, he would not have let his house be broken into (Luke 12:39).

Scripture: Luke 12:35-40
Song: "Soon and Very Soon"

The knock on my door that disturbed my sleep just before 2 AM was quite unwelcome. My dad always told me that nothing good happens after midnight and, at that point in my life, I had just started to agree with him. Still, the knock on the door of my seminary dorm room was persistent, and so I reluctantly answered it.

I soon discovered that the person knocking so loudly did indeed have bad news for me. My vehicle, along with several others, had been burglarized in the dormitory parking lot.

Questions flooded my mind. Why had I parked in that spot? What had been stolen? And . . . what could I have done to prevent this crime?

If only I had known that someone was planning to break into my truck, I could have been ready. It's like that with the second coming of Christ. His return will be unexpected, because no one knows the day or hour. The Scriptures promise it will come, but at a time that will take the world by surprise. Will you be ready for the unexpected when it comes?

Almighty and gracious Father, I thank You that, unlike me, You know the future, and nothing is a surprise to You. Help me to live a life that is honoring to You and always ready for the return of Your son, Jesus. In the holy name of Jesus, my Lord and Savior, I pray. Amen.

Stay Focused on His Leading

Thus you nullify the word of God by your tradition that you have handed down. And you do many things like that (Mark 7:13).

Scripture: Mark 7:9-13
Song: "Wonderful Words of Life"

The story has been told of a mother teaching her daughter how to cook the family ham for Christmas. In training her daughter, Mom instructed her to always cut off several inches of the end of the ham before she put it into the pan and then into the heated oven. The girl asked her mom why they always trimmed the end of the ham. The mom thought for a moment and finally replied, "I don't know; that is just what your grandmother taught me to do."

Later that day, Mom was still thinking about her daughter's question, so she called her elderly mother. "Why did we always cut off the end of the ham?" she asked. The answer she got surprised her: "Because our pan was too short."

Isn't it the same with many of our traditions? We carry out the old actions, the comfortable rituals, simply because "we've always done it that way before."

If we aren't careful, we can put human traditions—our beloved and well-meaning habits—in the place of heartfelt obedience to God's leading each day. No matter how well-meaning, nothing can replace that moment by moment following.

Dear God, help me to be sensitive to You and Your words. Guide me with Your Spirit and help me to discern between human tradition and Your inspired revelation. Keep my mind discerning and my faith sincere. In the name of my Savior, amen.

A Glimpse of God

Keep all my decrees and all my laws and follow them. I am the LORD (Leviticus 19:37).

Scripture: Leviticus 19:31-37
Song: "I Stand in Awe"

Most everyone can relate to this experience: You're driving down the road, minding your own business, and then it happens. As you round a curve, you see the black and white car with the red and blue lights. You may not even be speeding, but your heart begins to race; suddenly, there is a huge lump in your throat.

So why the sudden dread? Whether you are speeding or not, as you pass the police vehicle you still check your rearview mirror to see if you're being pulled over.

No doubt, this reaction occurs because of a respect and reverence for the power and authority in that police car. You know the officer can pull you over, give you a ticket, or even take you to jail. That kind of power demands respect—by our actions.

When we catch a glimpse of God's power, it should also influence our actions. It should make us attentive to the needs of others, form us into people of integrity, and keep us sincere followers of God's laws. But the great thing is that such "fear of the Lord" isn't the primary motive for our service to Him. No, ultimately, it's our deep gratitude for His love that moves us to give our whole life to Him.

Lord, You are wonderful, powerful, and Lord of all. I pray that I would see You for who You are and that it would change the way I live and treat my fellow human beings. In Jesus' name I pray. Amen.

Total Commitment

Calling his disciples to him, Jesus said, "I tell you the truth, this poor widow has put more into the treasury than all the others. They all gave out of their wealth; but she, out of her poverty, put in everything—all she had to live on" (Mark 12:43, 44).

Scripture: Mark 12:41-44
Song: "I Surrender All"

Secret Service agents are a unique set of individuals. They work every day knowing that, should the occasion arise, they will need to protect—with the possible sacrifice of their own lives—the life of the president of the United States. If there were to be an attempt on the life of the president, the job of a secret service agent is to do what is necessary to save him. If that means stepping in front of a bullet, so be it.

Complete and total commitment to their cause is the key to these agents' success. Their devotion to their mission means they can have no hesitation or pause when it comes time to fulfill their duties.

As followers of Christ, suppose our lives exhibited the same commitment? The poor widow gave what she had to the Lord—*everything* she had. There is a very real sense in which we are called to do the same. It means laying our most cherished wants and plans before the Lord, and asking Him to take them, shape them, mold them. We trust it all to Him.

Almighty God, I know that there are many things in my life that would prevent me from being totally committed to You and Your will for my life. Show me the thing that keeps me from walking close to You today. In Jesus' name, amen.

Why Sink Somebody?

Besides, they get into the habit of being idle and going about from house to house. And not only do they become idlers, but also gossips and busybodies, saying things they ought not to (1 Timothy 5:13).

Scripture: 1 Timothy 5:9-16
Song: "Now Let Every Tongue Adore Thee"

During the Second World War, the United States published a now famous poster. The poster showed a red sky above dark blue ocean, with a black ship sinking into the ocean. Smoke billowed up from the plummeting vessel. There were only four words underneath the image: "Loose Lips Sink Ships."

The poster reminded people that, particularly during war time, certain nefarious folks are always listening, hoping to hear someone spouting sensitive information. Someone being loose with their lips might let information slip that the enemy could then use to battlefield advantage.

These days, maybe we should hang such posters on the doorways to our churches! The devil is ready, willing, and eager to take advantage of our "loose lips" concerning brothers and sisters in Christ. It is human nature to enjoy having the inside story. But it is honoring to God not to pass such things along.

Today I'm going to think about some of the ways I could speak words that are edifying, words that won't sink the heart of anyone I know (or don't know).

Father, I confess to You that my mouth has spoken words that should never have been said. Enable me to become a more mature child of Yours in my speech. May I speak words that are useful and not harmful. In Jesus' name I pray. Amen.

Work: An Act of Faith

If anyone does not provide for his relatives, and especially for his immediate family, he has denied the faith and is worse than an unbeliever (1 Timothy 5:8).

Scripture: 1 Timothy 5:1-8, 17-22
Song: "Work, for the Night Is Coming"

As a child I never had to look far for an example of a solid work ethic. Both of my parents showcased it in spades. During my senior year in high school, my dad—who was a high school teacher, football coach, basketball coach, athletic director, church song leader, and Sunday school teacher—took a part-time job as a grocery checker at the local store where I worked as a bagger.

My dad didn't take on the extra job for his health, or because he needed a hobby. He took it because our family needed the money to make ends meet. My dad was an educated, intelligent, and hard working man. Yet we still ended up needing the few hours of minimum wage employment that he squeezed out every week.

Taking care of his family, even in a job that was far from pleasurable, was something that God had given him to do as a father. Eventually I would realize that my father's actions were really an extension of his faith.

O God, the King of glory, let me never take for granted the ways You provide for me. Bring those times to my mind often, and always make me grateful for the many people in my life who have provided for me when I could not provide for myself. And when it comes to providing for those who depend on me, keep me aware that it is a step of faith simply to do my work with honest effort. Through Christ, amen.

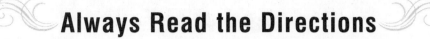

Always Read the Directions

You killed the author of life, but God raised him from the dead. We are witnesses of this (Acts 3:15).

Scripture: Acts 3:11-16
Song: "Day by Day"

I hope this will not be too indelicate for you, Dear Reader—but I find spiritual principles in the strangest places. Anyway, here's what happened . . . "You messed it up, Grandma," Sarah, age 7, accused me. "It's ruined."

We had stopped at a restroom in O'Hare International Airport before boarding. The newly installed commodes flushed automatically—and then automatically put in place a pristine tube of paper which wrapped itself around the entire seat. No germ spreading here! However, having failed to read all the directions, I tried to "help" the protective sleeve by pulling on it.

I thought about it later, in spiritual terms: Don't I sometimes allow the germs of sin to spread in my life? I have the protective covering Christ offers through His atoning blood. But unless I accept His grace, and walk in it daily, sin creeps in.

When I fail to read His word or commune with Him in song, quietness, or prayer, I once again kill the author of my spiritual life, as the Scripture says, and ignore His love for me. Then I need to go back, read all the directions . . . and follow them.

Dear Lord, jar me out of my rush to keep up with the things of this world. Mold me into a faithful servant who acknowledges Your love. In Jesus' name I pray. Amen.

March 28–31. **Margaret Steinacker**, of Winimac, Indiana, teaches a creative writing class and has served with her husband as ministers of music for over 40 years.

Grace Alone

Through him and for his name's sake, we received grace and apostleship to call people from among all the Gentiles to the obedience that comes from faith (Romans 1:5).

Scripture: Romans 1:1-7
Song: "Grace Alone"

As an adult education teacher for 30 years, I used acronyms to help students remember certain facts. Described as letters to jog one's memory, acronyms can be quite useful in the learning process. I still use HOMES. It helps me remember the Great Lakes—Huron, Ontario, Michigan, Erie, Superior. Online dictionaries offer as many as 600,000 acronyms.

Six years ago my husband and I received a call from a different church than the one where we had been ministers of music for over 30 years. On our first Sunday at the new church, the minister used this acronym for GRACE: God's Riches At Christ's Expense. I had been in church my entire life, but never heard this acronym. If we ponder *grace* with this explanation, it begins to sink into the depths of our souls. The Christ-paid expense cost Him everything—His very life.

Today's Scripture clearly conveys this idea. Through obedience that comes from faith, we receive grace—a grace only God can supply. This grace infuses our souls with encouragement, hope, and rightness in our relationship with God.

Father, I pray to comprehend the enormity of Your grace, for it is by the grace You provide that I gain strength to live in Your will. I thank You for being my cornerstone, for allowing me to go forth, even if in pain. And I thank You for helping me to turn my sorrows into praise. In Jesus' name, amen.

Renewed by Mercy

He saved us, not because of righteous things we had done, but because of his mercy. He saved us through the washing of rebirth and renewal by the Holy Spirit, whom he poured out on us generously through Jesus Christ our Savior (Titus 3:5, 6)

Scripture: Titus 3:1-7
Song: "At Calvary"

Many years ago an industry in our small town hired a new vice president named Urban. My friend, the human resources director, had to bow to numerous changes this man thought imperative to good business. Even if they were needed, his demanding methods turned employees toward mutiny. My friend, being a peacemaker, tried to joke about the changes by calling the man Urban Renewal. In the 70s and 80s this pun brought laughter and relieved some of the employees' stresses.

Urban's renewal methods left much to be desired. However, the method Christ uses to renew us in body, mind, and spirit comes by washing away our sins. Then He fills us with the Holy Spirit as we commit our lives totally to Him. We are saved only by His mercy, for we could do none of this for ourselves.

Mercy, best described as "compassion shown by one person to another" isn't practiced much in our world today. But heavenly Father practices it with His children every day of their lives.

Dear Lord, make me ever so grateful for Your amazing mercy. Open my eyes to the wonders You offer me as I accept Your salvation. Thank You for pouring out your Holy Spirit to lead and guide me daily. And give me opportunities to share Your mercy with those I meet today. I love You! In the holy name of Jesus, amen.

Communion with Christ

This is the blood of the covenant, which is poured out for many for the forgiveness of sins (Matthew 26:28).

Scripture: Matthew 26:17-30
Song: "Come, Share the Lord"

Generally speaking, a covenant is an agreement, a contract, a treaty, a promise, or a pledge. For many of us, marriage remains the best representation of a covenant we can imagine. However, the breakup of so many marriages causes us pain. When the covenant breaks, hurts abound for everyone involved.

None of the above definitions really does justice to the covenants God spoke of in His Word. Nor do they allow us to visualize the depths to which our Lord suffered to make His covenant with us. Our finite minds cannot imagine Christ's pain—especially in His "made himself nothing" to become fully human among us (see Philippians 2:7).

The movie *The Passion of the Christ* gives us a partial picture of His sufferings, but historians say the death by crucifixion defies understanding in today's world. Yet it was more than the physical suffering for Christ. Imagine the glories of Heaven that He gave up in order to align His nature of full diety with full humanity.

Christ, in His mercy, accepts our trust in forgiveness through His blood. Each time we partake of the Lord's supper we need to renew our covenant to follow Him in ever increasing faithfulness.

Father, at times I fail to connect with You as I should during communion. Help me to grasp Your hand and walk through the suffering with You, knowing that where You lead I will follow with a glad heart. Through Christ, amen.

DEVOTIONS®

April

/God . . . made his light shine in our hearts to give us the light of the knowledge of the glory of God in the face of Christ.

—2 Corinthians 4:6

Gary Allen, Editor   **Margaret Williams,** Project Editor   Photo © Rvs | Dreamstime.com

DEVOTIONS® is published quarterly by Standard Publishing, Cincinnati, Ohio, www.standardpub.com. © 2010 by Standard Publishing. All rights reserved. Topics based on the Home Daily Bible Readings, International Sunday School Lessons. © 2007 by the Committee on the Uniform Series. Printed in the U.S.A. All Scripture quotations, unless otherwise indicated, are taken from the *HOLY BIBLE, NEW INTERNATIONAL VERSION*®. *NIV*®. Copyright © 1973, 1978, 1984 by Biblica, Inc.™ Used by permission of Zondervan. All rights reserved. *New American Standard Bible (NASB),* © The Lockman Foundation, 1960, 1962, 1963, 1968, 1971, 1972, 1973, 1975, 1977, 1995.

Just a Name?

Whoever eats the bread or drinks the cup of the Lord in an unworthy manner will be guilty of sinning against the body and blood of the Lord. A man ought to examine himself before he eats of the bread and drinks of the cup (1 Corinthians 11:27, 28).

Scripture: 1 Corinthians 11:23-32
Song: "I Am His, and He Is Mine"

When the pregnancy occurred, he left Anya. "Being a husband is one thing, but I don't want the responsibility of being a father," he said. So Anya has raised Emily by herself.

Now that Emily is 5, her birth father has made contact with Anya. "Maybe I should get to know my daughter," he said. The clincher is this: He called to find out how to spell Emily's name—not so he could send a check, but so that he could get a tattoo! Emily's grandmother said, "You can wear someone's name, but it means nothing if you don't have a relationship."

This ties-in with today's Scripture, doesn't it? It says we are guilty of sinning if we take the bread and cup in an unworthy manner. If we have no personal relationship with Christ, we sin against His body and blood. Just wearing a cross, carrying a Bible, or attending church doesn't give us the relationship we need. Anytime we participate in Communion, let us closely examine our hearts.

Lord, as I come before You today, make me aware of any sins I have committed. May I come to Your Table with a clean heart. In Jesus' name, amen.

April 1–3. **Margaret Steinacker**, of Winimac, Indiana, teaches a creative writing class and has served with her husband as ministers of music for over 40 years.

GPS: God's Personalized Services

We put no stumbling block in anyone's path, so that our ministry will not be discredited (2 Corinthians 6:3).

Scripture: 2 Corinthians 6:1-10
Song: "Make Me a Blessing"

On our first trip using a new GPS, we ended up in front of a boulder. It blocked the frontage road beside the expressway we thought we should take. The GPS lady said, "Turn right."

"Sure," my husband said. He seems to delight in arguing with the GPS, as if she were interactive. Although new, our GPS hadn't been configured with the latest updates. So, we turned around, let the computer lady recalculate six times, and arrived on time for our friends' wedding.

If we want to serve God in the way He asks, we need to make sure we keep our spiritual GPS updated daily. Then we won't be a stumbling block to anyone. Instead, our ministry will be a credit to the love of Christ.

Years ago a friend taught me to go to the house of someone in need (due to sickness or bereavement, for instance) and say, "Would you like me to do the dishes, the laundry, or clean the bathrooms?"

My friend would never ask, "What can I do to help you?" Hearing specific choices, the person in need felt more comfortable accepting the offered help. This method turns us into blessings. Why not try it?

Lord, Keep me from being a stumbling block. Help me to stay so attuned to Your Word that my humble offerings of help will become a blessing. May I never forget, "Now is the time of God's favor, now is the day of salvation." In Jesus' name, amen.

Not Imprisoned, but Free

God's word is not chained (2 Timothy 2:9).

Scripture: 2 Timothy 2:8-19
Song: "Amazing Grace (My Chains Are Gone)"

Have you ever been physically housed in a jail or prison? Perhaps not, nor have I. However, I taught GED classes in two county jails for over 20 years. The feeling of being locked behind steel doors is daunting, even when you know that in three hours you will be released.

I chose to serve in a jail and endured the chained-in, imprisoned feelings for the sake of freeing the inmates' minds through education. But I also wanted to extend God's love for them.

I did not announce, "I am a Christian." They perceived it through my words and actions. Each week I reminded myself of John Bradford's statement, "There, but for the grace of God, go I."

Have you felt your spiritual life is, in a sense, in chains? Sometimes we allow ourselves to be bound by the world. Its schemes take our focus off Christ. Today's Scripture gives hope beyond measure: "God's word is not chained." No matter what our circumstances, God and His Word remain free—free to empower us for His work. So, "if the Son sets you free, you will be free indeed" (John 8:36).

Lord, when I recall how Corrie ten Boom walked into a prison camp with Your Word strapped to her back so she would be able to share it with others, I start to understand the depths of Your love and care. You must have blinded the eyes of the guards. Thank You for giving us Your Word, which may be physically imprisoned, but always available, never chained, and O, so freeing. In the name of Jesus, amen.

Dealing with Stoplights

We are hard pressed on every side, but not crushed; perplexed, but not in despair; persecuted, but not abandoned; struck down, but not destroyed. We always carry around in our body the death of Jesus, so that the life of Jesus may also be revealed in our body (2 Corinthians 4:8-10).

Scripture: 2 Corinthians 4:1-12
Song: "Yield Not to Temptation"

We live in a society afflicted by stoplights. I was in a hurry to get to my appointment, and I hadn't allowed any "wiggle room" before I left the house. It seemed that green lights turned red every time I came to an intersection. I would come to a halt and wait, frustrated by a stoplight that impeded my progress.

Life for us is mostly a matter of coping with the stoplights. We set out, full of hope, to accomplish something that we think is worthwhile. Yet, before we are well on our way, we run into a stoplight.

The way we deal with stoplights will witness to the significance of our faith. Why would we handle them with patience and good cheer? So that "the life of Jesus may also be revealed" in us. The quality of our faith is revealed in the way we cope with what we cannot avoid. Even inconvenient interruptions need not be total disasters—not if we practice the presence of God.

God of time and eternity, when the interruptions invade my day, help me to understand that You can take even the disruptions of my life and create a moment that honors You. In the spirit of Christ, amen.

April 4–10. **Drexel Rankin** served as an ordained minister for more than 35 years. He and his wife, Patty, live in Louisville, Kentucky.

Sand Prints

I have loved you with an everlasting love; I have drawn you with loving-kindness (Jeremiah 31:3).

Scripture: Jeremiah 31:2-9
Song: "O Love That Will Not Let Me Go"

When we are in Florida, my wife and I love to stroll the beach. Early one morning, we walked in the wet sand, the tide ebbing. Occasionally, the outgoing tide would catch me unawares and swirl around my ankles, leaving temporary footprints in the freshly washed sand.

Returning to our condo, I walked further from the water where the sand had begun to warm. As I looked down, I was amazed at all of the prints pushed into the sand. Some were made by bare feet, some made by shoes, some by children, some by heavier adults.

There were deep crosshatch tracks of tractor tires and shallower ruts of bicycles. I could make out the rhythmic-patterned prints of running dogs' paws and the fragile tripod patterns of shore birds that had been foraging washed-up shells.

So many of God's creatures going in so many directions! They each had a different tale, each one crossing the paths of other lives and forming new life stories.

Yet, God keeps an eye on us all. God not only created us, He knows each of us. We may not know where our various paths will lead, but the Lord does. And we can trust His guidance.

God of our lives, help me to trust in Your guidance and Your love for me. May I understand that, no matter what path I might take, Your watchful eye is upon me, keeping me safe in all of life's travels. In the name of Christ, amen.

Temptation!

"Everything is permissible"—but not everything is beneficial. "Everything is permissible"—but not everything is constructive (1 Corinthians 10:23).

Scripture: 1 Corinthians 10:23-31
Song: "Did You Think to Pray?"

Each day, my wife and I walked the 10 blocks from our hotel room to the convention center. We needed the exercise. Walking is both a healthy habit and a means of saving money.

Our route always took us past a chocolate factory. Until the last day, we resisted the temptation to take the advertised free tour. Nevertheless, we finally succumbed and visited the plant to see these wonderful chocolate creations. That was the safe part. We never walked into the manufacturing area. We stayed behind thick viewing windows.

We were determined not to buy anything. We didn't need the sugar, the fat grams, the calories. We wanted only to look from behind secure windows.

But when our tour ended, the doors opened into the sales area. The aroma was incredible. I knew at that moment that this must be what Heaven smelled like. And . . . you guessed it. We left with several boxes of chocolate. (Paul's words should have rung in my ears: "All things are lawful for me, but not all things are beneficial.")

God of strength, God of Glory, when I am weak and tempted, be my companion and my power, the one who moves me through those things that would pull me away from You and the path You want me to walk. In the name of the Father, the Son, and the Holy Spirit, I pray. Amen.

Building a Life

Now I commit you to God and to the word of his grace, which can build you up and give you an inheritance among all those who are sanctified (Acts 20:32).

Scripture: Acts 20:28-35
Song: "I'll Live for Him"

I remember the years when our kids were growing up. At Christmas time, my son would inevitably receive the gift of a kit that needed to be put together.

The instructions were always mind-boggling: put Peg A in Slot B; then fit AB into Groove C; take D and insert it into E; then fold H and line it up with I and J so that they are parallel with K and L. And then . . . well, you get the idea, right? Those kits were not only fascinating; they were supremely challenging. My guess is that such instructions have not become simpler in more recent years.

For me, construction kits are parables of life. I've come to see that God never gives us a completed life. He gives me the raw materials out of which to make life choices. He gives me gifts and abilities. He gives me the world with its beauty and bounty. He gives me the people I live with. And He gives me "the word of his grace."

Then, God invites me—*challenges* me—and says, "Out of these things, go and make life worthwhile. Enrich your life and liberate the lives of the people around you."

Ever-giving God, open my being to receive Your bountiful gifts. Give me the courage to reach for the resources You put before me. Then, fill me with the desire to enrich the lives of others in need of Your healing grace. In the name of Christ, amen.

Praying Effectively

I pray for them. I am not praying for the world, but for those you have given me, for they are yours (John 17:9).

Scripture: John 17:6-19
Song: "Blest Be the Tie That Binds"

Each day I try to pray for members of my family during my morning devotions: my wife, who has made an appointment for a second mammography after a dark spot showed up on her first test; our daughter in Oregon, who worries about her employment and a personal relationship; our son and his family in Indiana as they choose a church home and make decisions about parenting their two children; my cousin's husband, who is in the hospital in Pennsylvania following a recurrence of cancer . . . and the list goes on.

I sometimes feel that I'm not praying effectively for them because I'm not always sure what to pray about—not knowing what their specific needs really are. Occasionally, I finish with the regret that I've forgotten something important.

So, I attempt to remember Jesus' prayer at the last supper when He asked the Father for three things:
- Protect them from the evil one (v. 15)
- Sanctify them by the truth (v. 17)
- Unite them to God and to each other (v. 21)

Protect, sanctify, unite. Those are simple but powerful requests that are easy to remember. When I remember these things in my prayers, I hope I'm covering the bases.

God, You have placed precious people in my life. Help me to love them and be close to them, even as You love them and hold them close to You. In Jesus' name, amen.

Waiting for Life

Be sure to fear the LORD and serve him faithfully with all your heart; consider what great things he has done for you (1 Samuel 12:24).

Scripture: 1 Samuel 12:19-25
Song: "What Wondrous Love Is This?"

In the church where I worship, we are in the midst of Lent. Usually, the message is bleak and stern. Give up something. Forego doing something. Deny yourself. During the season of Lent, those thoughts are real, and they are important. They have been part of the Lenten tradition for centuries.

There is, however, another awareness that fills my spirit. It is exciting and hopeful because, in the agony of Lent, I also prepare for a great celebration. Lent does not mean waiting for death. It is a time of remembering what Christ has done for me—a time of getting ready for new, everlasting life.

Lent is a gift of time and self-awareness. It is a time to purify, to free us of all that gets in the way of the deeper spiritual experience, to remember the great thing that God has done for us. It is more than a time of sacrificing for a few days.

It is a time of knowing, again, that the waiting is not for death. We wait for the birth of the great promise of forgiveness, for remembering God's great gifts, and the signs of God's eternal love.

Gracious God, as I continue my Lenten journey, open my ears to hear Your good news for me and for all of the world. Open my eyes that I may see You in those whom I serve in Your name. Open my heart that I may faithfully believe in Your great gift of eternal life. In the name of Christ, I ask all of this. Amen.

Strength to See Us Through

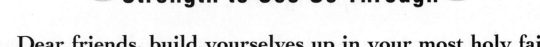

Dear friends, build yourselves up in your most holy faith and pray in the Holy Spirit (Jude 20).

Scripture: Jude 17-25
Song: "It Is Well with My Soul"

They said the trail was "moderate." Just what we wanted! But when my wife and I arrived at the trail head, the path went straight up. This was *moderate?*

Later, we arrived at the end of the trail and enjoyed the view across Jenny Lake from 7,200 feet. We were hot, sweaty, tired. But we had done it, and the exertion was worth it.

Along our way, we found bright yellow daisies blooming in a patch of sunlight. We discovered mountain hollyhocks, Indian paintbrush, alpine paintbrush. We found mushrooms like none we had ever seen. We watched a father and son fly fishing in a mountain stream.

Our hike reminded me that life and our Christian faith are never as simple as we would like. We get easy advice: "Read your Bible." "Pray about it." Those are part of our faith, but they are not talismans or charms. It would be wonderful if, simply by doing those things, we would have all problems solved.

No! It is the discipline of doing those things regularly that provides strength to see us through rough times. Once or twice doesn't cut it. But do those things faithfully, and we find something exhilarating for life and for times that try the soul.

Compassionate God, daily may my face reflect Your compassion, may my heart reflect Your love, may my life provide evidence of Your presence in and among us, through Jesus Christ our Lord, now and forevermore! In Jesus' name, amen.

Cast Your Burden

Cast your burden upon the LORD and He will sustain you; He will never allow the righteous to be shaken (Psalm 55:22, *New American Standard Bible*).

Scripture: Psalm 55:16-22
Song: "Lay It Down"

Mark was a young businessman full of ideals. The account that he had been working on was going to move his career to the next level. On the day he was set to give his presentation, a tragedy occurred within his family. He immediately requested a leave of absence to care for his loved ones. Upon returning to work, he was greeted with the news that his best friend had been promoted to partner. He soon learned that this same friend had taken his work—as well as the credit for it—and had made the presentation while he was away.

In any of our lives, situations can arise that create turmoil. We may become awash in sadness or explode in anger. Such feelings can gain control over our lives and steal our joy and peace in the Lord.

Jesus bids all to come to Him. The same Savior who bore our sins on the cross also asks that we cast our burdens upon Him. The one who has saved us will also sustain us, if we will simply trust in Him.

Father, in days of trial, give me strength to endure the journey set before me. Please help me to be gracious and forgiving, as I have been forgiven. Sustain me, please Lord, through the times of trial. Through Christ I pray. Amen.

April 11–17. **Jeff Short** is a military veteran and has a background in social work. He is a writer, artist, and musician, living in southwest Georgia.

Ever Present Light

Then Hezekiah took the letter from the hand of the messengers and read it, and he went up to the house of the LORD and spread it out before the LORD (2 Kings 19:14, *New American Standard Bible*).

Scripture: 2 Kings 19:14-19
Song: "Lamp of Our Feet, Whereby We Trace"

I had a friend who was a navy helicopter pilot. On one particular day the waves were choppy, and the ship that he was attempting to land on was being tossed violently about. As he was making his final approach, he took his eyes off the instruments for a little while.

Because of his training and experience, he knew this was a mistake, but in the uncertainty of the moment he decided to fly by his own instincts. Just before he nearly collided with the side of the ship, he pulled up sharply and made another pass.

The unpredictability we find in the world can lead us to feel as if we are standing on shifting sands—or trying to land on a wave-tossed ship! It is so important that we keep our minds and eyes focused on God.

The tough times in our lives are, in a sense, like cross roads. We have two choices: we can trust in our own limited judgment, or we can trust in God who cannot be moved or shaken. He alone is our ever-present light. As Hezekiah knew, it is best to bring everything to the Lord and spread it before Him.

Father, help me to spread my life out before You. In the good times and the difficult times, help me to trust in You. In doing so, may I grow ever closer to You, and may Your light shine through my life. Through Christ, amen.

Eternal Spring of Loving Kindness

For He stands at the right hand of the needy, to save him from those who judge his soul (Psalm 109:31, *New American Standard Bible*).

Scripture: Psalm 109:21-31
Song: "How Sweet the Name of Jesus Sounds"

Parents awake suddenly, hearing the frightened voice of their child. The husband reaches over and touches his wife's hand as he gets out of bed. He enters his daughter's room, turns on the lamp, and puts his arms around her. Rocking her gently, he whispers, "It's OK, Sweetheart, Daddy's here." Soon she lays her head back on the pillow. Comforted by her father's presence, she falls fast asleep.

As we travel through the pathways of life, it is certain we will experience trials and hardships. At times these experiences can leave us feeling broken, weak, and in great need. We may feel that the whole world is "down on us," judging us in some way.

We can find comfort in the fact that God is ever present in our lives. We are never alone, and there is absolutely nothing that can separate us from Him and His pleasure in us.

And let us hold this profound grace deep within our hearts and minds: We were not the ones who called out to our heavenly Father; instead, it was He who called out to us. For God so loved us, that He sent His only Son . . . (John 3:16) In the light of Christ, we find an eternal spring of loving-kindness.

Father, help me be ever mindful of Your presence in my life. Assure me that I need not fear or be anxious for anything. For You love me and will always be with me. In Jesus' name I pray. Amen.

Where Can I Go?

To You they cried out and were delivered; in You they trusted and were not disappointed (Psalm 22:5, *New American Standard Bible*).

Scripture: Psalm 22:1-8
Song: "In the Cross of Christ I Glory"

When difficult times come upon us, the experience can be overwhelming. This is especially true when the difficulties persist for long periods of time, perhaps even years. We may begin to focus on the earlier, more pleasant times—and we may well wonder if life will ever be the same. In desperation and in the deepest part of our being, we find ourselves crying out: Will this time of sorrows ever end?

Suffering affects every aspect of our existence. It is certainly personal, yet it also affects those around us. It can be a time of anguish, pain, and feeling of entrapment.

But remember this: Where can I go that God is no longer with me? There is no such place. Jesus said, "I am with you always" (Matthew 28:20).If we ascend to the greatest heights or if we descend to the greatest depths, He is there.

That is why the psalmist can tell us we'll never be disappointed in God, as we trust in Him. If He is near us—and He is omnipotent and all-loving—what should we fear?

Almighty and most merciful God, give me the strength of mind that I might trust You. I know that You are with me and that You alone know and understand the depths of my sorrow. Gracious Lord, give me Your peace until my time of deliverance comes to pass. In the name of Jesus, who lives and reigns with You and the Holy Spirit, one God, now and forever, amen.

Seek Him: All the Time

Seek the LORD and His strength; seek His face continually (1 Chronicles 16:11, *New American Standard Bible*).

Scripture: 1 Chronicles 16:8-18
Song: "The God of Abraham Praise"

For several weeks a mother had noticed her young son talking to himself. At first she thought that it was cute, but as time passed, she began to grow concerned. One morning, as they were walking to school, she asked him if he had an imaginary friend. "No, Mom," the little boy replied. "He isn't imaginary, but He is my friend: His name is Jesus."

As we look around we see the evidence of God's handiwork in His creation. With each breath, each movement, we experience a miracle. It is so easy for us to become distracted by a world that (we are told) holds no transcendent reality. For that reason it becomes even more important for us to spend time seeking and seeing God's face. Continuously we should seek Him, praising Him with joyful hearts for all that He reveals of himself around us.

I like the way Christian writer Frederick Buechner spoke of prayer as available to us all the time: "The odd silence you fall into when something very beautiful is happening or something very good or very bad . . . The stammer of pain at somebody else's pain. The stammer of joy at somebody else's joy. Whatever words or sounds you use for sighing with over your own life. These are all prayers in their way."

Father, thank You for the wonders You have created. May I live in a state of prayerful recognition and thanks, every single day. In the name of Jesus, amen.

Praise from All Places

Have you never read, "OUT OF THE MOUTH OF INFANTS AND NURSING BABES YOU HAVE PREPARED PRAISE FOR YOURSELF"? (Matthew 21:16, *New American Standard Bible*).

Scripture: Matthew 21:12-17
Song: "Blessed Be Your Name"

From the beginning of creation until this day, there remains the same amount of water in our world. To oversimplify the process: water is evaporated, pulled up toward the heavens, and then returns again in various forms of precipitation. This cycle is ongoing and continuous and provides sustenance for all life. This is a natural event, a part of God's plan that exists outside the control of humans.

Our God, who is a God of love, is deserving of all praise. He receives praise from angels in Heaven, from humans on earth, and even by His creation. "The heavens are telling of the glory of God; and their expanse is declaring the work of His hands" (Psalm 19:1, *NASB*). Like the rains that fall from the heavens, this natural event also occurs outside the control of humanity.

And even nursing babies praise Him. And well they should, for they, like us, were given the wonderful gift of life, created in the image and likeness of the creator. Thankfully, this praiseworthy Lord, when we were separated from Him by our sin, pursued us. He provided payment of our sin through the life of His beloved Son—the greatest reason of all to open our mouths in worship.

Father, help me to surrender and live my life in a way that glorifies You. May every thought, word, and deed be praise to You. Through Christ I pray. Amen.

The Fullness of the Gift

Those who went in front and those who followed were shouting, "Hosanna! Blessed is he who comes in the name of the Lord!" (Mark 11:9, *New American Standard Bible*).

Scripture: Mark 11:1-11
Song: "Take Time to Be Holy"

A great musician once admitted that if he missed three days of practice, his fans recognized it. If he missed two days of practice music critics were aware. If he only missed one day of practice, he himself could hear and feel the difference. When we love something, we must embrace it completely in order to experience the fullness of the gift.

It is so easy to get caught up in the day-to-day whirlwind of our lives. There is family, career, finances; the list goes on and on. In the midst of this swirling stew of callings, we may neglect what is most important.

God must take first place in our lives, and our faith must be nurtured. We are like instruments fashioned by our creator in His image. The way that we become what He has intended us to be is to spend time with Him. In doing so, we experience the fullness of the gift He has given.

The people on the road with Jesus made a priority of welcoming Him. What a gift He was! Yet to what extent did the individuals in that crowd truly embrace Him, truly love Him? Some few days later, many there would be in another crowd, shouting for His death.

Father, help me to open the innermost part of my being, so that You are welcome into every place of my heart and life. In the name of Jesus the Lord, amen.

Holding on for Life

By this gospel you are saved, if you hold firmly to the word I preached to you. Otherwise, you have believed in vain (1 Corinthians 15:2).

Scripture: 1 Corinthians 15:1-8
Song: "Tell Me the Story of Jesus"

Some years ago, one of my sons and I were practicing rock climbing at an indoor facility in Lexington, Kentucky. As I tried to make my way around an overhanging projection, I lost my grip and fell. Almost immediately, I felt the jolt of the safety harness and rope.

I dangled briefly between ceiling and floor, grateful that Ben had been paying attention and maintaining a firm grip on the belay. Without his alertness and response, I would have crashed onto the floor and demonstrated rather dramatically, in my own body, the forces of gravity, acceleration, and inertia! I much preferred my brief embarrassment to the alternative: a trip to the emergency room. "Thanks, Bud!" I called to Ben, and then resumed my climb.

If a nylon rope and web harness can spare us from serious injury while climbing mountains, of how much greater value is the word of truth that we have in the gospel? If we must grip firmly what saves our mortal bodies, how much more should we hold mightily to truth that saves our souls?

Help me, **O Lord,** to keep the word of the gospel firmly rooted in my heart. May it always anchor my thoughts and deeds. In Jesus' name, amen.

April 18–24. **Doc (Harold W.) Arnett** conducts institutional research for Highland Community College in Kansas. He and his wife, Randa, live in St. Joseph, Missouri, and have a dozen grandkids.

A Greater Good

[Jesus] said to his disciples, "As you know, the Passover is two days away—and the Son of Man will be handed over to be crucified" (Matthew 26:1, 2).

Scripture: Matthew 26:1-5
Song: "Trust and Obey"

A grandmother's stroke, a father's cancer, a spouse's dementia, a child's suicide—there are any number of announcements that tear into us with all the fury of this world's fears. We gasp for breath, we blanch in shock, we collapse in agony or lash out in anger. These are all deeply natural and completely understandable reactions. I suspect that the reactions of the disciples included all of those responses when Jesus again declared His inevitable suffering.

What He told them, and what He still speaks to us today, is that the will of our Father is not offered up conditioned on our approval or acceptance. Rather, it is our choice as to how we respond to His will. Can we respond in the manner of humble servants, eager above all things to please Him and glorify His name?

Satan moves against us in many ways. Our choices, and those of others around us, often take us onto the path of pain and evil. Yet, God is still at work, even in our worst choices, to bring about good.

Dear Lord and Savior, help me to remember Your choice of obedience and suffering. Help me to realize and to truly trust, that you are at work in every circumstance of my life, to bring about good. I do want to embrace Your will and celebrate Your work in my life. In the name of Jesus, Lord and Savior of all, I pray. Amen.

What Will Your Answer Be?

What shall I do, then, with Jesus who is called Christ? (Matthew 27:22).

Scripture: Matthew 27:15-26
Song: "I Am His, and He Is Mine"

I recently interviewed for an executive position with a small college. Throughout the day, I met with different groups, including the faculty, the search committee, cabinet members, and staff members. Nearly all of the groups had a prepared set of questions, asked in turn by different members of the group. Many of the questions were routine, exactly the sort of thing candidates expect to be asked. As I responded to the questions (hopefully, with thoughtful and effective answers), I couldn't help thinking that some of my answers would be crucial. I knew that some of them would be pivotal in the final recommendation made by each group.

We may ask and/or answer many important questions throughout our lives. But no question will ever rival the one Pilate asked: "What shall I do, then, with Jesus?"

Other questions may determine whether or not we get a job, a date, or even a mate. This question, though, determines whether or not we'll spend this life in the grace of God's fellowship. It will also determine whether or not we spend the next life in His eternal presence.

Dear Lord, You are the Christ, the Son of the Living God, the Lion of Judah, and the slain Lamb of God. You were crucified for my sins, buried and raised up again on the third day, and exalted to the right hand of God. Help me to serve You out of sheer gratitude and joy. I pray through my deliverer, Jesus. Amen.

Overcoming Ego

Those who passed by hurled insults at him (Matthew 27:39).

Scripture: Matthew 27:32-44
Song: "More Love, More Power"

From the time I was a kid, I have always taken pride in my work. Whether I was feeding calves, stacking hay in the barn, or working in the fields, I always tried to do a good job. At school, it was the same: I studied hard and always put a lot of effort into my homework.

Even now, in my career, I take pride in my data gathering, analyses, and reports. I have given numerous presentations over the years at regional, national, and even a few international conferences. I'm always a bit sensitive when someone challenges something I've stated or takes issue with my conclusions. My natural reaction is to become defensive or maybe strike back verbally.

What a contrast to my fleshly nature is Jesus! In spite of having legions of angels at His command, He endured the insults of the crowd. Mocked, spurned, reviled, and abused, He did not respond with accusations or even defensiveness. Instead, He prayed, "Father, forgive them, for they do not know what they are doing" (Luke 23:34). That is the example I need to remember when my ego wants to control my spirit.

Dear Lord, help me to remember Your love, Your patience, Your humility, Your obedience. Help me to choose forgiveness and forbearance instead of retaliation. Help me to bless those who challenge my opinions, who dispute my conclusions, and who argue with my judgment. Help me to choose to imitate You. In Jesus' name, amen.

The Glory of Small Things

Many women were there, watching from a distance. They had followed Jesus from Galilee to care for his needs (Matthew 27:55).

Scripture: Matthew 27:45-56
Song: "I Want to Be a Worker"

From time to time, some congregation, fellowship, or denomination will decide to write its own history. You'll find the names of their preachers, evangelists, elders, and others who have "played important roles" in the history of the group. In a few exceptional histories, you may find mention of influential women of the church.

There are women who taught Sunday school. Some raised sons who entered the ministry. Others played significant roles in the life of men who went on to have great ministries. But there are others, still.

It was Jesus himself who pointed out that whoever gives a cup of cold water in His name will receive a blessing. How much more those who have devoted their lives to encouraging another in service? For example, how long would the ministry of Jesus have lasted without those who followed him, caring for His needs and those of His disciples?

Many men and women receive little attention in this life, and very little mention. But in the kingdom to come, theirs will be the greater honor.

Dear Lord, make me mindful of the hidden ministries that make other ministries possible. Help me to notice the small things of duty and devotion. Help me to honor those less likely to receive honor. In the precious name of Jesus I pray. Amen.

Where Were the Others?

Mary Magdalene and the other Mary were sitting there opposite the tomb (Matthew 27:61).

Scripture: Matthew 27:57-61
Song: "In the Hour of Trial"

What a day of agony and grief it was! The Lord was betrayed, tortured, tried, and executed in the space of 24 hours. He was despised and scorned, crowned with thorns, mocked and beaten and lifted up on a cross like a common criminal! His disciples, filled with fear, had fled. Even bold Peter, who had declared his willingness to die for Jesus, had disappeared.

Where were the crowds who thronged around Him, yelling His praises and begging for healing? Where were the multitudes, eager for the show and the free food? Where were those who had known Him in the intimacy of the darkness, when no one else remained?

Of the thousands who had seen Him, followed Him, declared Him Son of David, only these three attended His burial: Joseph of Arimathea and these two women, Mary Magdalene and the other Mary.

Every disciple's life has seen its moments of determination and its moments of desertion. All have stood, and will stand, in need of the grace given in the Savior's blood. For it is not in the bold words of declaration but in the simple deeds of God-empowered devotion that our faith declares itself.

Dear Lord, help me find in every circumstance the courage and love I need to follow You. Help me when I am inundated by the ways of this world to still be true to You. Help me to be faithful. In the name of Jesus, amen.

When Faith and Fear Unite

So the women hurried away from the tomb, afraid yet filled with joy, and ran to tell his disciples (Matthew 28:8).

Scripture: Matthew 28
Song: "He Hideth My Soul"

The two women who attended Jesus' burial were the same two women who first witnessed His resurrection, according to Matthew's record. Mary Magdalene and the other Mary came to the tomb early on Sunday morning. After the angel told them that Jesus was risen, he sent them on a mission: "Go quickly and tell his disciples" (v. 7). As they hurried off, "afraid yet filled with joy" (v. 8) they encountered the Lord.

What a wonderful mixture of emotions—to be afraid and joyful at the same time! I think of the birth of my first child, of the incredible joy and . . . *responsibility*. As I held Michael, my little miracle, I felt that I would burst with unrestrained happiness. However, at the same time, I thought, "I hope I don't mess this up."

In our salvation, we experience an incredible joy; in our discipleship, we confront our awesome responsibility. We are called to be saved and to go and tell others. We are called to a life of joy and devotion, called to abandon this world and its ways of thinking. We are called to enjoy the love of our Lord and to give Him our whole life.

Dear Lord, I pray that You will so increase my faith that I may be filled with joy in spite of my fear. Help me to embrace the challenges of my life with joyful expectation. Help me to rely upon You and Your Holy Spirit more than my own strength. In the holy name of Jesus, my Lord and Savior, I pray. Amen.

God, Where Are You?

By his wounds you have been healed. For you were like sheep going astray, but now you have returned to the Shepherd and Overseer of your souls (1 Peter 2:24, 25).

Scripture: 1 Peter 2:18-25
Song: "I Need Thee Every Hour"

Little did I know, that as my husband offered devotions at the men's breakfast meeting, he was also telling about our walk through the "land of the unknown." For the second time in five years, our doctor spoke the frightening words "breast cancer" to us. As I moved through testing and surgery, I felt I was walking through a maze—wounded, lost, and alone. I could barely even say the words aloud. I held them close, hidden by my fear and anxiety. "God, where are you?"

Friends began calling to let us know they were praying for us. Our mailbox filled with notes from others willing to prepare meals, drive me to appointments, or even do our laundry. All of their willing hands and prayers brought my wounds to the surface, out into the open.

But my wounded spirit began to heal. The pain didn't go away, but having others walk with me made it all bearable. No more did I wonder where God had gone. Rather, I acknowledged the shepherd's presence in my life, the overseer of my soul.

God, at times I feel lost and alone. I am overwhelmed with fear and pain. Strengthen my weak spirit. Help me to recognize Your presence today. In Jesus' name, amen.

April 25–30. **Viola Ruelke Gommer** is a retired nurse, photographer, and contributing writer to several devotional books. She lives with her husband in Dallas, Pennsylvania.

Good, Flowing from Wisdom

Who is wise and understanding among you? Let him show it by his good life, by deeds done in the humility that comes from wisdom (James 3:13).

Scripture: James 3:13-18
Song: "Of All the Spirit's Gifts to Me"

Our university's school of nursing was in turmoil, as faculty and dean kept fighting. All the turbulence was infecting the classrooms and the students. So the president met with the dean, and then the faculty, with the result that the dean resigned. The new problem: Who would fill this position during the search for a replacement?

Professor Hogan, a seasoned faculty member, was consulted, and she agreed to serve as interim dean. The search began while the temporary dean "picked up the pieces."

Slowly, the environment changed as turmoil dissipated. Professor Hogan's quiet wisdom renewed respect among those whom she served. Openness and reason were applied to difficult situations in a spirit of quiet humility, bringing healing.

In other words, Professor Hogan brought more than knowledge and experience to the situation. She brought a wisdom from which emanated peace, mercy, and impartiality. If you were to ask the faculty or students, "Who is wise and understanding among you?" the unanimous answer would be: Professor Hogan.

Lord, help me treat the people around me with dignity and honor today. Make me a peacemaker for You, bringing harmony rather than discord, goodwill rather than hatred, and cooperation rather than conflict. In Your name I pray, amen.

Who's First?

Anyone who does not take up his cross and follow me is not worthy of me. Whoever finds his life will lose it, and whoever loses his life for my sake will find it (Matthew 10:38, 39).

Scripture: Matthew 10:34-39
Song: "Jesus Is All the World to Me"

My father's desk had a brass paperweight on it. He bought it the year I was born. When I sat playing at his desk, he would let me use it as a ruler to enhance my "art work." It had two words on it. They meant nothing to me then. What were the two words? "God first!"

My father's ministry to children took him away from home more than my mother, brother, and I liked. We grumbled and complained when he couldn't make it to our activities. Sometimes, jealousy caused angry words to sputter from my mouth when he'd say, "Honey-girl, I'm sorry. I wish I could be there." Did we . . . did *I* matter to him? I began to withhold my love from the father I cherished.

The paperweight's message was haunting me and calling me at the same time. Gradually, I realized my priorities needed to change. Slowly, the love I'd had for my father returned. One day he said, "Your love is a beautiful gift to me . . . and to the Lord." God changed my heart.

That paperweight now sits on a desk in my home. It reminds me to keep my priorities in line. It does not say, "God only"; rather, it says, "God first."

Lord, help me get my priorities in order. Give me courage to begin each day with "God first." When I put You first, everything else falls in line. In Jesus' name, amen.

A Worthy Life?

I urge you to live a life worthy of the calling you have received. Be completely humble and gentle; be patient, bearing with one another in love (Ephesians 4:1, 2).

Scripture: Ephesians 4:1-6
Song: "Breathe on Me, Breath of God"

Is Paul urging me to live a worthy life for the Lord? I want to, but I am not at all sure what that worthy life looks like. I am to be humble, gentle, loving, hope-filled, faithful, with a spirit of peace. Jesus embodied all of these qualities, in word and deed. But can I do the same?

Where can I see these characteristics of faith being lived out? Do I see them in the child who collects socks and underwear for the homeless? Or perhaps in a woman who calls to check on the homebound of her church and community. I think I might see them in a man who chauffeurs cancer patients to and from their treatments.

Oh yes, there's a man who gives his social security check to his church each month to maintain the food bank. A group of women knit shawls, delivering them to the ill, the elderly in nursing homes, and to newborn babies.

A volunteer cuddles and rocks newborn babies whose mothers don't want them. A teenager tutors elementary school children in reading. Lord, is this how Paul is encouraging me to live? If so, I'm willing to try. O, God, help me!

Dear Father, I want to live for You, as all these people do, just as Your Son shared His life of love. Grant me humility, gentleness, patience. In Jesus' name, amen.

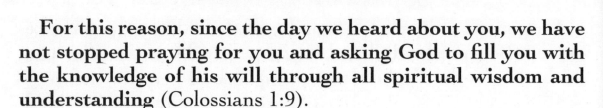

An Inheritance Shared

For this reason, since the day we heard about you, we have not stopped praying for you and asking God to fill you with the knowledge of his will through all spiritual wisdom and understanding (Colossians 1:9).

Scripture: Colossians 1:9-18
Song: "Happy the Home When God Is There"

My parents began praying for me from the day I was born. They stood at the altar, promising to nurture and guide me in the faith as they themselves lived according to Christ's example. They prayed for me throughout the various stages of my life, always asking God to give me patience, joy, and a heart of gratitude.

Their prayers for me remained constant through each stage of my life. On every remembrance of me, they did not stop praying, but rather continued asking God to fill me with the knowledge of His will. And when my children were born, my husband and I stood at the altar with the same desire to support our children in Christian growth.

It was not easy for my parents. It was not easy for us, either. But we are grateful to have this privilege of nurturing our children through our love and our prayers. Therefore, on every remembrance of them, we never stopped praying for them, asking God to fill them with the knowledge of His will. It is my earnest hope that our grandchildren will receive, with grateful hearts, that very same precious inheritance.

Lord, thanks for parents who nurtured me in the faith. I saw them live by Your will. I want to do the same with my children and their children. In Jesus' name, amen.

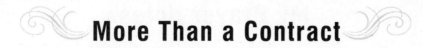

More Than a Contract

Whatever happens, conduct yourselves in a manner worthy of the gospel of Christ. Then . . . I will know that you stand firm in one spirit, contending as one man for the faith of the gospel without being frightened in any way by those who oppose you (Philippians 1:27, 28).

Scripture: Philippians 1:27-30
Song: "When Love Is Found"

Today is the wedding day they have dreamed and planned into reality. The church is filled with friends and family who'll witness these two dear ones stepping into their future. I wonder if they are aware of the deep significance of the words to be spoken.

The words are more than a contract. They are committing themselves to a holy covenant. No other ties are more tender, no other vows more sacred. They will live with each other and *for* each other. When struggles come, they will "stand firm in one spirit." They will remember their promises made today, "You can count on my love as we walk this new life together." Christian marriage is rooted in the promises written in their hearts, shared in their vows.

Weddings always remind me of my relationship to God. I promised to live my life to honor His name. I promised Him to care for my brothers and sisters in the fellowship. I told Him, "You can count on me. I will stand firm in times of struggle." My faith is rooted in the promises written in my heart, offered to God. It's not a contract, but a covenant.

God, I want to be an example as I live out my promise to You. May those I meet be able to count on me to stand firm. I know I can count on You. Through Christ, amen.

My Prayer Notes

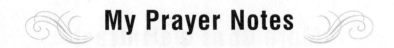

_____

_____

_____

_____

_____

_____

_____

_____

_____

_____

_____

_____

_____

_____

_____

_____

_____

_____

_____

_____

_____

_____

DEVOTIONS®

MAY

You were like sheep going astray, but now you have returned to the Shepherd and Overseer of your souls.

—*1 Peter 2:25*

Gary Allen, Editor **Margaret Williams,** Project Editor **Photo** © Formac | Dreamstime.com

DEVOTIONS® is published quarterly by Standard Publishing, Cincinnati, Ohio, www.standardpub.com. © 2010 by Standard Publishing. All rights reserved. Topics based on the Home Daily Bible Readings, International Sunday School Lessons. © 2007 by the Committee on the Uniform Series. Printed in the U.S.A. All Scripture quotations, unless otherwise indicated, are taken from the *HOLY BIBLE, NEW INTERNATIONAL VERSION®. NIV®.* Copyright © 1973, 1978, 1984 by Biblica, Inc.™ Used by permission of Zondervan. All rights reserved.

Breakfast Is Served

Your attitude should be the same as that of Christ Jesus (Philippians 2:5).

Scripture: Philippians 2:1-11
Song: "Take My Life, and Let It Be"

Two men had traveled to Ecuador to meet with missionaries there. The men hoped to address the needs of physically challenged people in that country. The older man directed a school for special needs kids. The younger man, Doug, was a physical therapist. Weary from their travels, they longed for sleep.

Morning found the director ready for the day. But Doug, not feeling well, asked to be excused from breakfast so he could return to sleep. Later, the older man quietly entered their room as Doug was taking a shower. The man placed a breakfast tray on the table and made Doug's bed. Stepping into the room, Doug immediately knew just who had been so kind and caring.

Shortly after their return home, the director lifted an envelope from his desk. Opening it, he read words written by his young traveling companion: "I can't begin to tell you how I felt when I saw that breakfast and my bed. All my weariness faded. You cared for me as a father. Your compassion made me recall our Savior's humble caring for others. This trip was a life-changing experience for me. Thank you."

Help me, **O God,** not to miss the "heart lessons" You offer to me on my journey through life. In Christ's name I pray. Amen.

May 1. **Viola Ruelke Gommer** is a retired nurse, photographer, and contributing writer to several devotional books. She lives with her husband in Dallas, Pennsylvania.

What We Can Do?

When the foundations are being destroyed, what can the righteous do? (Psalm 11:3).

Scripture: Psalm 11
Song: "The Solid Rock"

As I sip my morning coffee, I glance at headlines in the newspaper—"Unemployment Soars," "Terrorist Bombers at Large," "Stock Market Plunges," "Hospitals Close." Sighing, I feel overwhelmed once again; the foundations of my world seem to be crumbling before me.

Later, reading Psalm 11, I recalled that today's devastation has happened before and that my choice is the same as David's. Will I seek righteousness with God as my refuge? Or will I choose self-sufficiency and my own shelter? My self-made shelters do not usually work, though they do come easily. In fact, long ago, in my 5-year-old heart, I firmly determined: "I better do something because nobody else is going to help me."

But David' calls me to remember God, to be a true counter-revolutionary in this self-sufficient age—to trust God to act. Taking in David's words, my beaten-down heart begins to rise. Trusting God is what the righteous can do, what they have always done. And for today, at least, it is what I can do.

Almighty and gracious Father, I don't always find it easy to see my choices clearly. But I know that if I view the situation as You do, I will find the right way. Help me to do that and, in all things, to choose to trust You. In the name of the Father, the Son, and the Holy Spirit, I pray. Amen.

May 2–8. **GlenAnn Wood Egan** is a freelance writer, homemaker, and small-group Bible study leader. She lives in Centennial, Colorado, with her husband.

Two Men

In the year that King Uzziah died, I saw the Lord seated on a throne, high and exalted, and the train of his robe filled the temple . . . "Woe to me!" (Isaiah 6:1, 5).

Scripture: Isaiah 6:1-5
Song: "Holy, Holy, Holy"

Two men, two very different ends, yet God's holiness is at the center of both their stories. King Uzziah's death marked the end of a long and prosperous reign of military successes, impressive building operations, and agricultural advances. For the most part, he was a godly king. But then a consuming pride overtook him. He took to himself the priestly role of burning incense in the temple without authorization. For this, God struck him with fatal leprosy.

Isaiah was the greatest of the Old Testament prophets. Yet, when confronted by God, even he was completely undone. He was convicted, humbled, and broken as he faced his true condition. Having seen God, the prophet should have died. Instead he was transformed, more alive than ever.

As a believer, I relate to Isaiah. But today my heart struggles with Uzziah. It's hard to accept that the same holiness that cleanses and forgives also kills and maims. Such holiness seems unfair, and I don't understand.

In these times when my heart struggles, it helps me to remember that God is not only holy, but good. Trusting in His heart, my heart can find rest.

Lord, I am grateful for your goodness. Help me to be grateful too for your holiness in all its facets—for both judgment and mercy. In Christ's holy name I pray. Amen.

Living in the Question

God also said to Moses, "I am the LORD. I appeared to Abraham, to Isaac and to Jacob as God Almighty, but by my name the LORD I did not make myself known to them" (Exodus 6:2, 3).

Scripture: Exodus 6:2-8
Song: "Because He Lives"

Here God responds to the desperate, heart-cry questions that Moses had flung at Him in the previous chapter. But God doesn't really answer the questions. He simply reminds Moses of who He is.

Early in my Christian life, I believed (and still do believe) that nothing could touch me that had not first passed through God's fingers. That belief sustained me, until one day I realized: This God I was trusting had allowed me to have emotionally abusive parents.

Raging at God, I demanded explanations for this injustice. My heart began hardening, and I determined to wait for that answer before moving forward with life. A few weeks later, still sucking on my rage like a hard candy, I felt this question welling up within me: "Do you want an answer, or do you want the relationship?"

With tears of sorrow, my heart breaking, I chose relationship with Him. Like Moses, I never got an answer to my question. But I got more of the Lord. And that is enough.

Dear Lord, while I don't always get to have the answers, I thank you for loving me, the one who keeps asking. You keep sustaining me—in and through—all the unanswered questions of my life. Thank You, in Jesus' name. Amen.

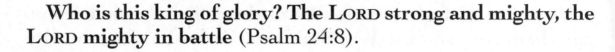

Ancient and Modern Gates

Who is this king of glory? The LORD strong and mighty, the LORD mighty in battle (Psalm 24:8).

Scripture: Psalm 24
Song: "Lift Up Your Heads, Ye Mighty Gates"

Reading my Bible's footnote on Psalm 24, I see that this psalm was often set to music, probably used in corporate worship, and may have been reenacted often in the temple. Imagine it! The people outside would call out to the temple gates to open up and let the king of glory in.

From inside, the priests or a chorus would ask, "Who is this king of glory?" Outside, the people would respond in unison, "The Lord strong and mighty, the Lord mighty in battle," proclaiming His great power and strength. The exchange was then repeated, and the temple gates would swing open. All of this would symbolize the people's desire to have God's presence among them.

This spirited and holy exchange continues today, I think. Only now it is between the Holy Spirit and our own hearts. "Who is this king of glory in your life?" He asks.

And we answer, each in our own way, reflecting what we know of God and how He has met us. And just as the temple gates swung open, the gates of our heart's temple swing open today. Will we then embrace His loving, mighty, and glorious presence?

O God, the king of glory, how grateful I am that You took a symbol and made it my reality, opening the gates of my heart and coming in. I pray this prayer in the name of Jesus, my merciful Savior and Lord. Amen.

Showing Up

You hear, O LORD, the desire of the afflicted; you encourage them, and you listen to their cry (Psalm 10:17).

Scripture: Psalm 10:12-16
Song: "A Mighty Fortress Is Our God"

How like the words of my own heart are the words of this psalm! I sometimes feel an overwhelming anguish, fear, and dread about what is happening around me, both in the world and in my home. Like the psalmist, I wonder where God is. Why doesn't He show himself?

My marriage has often been redemptive, sometimes glorious, but hard. One day recently, sensing in my husband a tension, I began to feel fear. Quickly, I began to pray for a change in him but was soon checked by the Holy Spirit. Why not bring my fear to the Lord, rather than my husband's behavior?

Like a mother cat—gently, but firmly, batting her kitten back into line with her paw—God was ushering me back into the truth. He seemed to be showing me that my fear wasn't even the major issue.

What was the major issue? It was this: My fear was blocking me from my heart's deepest desire—to know, love, and depend more upon God, whatever the situation. It was a subtle but needed reminder from the Holy Spirit. In both blessing and struggle we can invite God to "show up" for our encouragement.

Thank You, **Dear Father,** that the cares of this life do not overwhelm You or take You by surprise. And even in the worst of situations, You are there, You listen to my cry. In the name of Your Son, my Savior, I pray. Amen.

Our Weight of Glory

Ascribe to the LORD the glory due his name; bring an offering and come into his courts (Psalm 96:8).

Scripture: Psalm 96
Song: "And Can It Be That I Should Gain?"

One of the meanings of "glory" is: *weight*, like the heaviness of a warrior returning from battle, weighted down with the spoils of victory. We see the weight of God's glory in creation, but there is also a weight to our lives when we are His.

There is a story about a 19th-century circuit-riding evangelist named Peter Cartright. He was asked to preach at a conference led by a very proper seminary student. When Cartright gave the invitation to respond to the gospel, a mountain of a man came forward. This man threw himself down on the floor and began to pray.

He knew he was a sinner and told God so, loudly. The seminary student anxiously rushed up to him imploring, "Compose yourself, brother."

But Cartright pushed the student aside, slapped the man on the back, and said, "Pray on brother; there's no composure in hell where you're going." The man finally broke through to God and, leaping to his feet, howled with delight, dancing and praising God. The weight of God's glory in one man's life was brought to bear on another's that day. And worship became witness to those who watched.

Dear Heavenly Father, may I be bold! May I not hide my light because of what others might think; instead, may I choose to bring the weight of Your glory into a needy world. In the name of Jesus my Lord. Amen.

He Gives a Peek

You are worthy, our Lord and God, to receive glory and honor and power, for you created all things, and by your will they were created and have their being (Revelation 4:11).

Scripture: Revelation 4
Song: "Crown Him with Many Crowns"

In John's time, the phrase "You are worthy" was used to herald the entrance of an emperor when he entered in triumphal procession. Caesar's throne was the most powerful and glorious throne in the world. No expense was spared on the trappings of his court. But it paled in comparison to the bejeweled, rainbow-encircled, lamp-lit, sea of glass court John saw. Imagine the throne that called him to "Come up."

In our time, well-known preacher Jack Hayford tells a story about the early days of his ministry at Church On the Way in California. In January 1971, as he was leaving the church for home, he saw the room filled with a silvery mist. Finding no natural explanation for what he saw, he checked the room next door but found no mist there. Then he apparently heard the Lord speak: "It is what you think it is." God had filled the room with His glory.

We may never experience God's entry into our lives on earth as these men did. Yet this is Heaven's promise for us too. How good of God to give us a peek one in a while!

My most worthy Lord and God, thank You for the gifts of imagination and anticipation. Stir them up in me, Lord! Help me to use them well, as I live for that day I will meet You in Glory! In the name of Jesus, who lives and reigns with You and the Holy Spirit, one God, now and forever, amen.

Follow the Leader

Even though I walk through the valley of the shadow of death, I will fear no evil, for you are with me; your rod and your staff, they comfort me (Psalm 23:4).

Scripture: Psalm 23
Song: "He Leadeth Me"

Stretching about 140 miles between two mountain ranges—Sylvania in the north and Owlshead in the south—lies a daunting geographical obstacle: California's legendary Death Valley. Temperatures in this valley can range from 130 degrees in the summer to below freezing in the winter. Water from the salt flats is undrinkable, rainfall uncommon.

When you add the mountain lions, coyotes, bobcats, rattlesnakes, scorpions, tarantulas—it's easy to see how this valley earned its name. A foot traveler, facing these elements unprepared, would be in danger from the start. Obviously, a seasoned guide, a few maps, and a pathfinder compass would be helpful.

As Christians, we sometimes face daunting circumstances. These spiritual valleys contain perils and pitfalls that we cannot navigate by ourselves. Thankfully, we have an experienced guide who can lead us through these valleys unharmed. He carries the right equipment too: a shepherd's staff and hobnailed rod. What assurance and comfort!

Dear Shepherd, thanks for guarding my soul as I venture through the valleys. Most of all, thanks for leading me safely to pastures of eternal life. In Jesus' name, amen.

May 9–15. **Charles Harrel** served as a minister for more than 30 years before stepping aside to pursue writing. He enjoys digital photography, playing the guitar, and teaching from God's Word.

As Long As It Takes

As a shepherd looks after his scattered flock when he is with them, so will I look after my sheep. I will rescue them from all the places where they were scattered on a day of clouds and darkness (Ezekiel 34:12).

Scripture: Ezekiel 34:11-16
Song: "Rescue the Perishing"

We'd just finished loading our camp gear into the truck when the park ranger approached our now empty campsite. "Have you guys seen a small boy in a blue T-shirt and white shorts?" the ranger asked. "Well, he's wandered off, and his parents are worried."

Sadly, we all shook our heads "No." But as the ranger jogged to the next campsite, he noticed the L. A. County Fireman's sticker on my dad's Chevy Suburban. Even before he returned to ask, Dad had tightened his boots, grabbed a flashlight, and was heading down the canyon.

They both understood the urgency. In a few hours, temperatures would drop to near freezing. In the pitch darkness and rocky terrain, the little boy's chances of survival were slim. As Dad disappeared into the night, Mom called out, "How long will you be gone?" Dad yelled back, "As long as it takes."

Likewise, whenever we wander away from the flock, our faithful shepherd, Jesus, will find and rescue us—no matter how long it takes.

Precious Shepherd, sometimes clouds of discouragement sweep over my soul, causing me to feel lost, isolated from the flock. Please rescue me, Lord; bring me back to the fold and into Your loving embrace. In the name of Jesus, I pray.

Keeping Watch

The hired hand is not the shepherd who owns the sheep. So when he sees the wolf coming, he abandons the sheep and runs away. Then the wolf attacks the flock and scatters it (John 10:12).

Scripture: John 10:11-16
Song: "Jesus Loves Me"

Several years ago, I met a family who owned a small flock of sheep in the Midwest. Their flock numbered about 400. Although they were modern-day shepherds, with fenced pastures and trained sheep dogs, they still assigned family members to watch the flock during the nights.

One weekend, the family hired two men to take care of the flock while they were away on business. Instead of tending to their duties, these hirelings decided to throw a party. After a bout of drinking, they passed out and fell sound asleep.

Around midnight, three barking dogs entered the pasture. The sheep were terrified as they ran for their lives. These were not wild dogs; yet, by the time they finished, half the sheep lay dead. Some were killed in the fences trying to escape. Others died from exhaustion and fear. In the morning, the men awoke, saw the carnage, and fled the county.

Thank goodness, Jesus is not a hireling! He is the true shepherd who keeps watch over His flock. He never sleeps nor will He abandon us. We can always feel secure in Him.

Lord, I'm so glad to be in Your flock. When You came to me as Savior, You also became my faithful shepherd. How blessed I am! In You, I have salvation, protection, and a loving friend. Through Your precious name I pray. Amen.

The Healer Still Walks

Jesus went through all the towns and villages . . . healing every disease and sickness (Matthew 9:35).

Scripture: Matthew 9:35-38
Song: "The Healer"

Bev arrived late for church that morning. She slipped in during the worship service and sat quietly. Bev enjoyed attending church; she loved the joyful worship and hardly missed a Sunday. During the final song, she clapped her hands in joyful rhythm. But inside, her heart cried as she thought about Monday's doctor appointment: She was slowly going blind.

At the end of service, the minister asked everyone who was sick to stand. He told his congregation that Jesus still walked the aisles with healing in His hands. Bev rose to her feet, closed her eyes, and tried to believe for a miracle.

Next Sunday, Bev came early to church—two sets of test results were tucked into her Bible. After the service, she told the minister about her failing eyesight, then handed him both reports. He almost fell over. Bev's updated diagnosis: 20/20 vision, corrective lenses no longer needed, eye surgery unnecessary. The doctor had no explanation for her improvement.

The verse from Matthew holds true today. Jesus still walks through our land with healing hands. If you have a need, trust Him and believe.

Dearest Lord Christ, I believe You are passing by this moment. So, in simple faith, I reach out to You. My family and I need Your help, and I know Your touch will make all the difference. Praise to You, who reigns with the Father and the Holy Spirit, one God, now and forever. Amen.

One Tap

All the nations will be gathered before him, and he will separate the people one from another as a shepherd separates the sheep from the goats. He will put the sheep on his right and the goats on his left (Matthew 25:32, 33).

Scripture: Matthew 25:31-40
Song: "When We All Get to Heaven"

In Bible days, shepherds often tended combined flocks, but they knew it was necessary to separate the sheep from the goats at particular times. The goats were headstrong, unruly, and preferred grazing the rocky foothills throughout the day. The sheep, however, needed specific times for rest and loved feeding in grassy pastures.

Shepherds divided their flocks with a staff by tapping sheep to the right side and goats to the left. All the sheep would gather around the shepherd's right hand, while the goats moved to the left. The sheep found food and relaxation, while the goats continued to clamber restlessly.

With this word picture, Jesus portrayed a scene from the final judgment. The righteous inherit a kingdom filled with eternal rest, blessed by the right hand of promise. Since the left hand carries no such promise or blessing, the unrighteous depart to a kingdom of everlasting turmoil. On that day, we all receive one tap—on the right or the left. Apparently, the kingdom we inherit is our own choice.

Faithful Shepherd, I look forward to that final day when the flock is separated, and Your sheep enter the kingdom of Heaven. I can hardly wait to spend eternity with You. I pray through my deliverer, Jesus. Amen.

Hungry and Thirsty

Let them give thanks to the LORD for his unfailing love and his wonderful deeds for men, for he satisfies the thirsty and fills the hungry with good things (Psalm 107:8, 9).

Scripture: Psalm 107:1-9
Song: "Come and Dine"

At 19 years old, I was a new convert to Christianity, full of vigor but somewhat naive. One Sunday, after reading about the 40-day fast Jesus accomplished in the wilderness, I decided to try a fast of my own. Like Jesus, I would not eat or drink anything for 40 days. That night, I drank lots of water and consumed a huge meal to prepare myself for Monday.

When I arrived at work, the loading dock at W. T. Grants had two semi-trucks, both doubles, which needed unloading. By noon, my mouth had turned dry, and my stomach ached for anything edible. Our stock room crew usually ate lunch together at the food court. And wouldn't you know it—that day the menu offered one of my favorites—fried clams, all you could eat, including free refills on soft drinks. I just sat at my table, famished, watching my stockroom buddies chow down. I still remember that hungry feeling.

Hunger and thirst are powerful spiritual motivators. They push us toward God's kingdom and His righteousness. When we hunger after these things, God fills our lives to overflowing. And like nourishment for the body, the good things of God satisfy the soul.

God, Your unfailing love, divine mercy, and wonderful deeds are like food for a hungry spirit and water for a thirsty soul. Give me these things! In Jesus' name, amen.

The Best Water of All

For the Lamb at the center of the throne will be their shepherd; he will lead them to springs of living water. And God will wipe away every tear from their eyes (Revelation 7:17).

Scripture: Revelation 7:9-17
Song: "Springs of Living Water"

One afternoon, while hunting for a new camping spot in the Mammoth area of Central California, my father drove his truck into an alpine meadow. It was beautiful. The meadow offered the perfect place for pitching a tent, with level terrain and ponderosa pines to offer shade. However, one essential thing was missing—fresh water. After setting up our campsite, Dad hiked up the canyon to search for a mountain spring. In a few hours, he returned with a grin on his face, carrying a canteen of fresh spring water.

With each new trip, the path to the springs became more established and easier to traverse. In a few years, others were following the trail my father had blazed. Many campers now enjoy this meadow because someone first led the way to water.

One day, Jesus will lead His sheep to a heavenly water source. Much like the tree of life in Revelation, these precious waters have eternal properties. The springs are pure, limitless, and spiritually refreshing. At the springs of living water, we will always find safety, peace, and contentment—no tears allowed.

God and Father, not only is Your Son my shepherd in this lifetime, He will shepherd me throughout all eternity. I can hardly wait to see my Lord Christ in person and drink from the springs of living water. A long, satisfying drink will be worth the wait. I pray this prayer in the name of Jesus, my Savior and Lord. Amen.

Fresh Mercy

See, I am doing a new thing! Now it springs up; do you not perceive it? I am making a way in the desert and streams in the wasteland (Isaiah 43:19).

Scripture: Isaiah 43:15-21
Song: "Come, Thou Fount of Every Blessing"

A man in ragged clothes stumbles along in a parched desert in search of an oasis. Reaching out, strength failing, he now tries to run in the blazing sun toward what seems to be water surrounded by lush green palm trees. Suddenly it all disappears!

Do you ever feel like this spiritually? I do. When life throws me the toughest blast of heat and I need Him the most, it seems He appears as an allusion, a dream that I can't quite put my hands around. Then, like an underground spring that was there all the time, He shows up, bursting out, giving fresh nourishment to my parched life.

The former blessings of the past are sweet, but now He gives me fresh mercy and strength through His Son, Jesus. His presence is like a stream springing up in a parched wasteland.

Are you going through a parched and dry time right now? Hold on and be encouraged by His word. He will make a way in your desert and give you streams of living water.

Dear Father, I know You are with me, even in the wilderness times. Help me, Lord, to rely on what Your word says, not on how I feel during these times. I ask for Your strength and nourishment, while thanking You that You are making a way for me. Through Christ my Lord I pray. Amen.

May 16–22. **Kim McKinney** is writer who mentors other women in the faith. She loves her family and friends, hiking, writing, and planning fun events.

Enough Love Here!

A new command I give you: Love one another. As I have loved you, so you must love one another. By this all men will know that you are my disciples, if you love one another (John 13:34, 35).

Scripture: John 13:31-35
Song: "A New Commandment"

The doorbell rang repeatedly, a welcome sign that my daughter and two grandchildren had arrived. We were attending a Christian Kid's Conference, and we were excited. "Grandma!" Hope and JJ shouted. Catching my balance, I received their hugs. As we exchanged love and greetings, I was aware of the friend they'd invited. Dark brown hair with beautiful eyes to match, Sandra was a young girl who knew the hard side of life. She looked as if she were longingly peering into a snow globe of a picturesque home. I turned and included her in our hugs.

All weekend we brought Sandra into our family. And we watched her relax. One night, Hope even took Sandra's hand and knelt with her during worship, helping to draw her closer to God's family too.

Jesus' command to love one another must shape the way I live. People watch to see how I love and if I will share that love. I was tempted just to have an exclusive "Grandma weekend," but am so thankful God led us to include Sandra and be a part of her journey to Jesus. With Him, there is always enough love to go around.

Dear Heavenly Father, I thank You for Your love and for sharing the life of Your Son with me. Help me, Lord, to avoid self-centeredness, willing to give love the way You do. I cannot do this without You. In Jesus' name, amen.

High Treason

The hand of him who is going to betray me is with mine on the table (Luke 22:21).

Scripture: Luke 22:14-23
Song: "You Never Let Go"

My clinched fist held a crumpled note. I felt my cheeks burn and my heart breaking. I needed to find a place to read the note again. The bell rung for sixth-grade recess; my legs seemed too heavy to move me to the playground. Alone in the hallway, I carefully opened the note. It simply said, "I don't like you anymore. I like Tina now."

My boyfriend had betrayed me for my best friend. On the playground, I watched them swinging. The sting of betrayal felt like the sting of a wasp.

Betrayal hurts. Maybe you have known a much deeper level of betrayal than an early childhood romance that went bad. I know I have. But can you picture Jesus facing the cross and wanting to spend time breaking bread with His closest companions? He knew Judas would hand Him over for a mere 30 pieces of silver. That is high treason. Yet here He was, offering bread to His betrayer.

Jesus knows the pain of betrayal and can comfort and guide us through it. Eventually, the process of healing includes forgiveness. Is there someone you need to forgive? Is there a betrayal that you need the help of Jesus to overcome?

Jesus, I know You experienced betrayal. You understand the pain. Help me through the process of healing and help me to forgive, just as You forgave me. Thank You for breaking Your life open and pouring out Your blood for me. In Your name, amen.

Attitude Adjustment

You were taught, with regard to your former way of life, to put off your old self, which is being corrupted by its deceitful desires; to be made new in the attitude of your minds (Ephesians 4:22, 23).

Scripture: Ephesians 4:17-24
Song: "In Christ Alone"

"I need a new attitude." My husband wanted to go camping, but cold rain was in the forecast. I wanted to stay in my nice, warm house. Never mind that we have a heated camping trailer. I had a bad attitude. God's Word came to mind about being made new in the attitude of my mind. There was little particularly "new"—and nothing wholesome—about my attitude.

It required a choice if I were to take up a good attitude. "OK, let's go camping." We like to hike and have a campfire. I knew that would be out with the freezing rain. However, we found a shopping mall not too far from our camping spot, and we ate a nice dinner there! We talked inside our cozy trailer and enjoyed being away from routine. I could have missed out on all of this had I decided to keep my bad attitude.

God gave us a new nature. But our old nature keeps trying to pop its ugly head out of the grave. Our part is to obey His Spirit within us, and thus He gives us His power to live in that new nature. Thankfully, life lived with the attitude of Christ brings marvelous fulfillment.

Father, help me to live in the new attitude and nature that Christ died to give me. It is only through Your power that I can live in true holiness. I surrender my ways and ask You to take control of my heart and mind. Through the name of Jesus, amen.

The Radiant Bride

Come, I will show you the bride, the wife of the Lamb (Revelation 21:9).

Scripture: Revelation 21:9-14
Song: "Beautiful One"

Can you imagine a bride coming down the aisle with yellow teeth, torn and filthy dress, dirt on her face, and tangled hair? She's wailing and complaining about everything, causing guests to shrink back in embarrassment. No one wants to stand up in her honor. The groom's eyes widen in shock, and he dashes away in fear of the coming years.

That's not far from a description of God's people before Jesus lavished His love and grace on us, changing us to our very core. The bride of the Lamb is His people. Here in these Scriptures the church stands in a triumphant state, glowing in purity with the presence of the groom.

The Holy City shimmers and pulses with light, dazzling the eye with energy and color. The walls stand with strength, unassailable protection, and stability. God's light beams on the city, causing vibrant colors to reflect like a prism. Jewels and crystals sparkle and send out brilliant color rays. What a picture of God's church perfected, made radiant by His light and glory!

How can we prepare ourselves for the wedding day? I desire His love and presence to transform me into that pure and beautiful bride.

Father, I ask in Jesus' name for You to shine Your light and love on me. I pray I will prepare myself for You by prayer and obedience, giving You all the glory for Your amazing power and love. Through Your Son I pray. Amen.

Lost in a Maze

The city does not need the sun or the moon to shine on it, for the glory of God gives it light, and the Lamb is its lamp (Revelation 21:23).

Scripture: Revelation 21:22-27
Song: "City on a Hill"

My son Marc was part of what is called a "live analogy" at Bible School. Blindfolded and put in a maze with no instructions, 70 students bumbled around the room. The goal was to figure out the meaning of this activity.

No talking was allowed, though. Seven hours later most concluded that without light and someone to lead they had no clue as to how to find their way through life. Having been so hungry and frustrated, Marc has never forgotten how it felt to be without light, constantly bumping into people and blockades.

God himself is light, so there's no need in Heaven for light bulbs or the sun. Here on earth, we still need the physical sun; but spiritually we have no need for any other light but Him. His warmth will bring us comfort. His light will show us the way. Often it is tempting to try the latest human ideas on how to live, but we find those ways bringing us frustration.

God is the only light. He is brilliant. When life brings you unexpected turns, or blockades, to whom do you turn? Going to God first will give you the guidance you need.

O Eternal Lord God, I pray for Your guidance in my life. Help me to look only to Your Word to show me the way to live. Guide me through those dark times with Your brilliant light and hold me close so I will not stray. In the name of the Father, the Son, and the Holy Spirit, I pray. Amen.

Tears Unleashed

He will wipe every tear from their eyes. There will be no more death or mourning or crying or pain, for the old order of things has passed away (Revelation 21:4).

Scripture: Revelation 21:1-8
Song: "Garment of Praise"

My work companions and I walked into the crowded funeral home. The moment I positioned myself between my friends, our tears flowed freely. A 3-year-old boy in our preschool had died suddenly the week before. Sopping tissues began piling in our laps.

Knowing that the family didn't know Jesus made the funeral sadder for me. Little Chris, I knew, was playing with Jesus and happy as ever. I could see his infectious smile brightening the face of Jesus. Here, in our world, though, it was tears. The sadness loomed and seemed so heavy. Will tears ever stop? They seemed to flood forth as if through a broken dam. Memories of the carefree boy played on the screen.

Outside, my hands felt stiff after releasing a balloon. I said good-bye to Chris for the last time. The rising balloons reminded me of his playful personality and that God himself had already received Chris.

I am thankful that pain and sorrow won't be a part of our lives in Heaven. God will wipe away our desperate tears. Death will cease to exist as we embrace our Lord for eternity.

Father, I pray that You will comfort me in the times when I mourn; please heal my pain. Let me be so aware of Your presence during those times. And let me look forward with joy to the day when You wipe away my tears. In Jesus' name, amen.

Spirit Power

I pray that out of his glorious riches he may strengthen you with power through His Spirit in your inner being, so that Christ may dwell in your hearts through faith (Ephesians 3:16, 17).

Scripture: Ephesians 3:14-21
Song: "I Sing the Mighty Power of God"

In my 35 years as an employee, I've had two bosses who tried to lord it over me. One spent two hours telling me I was inefficient and disorganized. The other insisted—as I cried in his presence—that I no longer do so, because it put him at a disadvantage. Both episodes were intended to render me powerless.

We have much power-grabbing in this world: physical and emotional abuse, political maneuverings, dictatorial rule. The goal? Gain power through the helplessness of others.

God could crush us under His thumb if He wanted to. Instead, He reaches into His vast storehouses and distributes the Spirit's power to us poor citizens. This power doesn't corrupt and doesn't intimidate. It enables us to invite Christ to take up residence within us and to let Him clean up the mess we've made of our lives. That kind of power is beyond anything the world understands because the victory is on the inside.

God's power is a mighty thing. Let's appropriate it.

God, I'm tempted to use what little power I have for my own gains. I confess that too often I don't ask for Your power for daily living. Forgive me, in Jesus' name, amen.

May 23–29. **Bonnie Doran** lives in Denver, Colorado, with her husband of 27 years. Besides writing, she enjoys reading, cooking, and volunteering.

Known by Name

And the LORD said to Moses, "I will do the very thing you have asked, because I am pleased with you and I know you by name" (Exodus 33:17).

Scripture: Exodus 33:17-23
Song: "Even Me"

I can't remember people's names. I've tried repeating them. I've resorted to mnemonic tricks, such as Chuck the Chin and Amy the Amiable. For one company party, I begged the planner (Vicki) to use name tags. I've also learned to listen desperately for someone else to use the name that I'd quickly forgotten.

This common problem makes me wonder why we flounder with names. Don't we listen closely enough? Do we consider a person's name unimportant?

But names are important to God. Throughout Scripture, He uses people's names to call them for a special purpose—people like Jacob, Samuel, and Paul, for instance.

Today He calls us by name and knows us by name. We don't have to continually remind Him that it's George, not Jerry. And far from staying aloof, He speaks to us and says we please Him. The emotional connection goes beyond the superficial "what's-your-name-again"?

May we treasure that special connection God establishes with us. And may we treat others with the knowledge that they too are known by name.

Father, forgive me for showing a lack of care by not bothering to learn someone's name. Help me honor others while remembering the way You honor me by knowing my name. In the most precious name of all—Jesus the Christ. Amen.

He's Still the King

God reigns over the nations; God is seated on his holy throne (Psalm 47:8).

Scripture: Psalm 47:5-9
Song: "My Country, 'Tis of Thee"

Whether or not we voted for the current leaders in office, we hope they will do the best for our country. Sometimes it doesn't work out that way, or at least in our view. We debate, complain, or write letters to our congressmen when we approve or disapprove of a bill on the House floor.

Other nations make their laws under different rules. Some suffer under dictators. These tyrants often lead their people into ruin for the sake of their own greed. Then we despair this world will never recover from the wrongs we inflict upon ourselves.

A friend reminded me recently that even with politicians and governments that are far from God, and act accordingly, God is still in charge. I find that difficult to grasp, but it makes me want to pray all the more for our officials and for God to rule in their decisions.

God knows. God reigns. Current situations may disturb us, but ultimately God will prevail. He can use even evil men and women to accomplish His long-term goals, goals that we can't see when we're so bogged down in the here and now.

So . . . lift up your heads. God reigns.

Lord God, sometimes I wonder if You're really at work in this world. I'm great at worrying about national and international government, and not so great at acknowledging Your supremacy. Give me the long view, or at least a trust that You do reign over this world. May Your kingdom come! In the name of Jesus, amen.

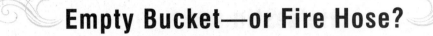

Empty Bucket—or Fire Hose?

"Sir," the woman said, "you have nothing to draw with and the well is deep. Where can you get this living water?" (John 4:11).

Scripture: John 4:7-15
Song: "Fill My Cup, Lord"

My parched soul keeps running to the well for water, but I have no bucket. I think I'm running to the wrong well. I want my faith to blossom, but it can't when I water it with dusty prayers and hymns sung by rote. Apparently, I need something more, right?

Like the Samaritan woman in this biblical account, I question how Jesus can draw water when He doesn't even have a bucket. What kind of water is this, anyway?

What Jesus offers is not the stuff that comes out of a tap, but He himself. It's a little more than I can fathom that the Lord of the universe wants to pour himself into me. And the woman at the well was pretty confused at first, as I often am. But she finally understood and asked Jesus for this living water that forever quenches.

All the sermons, Bible studies, and praise songs will do nothing unless I seek God first, until I ask Him to refresh me with His presence. He alone can satisfy my spiritual needs. (So why am I running around with an empty bucket when Jesus has a fire hose?)

Jesus, sometimes I'm a bit dense. I look longingly down the well and wonder how I can get to that religious refreshment at the bottom, when it's You I should be seeking. Fill my cup with Your living water as I lift it up. In Jesus' name, amen.

Testing 101

I know that you cannot tolerate wicked men, that you have tested those who claim to be apostles but are not, and have found them false (Revelation 2:2).

Scripture: Revelation 2:1-7
Song: "The Church's One Foundation"

As a volunteer at the Denver Museum of Nature and Science, I've learned to keep an eye out for disruptive kids. I am not to tolerate roughhousing or dangerous behavior. However, I can't just send the little ruffians to the security office. They come to the museum to learn and to have fun.

The preferred methods for dealing with those who are misbehaving are to either redirect their interest to another part of the exhibit or to quietly ask them to stop, explaining to them why. Roughhousing around sensitive equipment—or riding the escalator with dangling shoelaces—can result in injury.

Too often we tolerate Christian leaders who are obviously teaching false doctrine. It's easier to ignore the problem than to confront it, but their teaching could ultimately result in spiritual hurt to others.

The church in Ephesus had many faults, but the members there knew how to deal with disruptive behavior. I don't know what kind of discipline they imposed, but we need to be equally diligent in identifying false apostles, keeping their teachings from injuring fellow Christians.

Lord, I'm not very good at spotting those who spout false doctrines. When I do, I'm more likely to coexist with them in the name of peace. Give me the training I need to recognize false apostles and deal with them appropriately. In Jesus' name, amen.

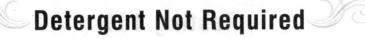

Detergent Not Required

Blessed are those who wash their robes, that they may have the right to the tree of life and may go through the gates into the city (Revelation 22:14).

Scripture: Revelation 22:10-21
Song: "There Is a Fountain"

On a recent vacation to Disney World, I packed plenty of clothes—or so I thought. My suitcase was heavy enough without stuffing another outfit into it. I was especially proud that each piece of clothing coordinated with the others.

I'd forgotten how hot and humid it was in Orlando, Florida, especially coming from cool and dry Denver. Waiting in line at theme-park attractions proved to be a test of my deodorant. I felt sure I was radiating the sweat sticking to my clothes. (I picked the cleanest outfit for the flight home, still worrying that my fellow passengers were downwind of me.)

When we get to Heaven, no doubt we'll have the same misgivings multiplied a thousand times. How can we approach God's city with the stench of sin on our very clothing?

By God's grace, He has already provided a way through the death of His Son. When we confess our sins, He takes our sin-stained clothes and washes them. Because of Jesus' sacrifice, we enjoy direct access to the Father. We can approach His dwelling-place with confidence.

Lord, thank You for providing the way to cleanse me from my sinful stains. I stand amazed at the privilege You've promised—to partake of everlasting life and enter Your holy city. I look forward to spending eternity with You, washed clean! I pray in Jesus' holy name. Amen.

Leave It to God

On each side of the river stood the tree of life, bearing twelve crops of fruit, yielding its fruit every month. And the leaves of the tree are for the healing of the nations (Revelation 22:2).

Scripture: Revelation 22:1-9
Song: "There's a Wideness in God's Mercy"

News reports constantly tell us of horrors around the world. Famine claims thousands of lives a day. AIDS decimates villages in Africa, leaving countless orphans. Genocide in Rwanda nearly wipes out a people group. Crime, drugs, sex slavery—the list goes on. In more "civilized" countries, unemployment runs rampant. Corruption allows criminals to escape prosecution. Greed destroys the life savings of retirees.

All of these atrocities affect people, of course, but they also affect nations. Sin has consequences when those in power turn a blind eye. In this country, the Civil War and its aftermath tore a hole in the fabric of individual lives and the nation's well-being. More recently, school shootings have contributed to the suffering of individuals and put a pall on the emotional atmosphere of these United States.

I think of God's heavenly city as a place of peace for God's people. In the coming age, the Lord's grace and healing will extend not only to the individual, but to nations, as well. We have reason to hope.

King of the nations, this world is hurting in so many ways. Forgive me for not responding to these hurts by either practical help or by prayer. Only You can soothe so much pain. Come bring healing to our wounds. In Jesus' name, amen.

Living Out God's Promises

Then Agrippa said to Paul, "You have permission to speak for yourself" (Acts 26:1).

Scripture: Acts 26:1-7
Song: "Believe and Obey"

How often do we lament "I wish I'd said this" or "If only I hadn't said that"? We can learn from Paul, for throughout his letters he provides powerful examples of how to speak. In lonely prison cells, he speaks of joy. Following beatings, shipwrecks, and betrayals, he speaks of thanksgiving. In today's Scripture, he stands before a king who has the power to pronounce life and death, and Paul speaks boldly of hope. You see, he believed God's promises.

Do we actually believe God's promises, or do we just say them on Sundays as a matter of habit? It's the words we speak daily that come from the depths of our heart: "I believed; therefore I have spoken" (2 Corinthians 4:13).

If our words convey joy, thanksgiving, and hope—regardless of our difficult circumstances—they bear witness to a dynamic belief. When we complain "Why me?" we also bear witness— but to a fear that "maybe God is falling down on His job." Could it be we need to focus more on being a devout believer than just a regular churchgoer?

Lord God in Heaven, please mold the meditations of my heart to Your design and strengthen my belief that it may spill freely from my lips. In Jesus' name, amen.

May 30–31. **Kitty Chappell,** of Chandler, Arizona, is a national speaker and author who has written an inspurrrrational book for cat lovers.

Weeping for the Lost

I have great sorrow and increasing anguish in my heart (Romans 9:2).

Scripture: Romans 9:1-5
Song: "People Need the Lord"

Paul grieved because his fellow Jews rejected Christ—to the point he would have traded places and born their curse if he could. I wonder if I could have that kind of love.

A friend's son once blurted: "Some people are so bad that I don't want them to come to Jesus." I understand. In my younger years I said of a child rapist-killer, "I'm glad there's a Hell!"

As I walked further with God, however, I began to see things from His viewpoint. It's not about an individual deserving Hell; it's about Christ deserving that individual's salvation. He shed His blood for everyone, including clearly evil people, and not one drop of His precious blood should be wasted. (In fact, there's one basic qualification to be saved: you must be lost, a sinner.)

It's not easy to love and pray for the unlovely, but Jesus did, and God commands us to. Not for the sinner's sake, but for Christ's sake.

And let us remember our own sinfulness. When we see a lost person, can we envision Christ standing above him, weeping for his soul, and for ours as well? No doubt Paul, the self-proclaimed "chief of sinners," had his own unworthiness ever before him. Thus he became the apostle of grace.

Dear Lord, forgive me for taking for granted Your precious blood shed for me, a sinner deserving only judgment. May I never be so selfish as to deliberately withhold my prayers for those still needing to know You. In Your name, I pray. Amen.

DEVOTIONS®

JUNE

"Fear God and keep his commandments, for this is the whole duty of man.

—*Ecclesiastes 12:13*

Gary Allen, Editor | **Margaret Williams,** Project Editor   Photo © Jonoman1 © Dreamstime.com

DEVOTIONS® is published quarterly by Standard Publishing, Cincinnati, Ohio, www.standardpub.com. © 2010 by Standard Publishing. All rights reserved. Topics based on the Home Daily Bible Readings, International Sunday School Lessons. © 2007 by the Committee on the Uniform Series. Printed in the U.S.A. All Scripture quotations, unless otherwise indicated, are taken from the *HOLY BIBLE, NEW INTERNATIONAL VERSION*®. *NIV*®. Copyright © 1973, 1978, 1984 by Biblica, Inc.™ Used by permission of Zondervan. All rights reserved.

God's Word Never Fails

It is not as though God's word had failed (Romans 9:6).

Scripture: Romans 9:6-12
Song: "Thy Word"

Years ago I had business dealings with a woman who was a staunch atheist. Over coffee she often brought up my Christianity. When she attacked my beliefs, I didn't try to defend God or disprove her views—I simply quoted Scripture. When she tried to debate them, I gently explained, "I didn't write the Bible, I just believe it." Almost a year later, I had seen no change in her attitude as our family began our move to another city. But how I had prayed for her!

In our modern world, we push lots of buttons. If we see nothing happen, we assume that something has failed. Similarly, we believe God's promises and push the button of prayer—for months, sometimes for years. We rejoice when we see results, but may become upset when we see nothing happen. (God always has the option of answering "No" or Wait.")

Several years later, we were back in town visiting our former church. To our delight, we met the atheist lady there. Noting my surprise, she said, "My husband and I are members here—we're Christians." She smiled and added, "You shouldn't look so amazed! After all, it was because of you—and the Scriptures you gave me."

Dear Lord, when my heart is tempted to doubt, please whisper Your promises in my ear. My soul can rest assured in Your fail-proof Word. In the name of Jesus. Amen.

June 1–5. **Kitty Chappell,** of Chandler, Arizona, is a national speaker and book author. She also pens Inspurrrational Stories for Cat Lovers.

Open Invitation

"I will call them 'my people' who are not my people; and I will call her 'my loved one' who is not my loved one" (Romans 9:25).

Scripture: Romans 9:22-26
Song: "Now I Belong to Jesus"

"God," I prayed, "if You really do exist, would You help me? I'm afraid—I don't want to do this!"

I was definitely an outsider—not one of God's people—but I had learned about Him from my maternal grandmother. As an abused teen, I had decided my family's only avenue of escape was for me to shoot my abusive father. What hope did I have of being heard by God, much less helped by Him?

Thankfully, my outsider status didn't stop Him from hearing my plea. Through Christ, God saved me at a crucial crossroads in my life—and He accepted me into His family. As one of His, I actually began praying for the salvation of the father whom I'd so hated—and had even planned to kill. Even more amazing, I discovered I could begin to forgive my father for serious crimes that sent him to prison.

I believe God will hear every outsider's prayer and call them "my loved one"(v. 25) just as He did for me—if they will just ask. After all, Paul—the great apostle of grace—assures us that it is not we who first choose God. It is the Lord of all who reaches down to choose us.

Lord, may I never take for granted my place in Your family. Remind me of Your gracious invitation to fellowship. Let Your grace spill from my heart to those still looking for You. May they too someday be called "my loved one." In Jesus' name, amen.

Equally Yoked

Do not be yoked together with unbelievers (2 Corinthians 6:14).

Scripture: 2 Corinthians 6:14–7:1
Song: "Return, O Wanderer, Return"

You knew better than to date a nonbeliever! I had recently broken up with my boyfriend and berated myself daily for having dated him. He was an ex-Marine who rarely attended church, but one Mother's Day he did. His mother introduced us and we began dating, just as friends—each of us sharing our plans for the future, which did not include each other.

And I spoke freely about never marrying a non-Christian. Quoting today's Scripture, I explained, "Marriage isn't easy. How can I ask God to work in a future husband's heart if it doesn't belong to Him?" Jerry wasn't offended, it was a nonissue—we weren't romantically interested in each other.

But he fell in love with me . . . and then I stopped dating him. I missed him terribly, suspecting I loved him too, but it didn't matter. I refused to be unequally yoked. When Jerry later said he wanted to become a Christian, I was suspicious. "It's the most important decision you'll make."

"My need for Christ is greater than my desire to marry you," he insisted. Shortly thereafter, he was baptized. At that time, only God knew we would eventually marry and be equally yoked together—until Jerry went to Heaven 47 years later.

Lord, through difficult times You counseled my heart with wisdom, enabling me to overcome countless trials. May I continue to seek wisdom and understanding from You. In the holy name of Jesus, amen.

Love—the Icebreaker

Accept one another, then, just as Christ accepted you, in order to bring praise to God (Romans 15:7).

Scripture: Romans 15:7-13
Song: "Lord, in Love Thou Didst Receive Us"

"Lord," I whined, "Mary doesn't like me, and I don't know why." Mary had recently joined our church after relocating from another city. Tall, statuesque, well-dressed, she was an attractive woman with a ready smile for everyone—except me. I tried to make all newcomers feel accepted, but it was obvious she didn't accept me. *Fine!* I decided. *It's her problem!*

"No it isn't," the Lord seemed to say. "It's also your problem. You two are supposed to love each other." Reluctantly, I began asking God to help me love Mary.

When, as a lecturer, I received an invitation to speak in Mary's former city, I sensed the Holy Spirit's nudging: "How about inviting Mary to go with you?"

What! Four hours' round-trip riding with someone who doesn't like me? But I fearfully went ahead and invited her, and she accepted. And on that trip Mary opened up. "I felt so intimidated by you," she said. "I thought: 'Kitty's so together—petite and classy—everything that I'm not. She must think she's really something!' But you're nothing like that—I really like you!"

That trip was the beginning of a lifelong friendship—and a lifelong lesson: Love is the key to acceptance.

Father, thank You for showing me the value of actively loving others. Too often I wait to receive love before I offer it. Help me to be more like You—love every individual without worrying whether or not my love will be returned. In Jesus' name, amen.

Stepping Out

"You and all these people, get ready to cross the Jordan River into the land I am about to give to them—to the Israelites. I will give you every place where you set your foot" (Joshua 1:2, 3).

Scripture: Joshua 1:1-6; 11:16-23
Song: "Wherever He Leads I'll Go"

Because Joshua obeyed God, his steps were blessed. God commissions our steps too. But do we follow where He leads?

Uncle Hal did. Hal was a widower who often walked down our street, loving us kids, hugging us, and praying for us—right there on the sidewalk. "Are you in trouble, again?" I once asked, teasingly. "Yep," he sighed. Hal belonged to a large church where some members were so unhappy with him that they refused to sit near him. "What happened?" we kids asked in unison.

"I took some more homeless folks to church yesterday," he answered. Wide-eyed, we listened as he again told of the lonely men on skid row needing Jesus. Each Saturday night, he scoured alleys, telling about Jesus' love. He often gave men a room at his house Then on Sunday morning, after showers and breakfast, he took them to church—smelly clothes and all.

Hal's steps down my street deeply affected me—an abused, forlorn child living on the wrong side of town. He never knew that I'd grow up to write and speak about God's love to thousands—because I learned to follow Jesus through his example.

Dear Lord, thank You for all of the uncle Hals who step off the beaten path to seek those who have been rejected by the world. May my feet faithfully follow Yours, regardless of the destination, heedless of what others think. Through Christ, amen.

A Heart Washed Clean

Oh, that their hearts would be inclined to fear me and keep all my commands always, so that it might go well with them and their children forever! (Deuteronomy 5:29).

Scripture: Deuteronomy 5:28-33
Song: "Teach Me, O Lord, Thy Holy Ways"

Seven-year-old Johnny was about to receive deserved discipline from his father when he asked, "Dad, do you know what a dark heart is?"

"Well, what do you think a dark heart is?" his father asked.

"It's this thing inside of you that makes you do bad things," Johnny said.

"Do you think you have a dark heart, Johnny?"

"Yeah, I do. I want to do what is right, but I disobey instead."

Johnny's father recognized this as a great time to share about God's desire to help Johnny obey. He told the little boy how Jesus obeyed His Father. He explained that Jesus could take his heart and wash it clean.

"How does God do that?" asked Johnny in amazement.

"I'm not sure, but now you know He can."

Almighty and gracious Father, thank You for Your amazing love. Show me the dark shadows of my heart and wash it clean. Help me obey You in every area of my life, and help me teach my children to do the same. I pray this prayer in the name of Jesus, my merciful Savior and Lord. Amen.

June 6–12. **Carol J. Sharp** is the wife of an accountant, mother of four, and grandmother of three. Living near Chanute, Kansas, she enjoys creative hobbies, missions, and traveling.

How Can They Hear?

Their children, who do not know this law, must hear it and learn to fear the LORD your God as long as you live in the land you are crossing the Jordan to possess (Deuteronomy 31:13).

Scripture: Deuteronomy 31:7-13
Song: "Here Am I, Send Me"

A few years ago, our neighbor Roy owned a white English bulldog. I thought the pudgy dog to be a little slow until I learned he was deaf since birth. I watched in amazement as Roy spoke to the dog in a way he could understand.

Roy knelt and pounded his hand on the hardened ground. The vibrations caused the dog to stop and turn his overgrown face toward his master. He cocked his head and watched. Roy said, "Sit," and the dog obeyed. He said, "Come," and the dog obeyed. He said, "Roll over," and the dog obeyed. Roy worked hard to teach his dog to read lips and overcome his wall of deafness.

Distractions in our culture, along with our busy lives, can make us deaf to the Lord's voice. He commands, we do not hear. Soon, our children are deafened by the wake of chaos we leave behind. Who will tell them God's plan is better? How can they learn what they never hear? How can they obey what they never learn? How can they fear what they do not know? Who will kneel and find a way to communicate the ways of the Lord with those who are mute to His promises?

Lord, forgive me for not listening to Your voice. Show me how I can I communicate Your love to others in a way they will understand. Please, help me find a way to reach children who have never really heard Your Word. Through Christ, amen.

Count Aloud

With my lips I recount all the laws that come from your mouth (Psalm 119:13).

Scripture: Psalm 119:9-16
Song: "Thy Word Have I Hid in My Heart"

Mrs. Stelplugh insisted I sing the notes aloud as I played the keys in my early years of piano lessons. Then she pushed me to count the beats in every measure. It took tremendous effort on my part to play notes, watch fingering, and count the rhythm aloud. Occasionally my thoughts wandered as I hammered out a new piece of music for my teacher. My concentration often drifted to dreams of playing outdoors after the lesson. I sometimes forgot to speak the quarter, eighth, and halfnote beats. A light tap on my shoulder reminded me: "Count out loud."

I still enjoy playing the piano. I enjoy music altogether, but my greatest joy is to sight-read music for the very first time. The counting and syncopation come easily.

My first glance at the chord goes right to my fingers before registering in my mind. I realize that this comes from the exercises Mrs. Stelplugh enforced in my early years.

We all recognize it is a good thing to memorize Scripture—to repeat God's Word aloud can only please Him. As I speak the Father's words with my lips, perhaps His Spirit becomes second nature to my heart. My faith can only rise.

Dear Father in Heaven, I want the truth of Your Word to be upon my lips. Tap me on the shoulder and remind me to speak Your Word aloud. Let Your Spirit lead and guide me. Let my confession echo Your Words of life. In the name of Jesus, who lives and reigns with You and the Holy Spirit, one God, now and forever, amen.

In His Steps

Walk in his ways, and keep his decrees and commands, his laws and requirements, as written in the Law of Moses, so that you may prosper in all you do and wherever you go (1 Kings 2:3).

Scripture: 1 Kings 2:1-4
Song: "Where He Leads Me"

My oldest son, Charlie, is an outdoor guy. He knows how to survive the rugged terrain and can tell you which plants to use for food or medicine.

My husband and I like to hike with Charlie and his wife in the Colorado mountains. With confidence they walk through thickets, climb rocky slides, and cross rivers. I follow behind, careful to step where Charlie stepped. The hike is made a little easier by his lead. He tells us which thorny bushes to avoid, where not to get your feet wet, and how to handle loose, rocky inclines.

He points out wondrous scenery. He pauses to enjoy the tiniest flowers and reminds us we are probably the only souls to witness their glory. Charlie leads us beyond our knowledge on a grand adventure. With another wonderful memory and lots of pictures, we arrive safely at our destination.

There's a reason that God tells me to walk in His way. It's for me. He wants my steps to follow His steps. He wants to show me the grandeur of His majesty and the simplest of His joys. Most of all, He wants me to prosper in this journey of life on earth.

Thank You, **Lord,** that You will always lead me and show me the path You want me to walk. Thank You for Your Word that lights my way. In the name of Jesus, amen.

Power Led to Pride

[King Uzziah] sought God during the days of Zechariah, who instructed him in the fear of God. As long as he sought the LORD, God gave him success (2 Chronicles 26:5).

Scripture: 2 Chronicles 26:1-5
Song: "O God, You Are My God"

Have you ever been arrested while reading your Bible? No, I don't mean by police officers. I mean arrested by the particular phrases the Lord uses to tell about the life of a man or woman. There are precious bits of information and godly instruction hidden in these curious phrases. My heart leaps when I stumble across them, as if I've found a treasure.

Here's a good example: "As long as he sought the Lord, God gave him success." I ponder this sentence and wonder why God included it in the Bible. Of course, it makes practical sense—as long as I seek the Lord and do His will, I'm a success. That's true no matter how circumstances unfold.

Uzziah was a godly king. He followed his father's steps, and all his deeds showed that he honored the Lord. So, he prospered.

That is, until his power led to pride. Ouch. You can read the rest of his story in 2 Chronicles 26. It's a surprise ending. Suffice it to say, this simple phrase is a strong warning to me. As I seek the Lord and as He causes my way to prosper, may I never forget just whose power has raised me up.

Lord, help me to seek You at all times, even in success. I know You are my source of strength, and that only in You will I prosper. Therefore, You alone are worthy of praise. Through Christ my Lord I pray. Amen.

Look at Me!

Turn my eyes away from worthless things; preserve my life according to your word (Psalm 119:37).

Scripture: Psalm 119:33-40
Song: "Looking Upward Every Day"

My father worked in the coal mines of Missouri for a living. He came home covered in coal dust and sweat. He always took a bath first, then ate dinner. When he finally settled in his chair with newspaper in hand, I climbed up on his lap, anxious for his undivided attention.

He liked this game. He often let me squirm with impatience and pretended to ignore my endless chatter. Finally, I would take his strong, tanned face between my tiny hands and turn his head to look at me. "Daddy, I'm talking to you!" His pretense turned to seriousness, and with a smile he gave his heart to my little girl stories.

The verse for today doesn't speak of turning eyes from evil things, in particular. It says worthless things. And, as a little girl with my father, I considered his newspaper worthless and took matters into my own hands.

The psalmist's prayer is for God to take him in hand and turn his eyes away from things that have little value. The magnetic attractions of this earthly realm require a stronger power to fight against their pull. The psalmist knew where to ask for help.

Father, often my schedule swirls to overflowing with things that are of little value in the eternal sense. Help me to discern which things I need to leave behind and focus more attention on things that will count forever. Thank You, Lord. In the holy name of Jesus, my Lord and Savior, I pray. Amen.

Get Ready

Go through the camp and tell the people, "Get your supplies ready. Three days from now you will cross the Jordan" (Joshua 1:11).

Scripture: Joshua 1:7-18
Song: "Be Bold, Be Strong"

My husband is a list maker. He creates lists for every activity under the sun. When we get ready to go on a trip, the list is a must. Items are checked until the list is complete, so nothing is forgotten.

What about a list for our journey to eternity? Have you ever considered what items should be on such a list?

What supplies will we need for this journey? We will never make it without faith, perseverance, hope, and trust.

What should we embrace along the way? Maybe forgiveness, love, and compassion need to be listed.

What about the list of things to take care of before we leave? My husband never leaves town without telling the people we love where we are going. He lets them know, so they won't worry. In the same way, we can tell others that we are journeying toward our inheritance—our heavenly home (see Ephesians 1:14). In other words, we can let them know we're servants of Christ, both by what we say and how we act. (Let's put that on our list too!)

Help me, **Lord,** to share my faith so that no one will wonder about my eternal Savior and the place He has prepared for me. Let my testimony encourage others to prepare for their journey, as well. Show me the things I should put on my list, and help me to check off each one. In Jesus' name I pray. Amen.

Omnipotent Guarantee

No matter how many promises God has made, they are "Yes" in Christ (2 Corinthians 1:20a).

Scripture: 2 Corinthians 1:16-20
Song: "Great Is Thy Faithfulness"

"But, Mom, you promised!" wailed my young son when I told him a long-planned outing had to be canceled, or at least postponed. While it is true that sometimes we are unable to keep our promises for good reasons, it is also true that we live in a society where too often people take promises lightly. Wedding vows are broken, business contracts violated, and commitments to family members pushed aside.

We can find in the Old Testament many promises that God made to His people, foretelling the coming of His Son into the world. Then, when Jesus came, He fulfilled those promises to the letter in His preaching, healing, crucifixion, and resurrection.

Moreover, Jesus continued to make promises to His followers that still challenge, comfort, and guide us in our Christian lives today. We can trust His every "yes" for this one great reason: His unique nature. You see, Jesus is both man and God, one person in two natures. When He makes a promise, omnipotent power will make it happen.

Dear Heavenly Father, thank You for reminding me that all of Your promises are always "yes" in Your Son. And help me to follow His example by working harder to keep the promises I make. Through Christ I pray. Amen.

June 13–19. **Doris Mueller** is a teacher and writer who enjoys traveling and hiking. She lives in suburban St. Louis with her husband, Jack.

Inconvenient Obedience

Love the LORD your God . . . serve him with all your heart and all your soul (Joshua 22:5).

Scripture: Joshua 21:43–22:6
Song: "In the Service of the King"

I must confess that I was a willful child. When Mom would ask me to do something, I didn't always obey. Instead I dallied, hoping she'd forget. Or maybe I'd just make the job easier by doing it halfway. Of course, my schemes usually didn't work.

But don't we children of God sometimes try to delay or "modify" our obedience to Him? Not that we don't understand what is right—it's just quite often so . . . *inconvenient*.

The Ten Commandments had given clear guidance to God's people. Yet Joshua felt it necessary to remind the people to be very careful to keep His commandments. Later, the prophet Micah said, "And what does the Lord require of you? To act justly and to love mercy and to walk humbly with your God" (Micah 6:8). And when Jesus came, He reinforced the commandments many times, such as when He said, "'Love the Lord your God with all your heart and with all your soul and with all your mind.' This is the first and greatest commandment" (Matthew 22:37, 38).

My point is simply this: In spite of such constant, heavenly reminders, God's people often turned away. We can set a new precedent today, however. Let us take the first step, the step of inconvenient obedience.

Dear Father in Heaven, forgive me when I fail to serve You. Help me to understand that if I trust and obey, I will be much happier. In the name of the Father, the Son, and the Holy Spirit, I pray. Amen.

A Reminder to Worriers

For the LORD your God is God in heaven above and on the earth below (Joshua 2:11).

Scripture: Joshua 2:10-14
Song: "Give to Our God Immortal Praise"

Sometimes I think I must be a natural-born worrywart. I can be anxious about major problems or even tiny concerns. I fret over my son's job-searching; I am fearful when my husband loses sleep because of heart-related breathing problems. I toss and turn, dreading the direst outcome when a close friend finds out she has cancer. And how nervewracking to face the prospect of a speech I've promised to give!

But on each such occasion, after a time, I finally remind myself—or am reminded—that I belong to God, that He is all-powerful, and that He can handle any problem I lay at His feet.

I once saw a greeting card that spoke directly to my heart. On the front it said: "A message from God." Inside were the words, "You don't have to worry about anything today. I've got it all under control, and I'll take care of everything."

If you too are a worrywart—if you ever stew over world conflicts, family problems, or personal fears—I hope you will be comforted, as I am. I've come to see that our heavenly Father "is God in Heaven above and on the earth below." He will provide whatever is needed.

O God, Creator of Heaven and earth, keep reminding me that You have everything under control. Thank You that all my concerns, small and large, pose no problem for You. Most of all, I thank You for always having my best in mind. In the name of Jesus, who lives and reigns with You and the Holy Spirit, one God, now and forever, amen.

Prayer Overcomes Fear

Do not be afraid; do not be discouraged (Joshua 8:1).

Scripture: Joshua 2:17-21
Song: "Courage, Brother, Do Not Stumble"

If you haven't yet read the book of Joshua, I encourage you to do so. It reads like an exciting adventure story, with colorful descriptions of battles and conquests, challenges and obstacles. In one exciting episode, spies go out to explore the land of Canaan. And they're assisted by a most unlikely coconspirator—a local harlot named Rahab. In another oft-told event, the Israelites march around the city of Jericho once each day, for six days; on the seventh day they march around it seven times, and the city walls collapse, clearing the way for conquest.

Time and again, however, the conquering Israelites failed to remain faithful to God. At such times, it fell to Joshua to reassure, confront, or even discipline them. In his leadership role, Joshua had many ups and downs and often became discouraged. But when he knelt and prayed for guidance, God told him, "Do not be afraid . . ." Each time Joshua arose, reassured his men with those comforting words, and urged them to "be strong and courageous."

We too, whether or not we are in positions of leadership, often face disappointment, discouragement, and perhaps even despair. But, like Joshua, we can turn to God and listen for His words of encouragement and renewal.

Almighty and gracious Father, thank You for Your promises of deliverance. When I am overtaken by doubt or dismay, lift me up and help me get started again. In the name of Your Son, my Savior, I pray. Amen.

Walking by Faith

We live by faith, not by sight. . . . So we make it our goal to please him, whether we are at home in the body or away from it (2 Corinthians 5:7, 9).

Scripture: Joshua 6:22-25
Song: "God Is My Strong Salvation"

Radio announcer Paul Harvey was famous for telling his audience "the rest of the story." Today's Scripture reading belongs in that category as well. Earlier we read in the book of Joshua that the courageous prostitute Rahab, when the Israelite spies came and sought her help, chose to repudiate her heathen gods and place her faith in the one true God. What a daring commitment she made! (Would you or I have been willing to take such a risk?)

Now, in today's reading, we get the rest of the story. Here we learn that, because of her brave stand, she and her family were the only ones saved from destruction at the hands of the Israelites. Moreover, long after her death, Rahab continued to be cited by New Testament writers for her commendable faith.

You and I will always face choices that may make dramatic changes in our lives. At such a crossroads, we can't be certain of the outcomes. But what we *can* do is determine to please Him in every situation. Then we pray for guidance and step out boldly, trusting in His grace.

O God, the king of glory, I know You hold the past, present, and future in Your hands, and that nothing takes You by surprise. When decisions are to be made, help me to choose wisely, and to trust in You for the outcomes. In the holy name of Jesus, my Lord and Savior I pray. Amen.

Show Me!

Show me your faith without deeds, and I will show you my faith by what I do. . . . faith without deeds is useless (James 2:18, 20).

Scripture: James 2:18-25
Song: "They'll Know We Are Christians by Our Love"

I live in what's called the Show-Me State, and we Missourians have a saying: "Don't just talk about it—show me." And there's an old axiom that declares, "Your actions speak so loudly I can't hear what you're saying." Again—show me.

James's admonitions on faith and works are often debated: Is he saying that doing good works is a requirement for salvation . . . or that good deeds simply demonstrate the genuineness of one's faith?

Surely it's the latter. If we have have received God's gift of salvation, we will choose to engage in good deeds out of thankfulness. In other words, James tells us that we witness to our genuine faith through our actions.

I remember an old poem from my childhood in which four children declared their love for their mother. Then three of them went blissfully on their way. Only one added, "Today I'll help you all I can," and then did so. The poem ends like this—

How do you think the mother guessed
which one really loved her best?

Dear God, I know I'm redeemed by faith. But help me, out of my great gratitude for Your grace, to act out my faith through daily deeds of kindness. In the name of Jesus, my Redeemer and friend, I pray. Amen.

Land of Promise

They said to Joshua, "The LORD has surely given the whole land into our hands; all the people are melting in fear because of us" (Joshua 2:24).

Scripture: Joshua 2:2-9, 15, 16, 22-24
Song: "This Is My Father's World"

Today's Scripture passage is another scene in the story of how the children of Israel came to acquire the promised land. It tells how Rahab deliberately misled the king of Jericho. She told him that the Hebrew spies had left the city at nightfall, when in fact she had hidden them on her roof under stalks of flax. When she returned home, she recounted to the spies that her fellow countrymen were in "great fear" of the invaders. Moreover, she declared to them her own new-found faith in the true God, begging for mercy for herself and her family.

The spies responded to her plea. They went back to Joshua, reporting that "all the people are melting in fear."

Before long you and I will be celebrating Independence Day. Americans everywhere will rejoice in the privilege of living in a country that enjoys freedom. But how many of our citizens remember to stop and thank God for this golden land He has given us? And do we always act as good stewards of the bounty we so enjoy? Let us remember that the psalmist wrote, "Blessed is the nation whose God is the Lord" (Psalm 33:12).

Almighty and gracious Father, thank You for the opportunity to live in freedom. It is so easy to take this liberty for granted. So I pause right now and offer heartfelt gratitude. In the name of Jesus, who lives and reigns with You and the Holy Spirit, one God, now and forever, amen.

Our Marvelous God

Sing to the LORD a new song, for he has done marvelous things (Psalm 98:1).

Scripture: Psalm 98:1-6
Song: "What a Wonderful Savior!"

How do I get out of this one? I mused. It was time for a season of serious prayer again. I seemed to have hit another brick wall. There were no immediate answers to my dilemma, but I needed to find an answer quickly.

I don't know if you have been in such situations, but I have, many a time. And it happens over and over again, especially when I begin to think that the worst is over. I fret, I worry, and then I crawl back to God because I realize that He alone can cure the ills I face every day.

The psalmist David reminds us that one way to handle our dilemmas is to look back at the wonderful things God has already done for us. When we do that, we will be encouraged. We will remember that the God who helped us in the past will surely do so again. For He is a God who "has done marvelous things"—over and over again.

The trouble is, when our problems are behind us, it is easy to forget how the Lord came through for us. David calls us to remember and to keep offering God the praise He deserves.

Dear Heavenly Father, help me to remember all the good things You have done for me. May my heart sing with praise whenever I recall Your goodness and grace! Through Christ the Lord, amen.

June 20–26. **A. Koshy Muthalaly** is an ordained minister currently serving as professor in the Department of Professional Studies at Southern Nazarene University in Bethany, Oklahoma.

No End in Sight?

The Sovereign LORD will wipe away the tears from all faces (Isaiah 25:8).

Scripture: Isaiah 25:6-10
Song: "Far from My Heavenly Home"

It seemed as if the problems would never end. First it was Jim's asthma, then Craig's diabetes, and then the accident. Yes, Jean was badly injured in that accident, and the medical bills were piling up. And then to top it all, the credit card bills came due, and there was no money left to pay them.

The family was driven to despair, knowing nothing but sorrow, as Mary, Jim's wife, cried her heart out to God for answers.

Can you relate? We all go through tough times. Sometimes it feels to us as if we're living the story of Job all over again, one tragedy after another coming at us in quick succession. As one friend told me: "It seems as if the Devil has my name and number on his speed dial!"

When we go through life's trials, God gives us the power to endure them here. But Isaiah tells his people that a new day would come—a day where sorrow and tears would be wiped away.

We believers today are called to live life with our feet firmly planted on this earth. But our eyes are to be trained on Heaven. There, handkerchief in hand, our God waits to comfort us.

O Lord, help me to live this day knowing You are my ultimate source of comfort. When earthly life overwhelms me, let me remember that you are waiting to comfort me. In Christ I pray. Amen.

Standing Victorious in Struggle

The sting of death is sin, and the power of sin is the law. But thanks be to God! He gives us the victory through our Lord Jesus Christ (1 Corinthians 15:56, 57).

Scripture: 1 Corinthians 15:50-57
Song: "Faith Is the Victory"

If you have ever come face to face with death and were scared by it, then this story is for you.

Ron was only 13 years old, but I saw him in the hospital as he lay dying. He knew he was dying, yet every time I went to see him, he was cheerful.

How could he have that attitude? For one thing, Ron told me that he was going to Heaven. "Even though it's gonna be hard to leave my mother and brothers, I know I'm going to see them again."

There was something quite calming about listening to Ron. He encouraged me. And when I got back into my chaplain's office at the hospital, I would shed tears—not so much for Ron, but for myself and the lack of joy I seemed to have in the face of life's crises. Ron taught me to trust in the Lord a little bit more each day.

Are you facing some serious struggle today? Paul reminds us that Jesus is our victor. No matter how hard life seems to be right now, as Ron knew, in Him we have already won the battle.

Dear Lord God, help me to see that no matter what I face today, you have already gone before me to prepare the way. Even death has no power over You. So help me to trust You completely in every situation. Through my precious Savior, amen.

Believe . . . and Overcome

This is the victory that has overcome the world, even our faith. Who is it that overcomes the world? Only he who believes that Jesus is the Son of God (1 John 5:4, 5).

Scripture: 1 John 5:1-5
Song: "The Strife Is O'er, the Battle Done"

Tired of failure and defeat? You try so hard, and you fall flat on your face again and again. You want to do what is right, but you never win! Sound familiar?

Among other things that I do at the Christian university where I now work is teach World Religions. It is simply fascinating to see what people will do to "get to Heaven" (or their idea of it). Most of the devotees will do good works and follow the rules of their particular faith, and we certainly have to admire them for their steadfast devotion. But what I see in their lives is: They never know when they have done enough.

In Christianity, however, things are different. *Enough* was accomplished upon the cross. There Jesus offered the perfect and complete work to gain us fellowship with the Father and entry into His Heaven.

We don't have to earn an A+ on our own, for our Lord knows that is not possible. What He offers instead is to indwell us by His Spirit. Our dependence is on Him. He is the overcomer — Jesus, the Son of God. His perfect life and perfect sacrifice make us overcomers too. Do you believe it?

Lord God Almighty, I am weary of failures. I need your strength to win today's battles. Walk with me, dear Lord, and I know I am a winner. I pray this prayer in the name of Jesus, my merciful Savior and Lord. Amen.

What Is Your Heart's Desire?

May he give you the desire of your heart and make all your plans succeed (Psalm 20:4).

Scripture: Psalm 20
Song: "Guide Me, O Thou Great Jehovah"

What is your heart's longing? Did you know that God wants to give that desire to you?

I grew up in a simple, poor home in India. We didn't have very much. But my brother and I had godly parents who taught us to put the Lord first and to follow His leading. And what did I want to be when I grew up? A minister. Looking back now, after several decades, I see that God has given me much more along with fulfilling that childhood desire. Thus I've come to see that God wants to bless us to our heart's content and beyond what we could have imagined.

Yet some Christians seem to think that God is in battle against all their prayers and desires. They imagine having to pry God's reluctant hands open for His blessings. It's just the opposite! And we discover this when we realize that He is the source of *every* blessing.

So let us pay attention to our deepest longings. They can teach us, and if handled rightly, can even lead us closer to God. As A. W. Tozier put it, "The desire to fulfill the purpose for which we were created is a gift from God." God uses our longings to lead us to His purpose for our lives.

Almighty Father, You know exactly what I want, for You already know what is in my heart. I surrender those desires to You, because You alone can make all my plans succeed. I seek Your blessing today, in the name of Jesus. Amen.

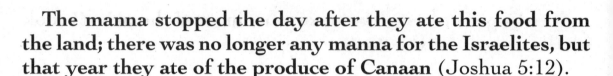

The Miracle Next Door

The manna stopped the day after they ate this food from the land; there was no longer any manna for the Israelites, but that year they ate of the produce of Canaan (Joshua 5:12).

Scripture: Joshua 5:10-15
Song: "The Care the Eagle Gives Her Young"

Has God stopped doing miracles? Consider: Jimmy had a lump on his neck that was growing larger every day. He prayed and prayed for the lump to go away, but every morning when he awoke the lump was still there.

No miraculous healing had occurred, but sometimes God forces us to think of alternatives that are waiting for us, just next door. You see, Jimmy's mother took him to the doctor. The lump was removed, and the problem was resolved.

Here God had already provided for the answer, and it was closer than expected. This does not mean that we do not call on Him. He loves to hear from us all the time. And He chooses many creative ways to answer (while sometimes saying No).

The Israelites ate every day in the wilderness. Where there were no grocery stores, God gave them miraculous manna. On the other hand, when they reached Canaan, God told them to go into the community and buy what they needed.

Do you need a miracle from God today? The answer may be next door. Or . . . if heavenly manna is the answer, God will open all of Heaven for you.

Dear Heavenly Father, enable me to see Your providence all around me today. I depend on You for all my needs, and I know You will provide. And if that includes a shower of heavenly manna, I am ready! Through the name of Jesus, amen.

First Things First

Joshua got up early the next morning and the priests took up the ark of the LORD (Joshua 6:12).

Scripture: Joshua 6:2-4, 12-20
Song: "Victory in Jesus"

What do you do first when you find yourself in a big mess? Who is your resource?

Jerry and Jane faced a mountain of debt for the third time that year. They had vowed never to get into debt again, but it kept happening. Now it loomed over them like a dark cloud. Their family was in turmoil.

Jerry took out another loan on his retirement account and paid off their pending bills. The problem was hardly solved, however. They did not have a plan in place for the future.

In these troubled times, we need a solid rock foundation to keep us anchored amidst raging storms. When faced with the formidable walls of Jericho, Joshua got up very early in the morning and took up the ark of the Lord. In today's terms, we might translate that to mean: He went first into the presence of the Lord to seek Him.

Where do you go in a crisis? Joshua's seeking after God teaches us that the walls will come down when we seek God. Like Joshua, Jerry and Jane can learn to turn to God first. From the days of Joshua to the present day, it is still a good thing for any of us to learn.

Lord, help me know today that You are there for me. When I face today's challenges, nudge me towards You, for You have all the resources I need in order to persevere with my faith intact. I pray through my deliverer, Jesus. Amen.

We Reap What We Sow

O LORD, what can I say, now that Israel has been routed by its enemies? (Joshua 7:8).

Scripture: Joshua 7:2-9
Song: "O How Happy Are They Who the Savior Obey"

One day Marcy's mother took her along to shop for groceries. Marcy decided to take a candy bar and put it in her purse. She and her mother left the store without any alarms going off, but later that evening her mother received a phone call. The store manager said that Marcy had been spotted, on a security camera, taking candy. When confronted, the young teen denied the theft. However, Mom eventually suffered through a court appearance, a fine, and much embarrassment.

Similarly, Achan's choices caused serious consequences. Warriors lay dead, and Joshua's faith wavered. But God revealed the source of the problem to Joshua and the people. After it became clear who the culprit was, Achan and his family were stoned to death. His theft brought an end to his life and created a legacy of shame.

What can we can learn from this story? For one thing, let us trust that God will indeed reveal evil deeds that are hidden. Secondly, we can be sure we'll reap what we sow—whether in this life or the next.

Heavenly Father, I approach You with gratitude and humility. Thank You for Your mercy and undying love. Please help me to count the cost prior to saying or doing anything that may be contrary to Your will. In Jesus' holy name. Amen.

June 27–30. **Le Lang,** who lives in Moultrie, Georgia, uses her doctorate in education to help guide and counsel schoolchildren.

Get Rid of the Ungodly Stuff

That is why the Israelites cannot stand against their enemies; they turn their backs and run because they have been made liable to destruction. I will not be with you anymore unless you destroy whatever among you is devoted to destruction (Joshua 7:12).

Scripture: Joshua 7:12-15
Song: "Immortal, Invisible, God Only Wise"

Achan had tangible things in his possession—a robe, silver coins, and a bar of gold. Those were the things God had wanted destroyed.

Even today people carry around "things" God wants destroyed. The difference is that we can't touch them with our hands, but we can surely see the manifestations of them in our behaviors. We are clearly told in Ephesians 4:31, to get rid of bitterness, rage, anger, harsh words, slander and all other types of malicious behavior. Romans 8:13 says, "If you live according to the sinful nature, you will die; but if by the Spirit you put to death the misdeeds of the body, you will live." Yes, we are to destroy the things that will be destructive to us. That is the way of God's love for us.

So when we are out facing the storms of life, and it seems we are all alone, a good question to ask is: "What things do I have that I need to get rid of?"

Heavenly Father, there have been times when I've felt as if everything was going wrong. Please help me learn from those times and to examine myself to see if I'm harboring a cherished sin. Especially, give me the courage to get rid of the things in my life that You know will hurt me or others. In Jesus' name, amen.

Don't Get Tangled!

Joshua said to Achan, "My son, give glory to the LORD, the God of Israel, and give him the praise. Tell me what you have done; do not hide it from me" (Joshua 7:19).

Scripture: Joshua 7:16-21
Song: "Hold to God's Unchanging Hand"

Every mother has pet peeves when it comes to her children. When I was growing up, number one on my own mother's list was dishonesty. "You'll always come out better by telling the truth," she'd say. And after testing that theory once—and dealing with the very unpleasant results—I was afraid ever to tell Mom something that wasn't quite true. (Now that I'm a mother myself, dishonesty is one thing I simply don't tolerate from my children.)

God wants us to be honest, as well. We can start by being honest with ourselves first, since He already knows every thought we have. And we can all strive to help and pray for each other in this area. That's important, because James 5:16 reads: "Confess your sins to each other and pray for each other so that you may be healed."

As a general rule of thumb, honesty in all things will give us a better life. We won't have a need to keep trying to remember what lies we've told in order to remain "consistent." I like the way Sir Walter Scott put it: "Oh, what a tangled web we weave, when first we practice to deceive!"

Dear God, I marvel at Your guidance. Surely You knew every snare that would beset me before I was even born. May I never weave my own web-like snares through practiced deception. In the precious name of Jesus I pray. Amen.

Freedom Tastes Good

You have been set free from sin and have become slaves to righteousness (Romans 6:18).

Scripture: Romans 6:15-23
Song: "Free from the Law"

When did you get your first taste of real freedom? When you left for college? When you moved into your own place? Think back to what it was like: "Nobody's going to tell me what time to be back home anymore! I can do whatever I want." You could hardly imagine the end of family curfew, right? What youthful elation!

But consider another kind of freedom and rejoice. It's freedom from eternal doom and destruction—freedom from being a slave to sin. The apostle Paul must have felt such relief to be delivered from the path he was on when his name was still Saul.

Remember, he'd been known for persecuting Christian believers. After his conversion and regaining his sight, he could finally see the light—physically and spiritually. He chose to become a servant of Christ, and he was quite happy about the freedom that would mean for him. In fact, for Paul, being a slave to righteousness was the greatest freedom of all.

It's amazing what liberty we have in living close to the Lord. We can shun bad habits that will put us in chains. We can let go of poisonous attitudes that will bind our spirit. We can run from questionable associations that will put our reputations in the cellar. Thank God, in Christ we're free!

O Sovereign God, help me to value and appreciate my freedom to love and serve You. Thank You for the cross of Christ that made it possible. In His name, amen.

My Prayer Notes

DEVOTIONS®

JULY

"Tell the next generation the praiseworthy deeds of the LORD, his power, and the wonders he has done.

—*Psalm 78:4*

Gary Allen, Editor   **Margaret Williams,** Project Editor   Photo © Michaeljung | Dreamstime.com

DEVOTIONS® is published quarterly by Standard Publishing, Cincinnati, Ohio, www.standardpub.com. © 2010 by Standard Publishing. All rights reserved. Topics based on the Home Daily Bible Readings, International Sunday School Lessons. © 2007 by the Committee on the Uniform Series. Printed in the U.S.A. All Scripture quotations, unless otherwise indicated, are taken from the *HOLY BIBLE, NEW INTERNATIONAL VERSION®. NIV®.* Copyright © 1973, 1978, 1984 by Biblica, Inc. ™ Used by permission of Zondervan. All rights reserved. *Holy Bible, New Living Translation (NLT),* © 1996, 2004. Tyndale House Publishers. *The Revised Standard Version of the Bible (RSV),* copyrighted 1946, 1952, © 1971, 1973.

So Who's to Judge?

The world's sin is that it refuses to believe in me (John 16:9, *New Living Translation*).

Scripture: John 16:4b-11
Song: "O Why Not Tonight?"

Today we seem to live in a world of relativism. I see followers of countless belief systems imaginable, from A to Z (Atheism to Zoroastrianism, for example). And many folks assume that each belief is as valid as the next. "Who's to judge?" they ask, with wide-eyed innocence.

A friend once shared a story about a teenager she knew who ended up "following the crowd." They were playing a game in which they tried to make themselves pass out for lack of oxygen and then revive themselves, just in time. What danger! One of the kids ended up not coming back.

I suppose these kids believed they could have fun in any way they wanted. But certain laws—absolutes about human physiology—demanded their respect. So it is in the moral realm. There really are absolutes there too. When we disregard that basic fact, we find ourselves short of life-giving spiritual sustenance. Bottomline: It would truly be a pity for us to be without God in our lives for too long and end up dying without Him.

Most High God, You have spared my life more times than I may know. For reasons only You know of I'm alive and well enough to read and learn more about You and your unconditional love. Please help me to increase my knowledge by reading and studying your Word more often. This is my prayer, in Jesus' name. Amen.

July 1–3. **Le Lang,** who lives in Moultrie, Georgia, uses her doctorate in education to help guide and counsel schoolchildren.

It's All Good from God

So you also should consider yourselves to be dead to the power of sin and alive to God through Christ Jesus (Romans 6:11, *New Living Translation*).

Scripture: Romans 6:1-11
Song: "Never Could Have Made It"

My teacher-friend's principal asked her to work with a lead teacher on plans to improve students' math scores. My friend always goes above and beyond to help her students excel. So she created a plan, at the request of the lead teacher, and presented it at the next faculty meeting. Everyone loved it and decided to implement it.

Finally, it was test time, and the students did extremely well. So the principal decided to invite the Central Office staff to the school for a meeting to showcase the achievement. Not only was my teacher friend not informed of, or invited to, the meeting—she received absolutely no credit for her plan, presentation, or hard work.

That is exactly how some people treat their Lord and Savior. Yet the apostle Paul reminds us again and again that if we have any life at all—it comes from God. If we are saved, we are saved by His grace. If we are blessed, we are blessed from above.

God should receive the glory in our lives. We have life and victory in Him alone. Everything good comes from His hand.

Lord, I realize that this world is far from perfect. My heart fills with gratitude when I think of how awesome You are and what power You possess. Please help me to remember from whom all blessings flow in my life. It's all from You, so may I lift up my heart in praise each day. In the name of Jesus I pray. Amen.

With the Lord, Stay on Your Feet

The LORD said to Joshua, "Get up! Why are you lying on your face like this? Israel has sinned and broken my covenant!" (Joshua 7:10, 11, *New Living Translation*).

Scripture: Joshua 7:1, 10-12, 22-26
Song: "A Shelter in the Time of a Storm"

Ever been knocked off your feet? It can happen literally, of course. But the feeling can also come wrapped in sudden, shocking news—death of a loved one, loss of a job, a bleak prognosis from the doctor. What do you do when you lose your footing?

Joshua was surely knocked off his feet by news of his army's thoroughly unexpected, defeat. What anguish he felt as he considered his soldiers' lost lives. Joshua and his leaders tore their clothing, threw dust on their heads, and bowed down in dismay.

Then Joshua went to God about the matter. And we learn that God revealed everything the general needed to know: He gave Joshua clear instructions on solving the problem.

As I meditated on this Scripture, I had to ask myself: Do I consistently look to God when trouble tumbles into my life? Or do I tend to sink in despair?

I'd like to grow in my ability to remember who I am in those tough times—a child of the king. I'd like to remember that my Lord, the king, can do far more than I could ever ask or think to deliver me and give me peace.

O, **Lord,** help me to remember to run to you in the day of trouble. Help me to stand up, and then keep me on my feet! How I need Your guidance daily! In the holy and divine name of Jesus I pray. Amen.

Just Get Me Home

See, I am sending an angel ahead of you to guard you along the way and to bring you to the place I have prepared (Exodus 23:20).

Scripture: Exodus 23:20-33
Song: "O God, Our Help in Ages Past"

My 1980 Chevrolet Citation had landed a solid position in the unreliable category. But until I could convince my parents of this, I was stuck driving the old beater during my high school years in the mid-90s.

This car frequently left me stranded, so I developed a kind of protocol. First, call my parents to tell them I was heading for home and letting them know which route I'd take. Second, always make sure someone waited until my car started. I didn't want to be alone when my car didn't start. The third step in my routine (and most important): I prayed the entire way home that God would send angels to protect and guide me.

Those days of unreliable transportation are behind me. But I still cling to the idea that God may well send angels to prepare the way for me throughout my daily life. It's nice to know when I reach a spiritual, physical, or emotional destination that I am in a friendly place. In some marvelous way, the eternal God is there already, waiting for me.

Lord God Almighty, thank You for Your constant presence in my life. I am grateful that You care for me amidst every situation I face. Thank You for Your guidance and provision. I humbly accept this gift and praise You in Jesus' name. Amen.

July 4–10. **J. Renee Arche**r is a wife, mother, writer, and piano teacher. She and her husband enjoy working in their yard and fixing up their 100-year-old home.

I Need a Witness

"See!" he said to all the people. "This stone will be a witness against us. It has heard all the words the LORD has said to us. It will be a witness against you if you are untrue to your God" (Joshua 24: 27).

Scripture: Joshua 24:19-27
Song: "Remember in Youth Thy Creator"

I forget easily. In order to minimize my lapses in memory, I write lists, make mental notes, and ask for reminders frequently. I've even been known to put my car keys in the refrigerator so I wouldn't forget to take my lunch to work! Leaving notes on the counter and mirror has also served me well. I put items in my way so I'll see them, reminding me of what I'm supposed to do.

In other words, a visual reminder helps me follow through. For several years I wore a cross necklace every day. I wore it more as a reminder to myself than a proclamation to others. It was a small, but effective way to keep me accountable to the one who gave His life for me.

When I struggle in my spiritual journey, I do what I can to foster growth and improvement. For example, to develop my habit of reading the Scripture every day, I knew I couldn't leave my Bible on a high shelf in the living room. So now it resides on my bedside table. That Bible serves as a "witness" when I decide that a few minutes more sleep is more important than reading God's precious Word.

Thank You, **Dear Lord,** for Your steadfast love, even when I am untrue to You. Lord, reveal to me when and where I need visual witnesses to keep me close to You, and forgive me when I fall short of Your will. In Christ's name I pray, amen.

Did You Really Obey?

"But I did obey the LORD," Saul said. **"I went on the mission the LORD assigned me"** (1 Samuel 15:20).

Scripture: 1 Samuel 15:17-23
Song: "Obey My Voice"

I didn't purposefully disobey. In fact, I thought I *was* obeying. After listening to the instructions, I did what I thought was right, only to find out later I'd clearly done the wrong thing. I misunderstood the instructions.

Has this happened to you? Have you ever felt that you did the right thing, only to find out you did what was wrong and even made matters worse? Mistakes happen—it's called being human. But it can be difficult to get past our shortcomings, especially if we were trying our best to do the job correctly. We're left feeling defeated and inadequate.

Now think about Saul in our Scripture today. It must have been devastating to discover he'd misunderstood the assignment God gave him, though the Scripture implies a significant strain of rebellion in the king as well. There was also the fact that he "was afraid of the people and so [he] gave in to them" (v. 24). Yes, deep inside he knew he was at fault.

When this happens to me, I remind myself that a failure isn't the end of the world. And I hold fast to the mercy and grace of my Father in Heaven. If there is sin, I can confess it. God knows my heart, and He knows when I intend to obey.

Heavenly Father, thank You for Your grace and mercy when I misread Your will for my life or when I simply choose to ignore it. Thank You for not giving up on me at those times! In the name of my gracious Savior, I pray. Amen.

Meeting God Through Music

Speak to one another with psalms, hymns and spiritual songs. Sing and make music in your heart to the Lord (Ephesians 5:19).

Scripture: Ephesians 5:6-20
Song: "Open the Eyes of My Heart"

The campfire in front of me captivated my sight, but my mind and soul were focused elsewhere. The young voices, including mine, were praising God through song. God in return was capturing our hearts.

The sacredness of that experience was awesome. It wasn't the people who shared it with me, the camp setting, or the spoken words. The holiness of those moments was a result of my *complete* focus on God. I truly desired to worship Him and offer myself to Him in service.

The songs we sang led me to God and provided an atmosphere for such a worship experience. In fact, I feel that I first met God through song, and I continue to meet Him through music today. When I long for that pouring-out-my-heart in pure worship, I can depend on music to lead me. I love meeting God this way. It's our special thing we do together.

God is ready to meet us wherever we are ready for that special time together. He wants to spend time with each of us. He desires our worship. Meet God with an open heart and meet Him frequently.

Thank You, **Lord,** for connecting with me through worship. I thank You for the musical gifts You have given me, and I pray to use them for Your honor and glory. May I always desire to meet you in fellowship and worship. In Christ's name, I pray. Amen.

And Your Legacy?

After that whole generation had been gathered to their fathers, another generation grew up, who knew neither the LORD nor what he had done for Israel (Judges 2:10).

Scripture: Judges 2:1-10
Song: "I'll Fly Away"

Sometimes I wonder what people will remember about me after I die. What memories and stories will people tell at my funeral? I may sound morbid, but it's worth giving it some thought.

My brothers could share stories of the times I tattled on them, or they could tell about the heart-to-heart conversations we had while they fixed my car. My childhood best friend could tell about the time I lost her favorite flip-flops in a manure pile. Or she could reminisce about the high school trials we helped each other survive. And my parents! Would they spend time rehashing all the times I nagged them? Or would they just smile and tell about the times I made them proud?

Although I can't control what people will remember about me, I can live in such a way that leaves people blessed to have known me. There are certain characteristics I hope people see portrayed throughout my life—like love, joy, generosity, and self-control.

Most of all, I hope people will remember that I lived my life for my Savior, Jesus Christ. I want my legacy to shine with His radiant beauty—right through to the next generation.

God, help me live in a way that will reflect Your greatness in my legacy. I want future generations to know Your ways. Give me opportunities to share the hope that is in me, as I do and say the things that will bring You glory. Through Christ, amen.

No Hush-Hush Faith!

We will not hide them from their children; we will tell the next generation the praiseworthy deeds of the LORD, his power, and the wonders he has done (Psalm 78:4).

Scripture: Psalm 78:1-8
Song: "Pass It On"

What's your secret? What part of your life do you try to keep under cover? Is it your weight? your age? your past? your in-laws? your faith? I suppose we all have a skeleton in the closet of some kind.

I don't want everyone to know everything about me. Some details in my life I'd rather keep to myself! And thankfully, most people appreciate such social boundaries. It's not that I have a lot to hide, but some things should be left private.

However, according to Scripture, my faith isn't meant to be a hush-hush aspect of my life. Who I live my life for shouldn't be the best kept secret. I want people to see and know the joy I have in Christ. Especially, I want my son to witness my relationship with my Savior. I know I'm called to introduce and lead my child to Christ, and I can't do this secretly.

Besides, how can any of us keep the best things in our lives from our children? As the psalmist knew, God has done, is doing, and will continue to do awesome things in the lives of His people. That's no secret. Go spread the word!

Almighty God of glory, You are worthy of all my praise and devotion. Give me the courage to tell of Your goodness to the next generation. May I resist the temptation to keep my faith a secret and forgive me when I stay silent in the face of opportunities to speak of Your salvation. I thank You in the name of Jesus. Amen.

When the Cat's Away

When the judge died, the people returned to ways even more corrupt than those of their fathers, following other gods and serving and worshiping them. They refused to give up their evil practices and stubborn ways (Judges 2:19).

Scripture: Judges 2:11-19
Song: "Higher Ground"

Every classroom of kids is the same. When the teacher leaves the room, the mischief begins. It only takes one ornery student to rile the others. A few moments in that teacher-less state and the old rule of thumb kicks in: "When the cat's away, the mice will play."

According to our Scripture today, it happened in ancient Israel whenever the people felt free of a godly leader. Even we Christians today can backslide into old behaviors—especially when we think no one is watching. It's easy to let our standards slip then, as if we can only be good for so long.

God knows we have this tendency. No doubt that's why He puts people in our lives like judges, ministers, teachers, and accountability partners to help us walk in the light. Yet such folks come and go throughout our lives. We need to develop the inner resolve and strength to live right, even when external boundaries loosen. It is the Holy Spirit within us who leads us into righteous living. Relying on Him is the way through all temptations—even when no one else could ever know of our sin.

Lord, thank You for Your unconditional love, even when I succumb to self-destructive behaviors. Help me stay accountable to the way of life You desire for me, relying on Your indwelling Spirit to see me through. In Jesus' name I pray. Amen.

Beyond Betrayal

Now my head shall be lifted up above my enemies round about me (Psalm 27:6, *Revised Standard Version*).

Scripture: Psalm 27:1-6
Song: "Lift Up Your Head"

Anne sat in her minister's study, head bowed, as she told her story. She and Jeff, her husband of 23 years, had befriended Sandi, a troubled young woman. Together they had reached out to Sandi. They had even taken her into their home to help her gain a new start in life, spending hours counseling with her.

Gradually, good intentions turned to temptation. Jeff spent more time with Sandi. His counselor role became something else—something more intimate. Sandi had usurped Anne's place.

Anne's life as wife, partner, and best friend had disappeared. She was alone and embittered. How could she go on? How could she ever trust again and hold her head high?

David, the psalmist, knew about betrayal. Saul pursued him unmercifully and without just cause. And his own son, Absalom, led a revolt against his kingship. David also agonized over lost relationships through the treachery of those he had loved. Yet David put all his hope in God who would lift his head.

Enemies may seek our destruction, and loved ones may fail us. But our promise-keeping God remains ever faithful.

Lord, in the despair of human betrayal I will trust You to lift my head. Trusting You, I will reject the bitterness that could enslave me. In Jesus' name, amen.

January 11–17. **Jan Pierce,** a freelance writer living in Vancouver, Washington, is a retired school-teacher. She spends several months each year doing missions work in India with her husband.

Determined Dandelion

I am still confident of this: I will see the goodness of the Lord in the land of the living (Psalm 27:13).

Scripture: Psalm 27:7-14
Song: "Now to God, Our Strength and Saviour"

You have to admire the lowly dandelion. For sheer determination to thrive under all conditions, it has no rival. Its long taproots can grow 10 inches deep into the ground. And its sunny yellow flower develops into fluffy seedpods overnight. Ask any gardener—dandelions are nearly impossible to eradicate.

Literally translated from Old French, the *dent-de-lion*, or "lion's tooth," takes its name from its long, lance-shaped leaves. Dandelions grow in virtually all climates all over the world. Who hasn't seen one poking its head up through asphalt, seemingly invincible?

You and I would benefit from that same degree of hardy strength and perseverance in the face of life's adversities. Even as David cried out to God for help in the midst of trouble, he also voiced a determined confidence in the goodness of God. He chose to see that goodness and grace in all circumstances, focusing on a victory beyond the troubles of the day.

As that dandelion plant sinks its roots deep and pushes straight up through all obstacles toward the light, so we can deepen our roots in the Lord. Let us be absolutely determined to put our trust in Him, no matter what.

Almighty Father in Heaven, when my days swirl with troubles, may I put down deep roots into Your Word. Help me turn my face up to Your life-giving light. In the name of Your Son, my Savior, I pray. Amen.

The End of the Story

Why do you make me look at injustice? Why do you tolerate wrong? (Habakkuk 1:3).

Scripture: Habakkuk 1:1-5
Song: "Come, Thou Almighty King"

In C. S. Lewis's classic book, *The Lion, the Witch, and the Wardrobe,* there is a scene of tremendous sorrow. Aslan has submitted himself to the deep magic. He has been shorn of his beautiful mane, humiliated by the evil horde, tied upon the stone table, and killed. Susan and Lucy witnessed these heinous acts. Heartbroken, they have cried all through the long night.

We too can be pulled down by the whirlpool-force of evil in the world around us. Everywhere we turn we see violence and injustice. The evening news drones on with its reports of bombings, robberies, and financial disintegration. We become heartsick with the continual vision of man's inhumanity to man.

In Narnia, though, Susan and Lucy soon witness a miracle. At the appointed time, just at sunrise, the girls hear a deafening noise. The stone table breaks in two. As the girls stare in wonder, Aslan reappears as golden and beautiful as ever. There is pure joy as Susan and Lucy ride on Aslan's back to the final battle. There evil goes down to defeat — once and for all.

You and I know the end of this world's story. It's the perfect ending. Get ready for the ride of your life!

Gracious God, give me the courage to live victoriously in a world overcome with evil. And may I have the patience to wait for the conclusion of Your great restoration. Your promises remain true, and they never fail. Thank You, great King of kings! I pray this prayer in the name of Jesus, my Savior and Lord. Amen.

The Homecoming

In God, whose word I praise, in God I trust; I will not be afraid. What can mortal man do to me? (Psalm 56:4).

Scripture: Psalm 56:1-11
Song: "Heaven Is My Home"

The letter of August 15, 1900, read, "We've tried to get away to the hills, but the plans do not work. Our things are being stolen right and left, for the people know we are condemned."

The author was Mrs. Elizabeth Graham Atwater. She and her husband, Ernest, with their four daughters, were serving as missionaries in Shan-si province, China. The Boxer Rebellion was in full swing, its participants intent on killing all foreigners, including Chinese Christian converts. Roving bands of rebels had been threatening them for months, and government forces were unable to quell the violence.

The letter continued, "I am preparing for the end very quietly and calmly. The Lord is wonderfully near . . . I was very restless and excited while there seemed a chance of life. But God has taken away that feeling, and now I just pray for grace to meet the terrible end bravely. Lizzie."

As the family left by oxcart, Elizabeth, her husband, and two of their daughters did, indeed, lose their lives at the hands of rebels. Yet Elizabeth had come to peace with her imminent death. At the end of her letter she wrote, "The pain will soon be over—and Oh!—the sweetness of the welcome above."

Heavenly Father, may I live courageously as so many before me have done. Though my body is fragile, my spirit is eternal. I look forward to my heavenly homecoming. In the name of Jesus, Lord and Savior of all, I pray. Amen.

We'll All See His Power

Ascribe to the LORD the glory due his name; worship the LORD in the splendor of his holiness (Psalm 29:2).

Scripture: Psalm 29
Song: "All Hail the Power of Jesus' Name"

It was a Sunday in May of 1980 when Mt. St. Helen's erupted, forever changing the landscape of southwestern Washington State. Even though scientists had been tracking the increasing pressure of the lava dome and newscasters monitored daily tremors, the devastating eruption still came as a shock. The blast's sheer power was astounding.

Fifty-seven men and women lost their lives that day. An area of 200 square miles was rendered lifeless, and 1,300 feet of the mountain simply disappeared. Millions of animals, birds, and fish died instantly, and miles of huge trees were stripped and laid flat like toothpicks.

All eyes stayed glued to the television coverage. But why did people marvel at an event predicted for months? The answer is easy—it's hard to merely *imagine* such power; people wanted to actually *see* it. In like fashion, before humans see God's power, they tend to underestimate it. Natural phenomenon, such as the crack of thunder or the roar of tornado winds, hint at a heavenly power far beyond our capacity to fathom.

How blessed we'll be if we bow our knee today and humbly worship Almighty God by our own choosing.

O God, I praise You in Your might and Your power. I honor You as king. You are the source of my strength, and You are king forever! In Jesus' name, amen.

Finding Family

The Egyptians are men and not God; their horses are flesh and not spirit (Isaiah 31:3).

Scripture: Isaiah 31:1-5
Song: "The Family of God"

One of the saddest realities of life in today's urban centers is the presence of youth gangs. Mere children take part in violent, senseless acts as rites of passage, hoping to gain personal protection. The streets are dangerous, family structures are weak or nonexistent, and young people want connection with something bigger than themselves. They need a "family."

Hezekiah, king of Judah, was under siege by Assyrian forces. Though Isaiah counseled him to trust only in God—and not in the horses and chariots of mere men—Hezekiah allied with Egypt, an ungodly nation. There would be strength in numbers, he thought.

Fueled with a false sense of well-being, Hezekiah attacked the Assyrians. The result: over 40 walled cities lost, and 200,000 people of God taken captive.

Our young men and women, deep in the pit of gang activity, will also experience profound loss. Their search for a family is valid. But like Hezekiah, they're looking in the wrong place. There's an ultimate safety in belonging to the family of God. There's protection in finding identity in the Father of all mankind. Let us proclaim it, loud and clear.

O, **God,** my rock and my salvation, I choose to trust You in the battles of my life. I look to You only for victory, and I claim You only as my protection. Thank You, Father, in the precious name of Jesus. Amen.

Playing Both Sides?

Again the Israelites cried out to the LORD, and he gave them a deliverer (Judges 3:15).

Scripture: Judges 3:15-25, 29, 30
Song: "Undivided Heart"

As a child at school, I loved recess. At recess we could roller-skate, swing, or spy on boys. Spying was by far my favorite game. I can still recall the thrill of sneaking around the corners of buildings, catching a glimpse of "the enemy," and running back to report to my girl-spy friends. Alas, my spying ran amuck when I realized I could double the intrigue by sometimes spying *for* the boys—a miniature Mata Hari was born!

Where was my allegiance? To whom would I be faithful? It was all confusing until a new game came along and spying became passé.

The children of Israel faced a similar quandary, but with grown-up consequences. They loved the Lord their God. They kept the laws and celebrated the holy days. But they also bent their ears to local culture and false gods. They went to the shrines of Ashtoreth and Baal, celebrating fertility rites for the successful crops. Time after time they did evil and then repented, crying out to God for deliverance.

God hates a divided heart. We need to know where our allegiance lies, serving the Lord purely and faithfully. It is in our sin nature to play both sides, but the benefit of a devoted heart is beyond compare.

O God, purify my heart that I might serve You, and You only, all of my days. Give me an undivided heart. In Jesus' name, amen.

Prayer Power

Then Hannah prayed and said: "My heart rejoices in the LORD; in the LORD my horn is lifted high. My mouth boasts over my enemies, for I delight in your deliverance" (1 Samuel 2:1).

Scripture: 1 Samuel 2:1-10
Song: "Sweet Hour of Prayer"

Hannah knew the deal. And had she not known, her rival, Peninnah (her husband Elkanah's other wife), would gladly remind her (see 1 Samuel 1:6). Nothing other than having a child could fulfill Hannah's deepest longing. She cried out to God, and God answered her prayer. Yet Hannah gave her son, Samuel, back to God as she had promised.

My friend Cynthia, who gave birth to her first child at age 43, had also fervently prayed to God. "The Bible tells me that nothing is too hard for God," said Cynthia. "And I believe it!"

Cynthia knew that many others were praying for her too. "I remember how my aunt Della used to call me at 5:30 in the morning so we could pray together," said Cynthia. "She told me not to give up, and I didn't."

Hannah didn't give up in her prayer for a child, and her praise for God's answer can be an encouragement to others. As another friend of mine, Dottie, would say, "Those who don't pray don't know what they're missing."

Lord, help me learn more about the power of prayer and to pray more often. In the name of Jesus, my Savior, amen.

July 18–24. **Jimmie Oliver Fleming,** of Chester, Virginia, spends her days writing, caring for her grandchildren, and making local nursing home visits.

Just Follow Instructions

It is the LORD your God you must follow, and him you must revere (Deuteronomy 13:4).

Scripture: Deuteronomy 13:1-5
Song: "Follow Me, the Master Said"

Following instructions can save your life. This applies both spiritually and physically. For example, the words in the familiar verse John 3:16 are quite clear. Follow them and receive eternal life.

Similarly, the second half of Deuteronomy 13:4 states, "Keep his commands and obey him; serve him and hold fast to him." Following instructions like this will create a life of goodness and blessing. The alternative is indeed a form of spiritual death.

In our Scripture today, as God warned the Israelites about worshiping other gods, He warns us in the same way today. False prophets still lurk among us in the world, and we can sometimes get caught off guard. That's when we need to ask ourselves: "Is the true God, the Father of my Lord Jesus Christ, always first in my life?"

I like the way writer Frederick Buechner described the problem in his book *Wishful Thinking:* "Idolatry is the practice of ascribing absolute value to things of relative worth." It is always a temptation, isn't it? When we let anything of finite value claim the place of our infinite Lord . . . well, we've stopped following instructions, haven't we?

Almighty God, thank You for everything that You have given me. Help me to serve You with sincerity and oneness of heart. My life would be nothing without You, so may I pass the test of devoted love to You always. In Jesus' name, amen.

At It Again!

Midian so impoverished the Israelites that they cried out to the LORD for help (Judges 6:6).

Scripture: Judges 6:1-10
Song: "The Trusting Heart to Jesus Clings"

A familiar scene took place in a certain household one Wednesday afternoon when 10-year-old Michael arrived home from school. His parents had already gotten word that Michael had been "at it again." He had not only caused trouble in the classroom but on the school bus as well.

The Israelites had a similar relationship with God: they too were often "at it again." They faithfully served Him for a while but then turned once again to their old, idolatrous ways. Yet in today's Scripture we see them crying out for help because of their severe plight. The Lord was all too familiar with their fickle attitudes.

We can look down on that ancient community and wonder how it could vacillate so easily between faithfulness and sin. But aren't we too often fickle in our relationship with God? Yet let us not hesitate to cry out for help, just as the Israelites did, time after time. After all, our God is long suffering and merciful.

Ten-year-old Michael certainly learned his lesson, and all by way of firsthand experience. His parents loved him enough to discipline him. He grew up knowing he was loved and decided to become a school bus driver.

Heavenly Father, please forgive my fickleness. In my weakness, I don't trust You as I should. Yet I'm praying for a closer daily relationship with You. I pray that this will be so with my fellow believers, as well. In Jesus' name, amen.

Words from an Angel

When the angel of the LORD appeared to Gideon, he said, "The LORD is with you, mighty warrior" (Judges 6:12).

Scripture: Judges 6:11-16
Song: "The Battle Belongs to the Lord"

I had far more questions about my situation than Gideon had about his, even if I hadn't voiced them. I also knew I was already deep into a battle.

As I tried to make my decision, questions had been swirling in my mind for several weeks. How would this affect my writing career? How would it affect my marriage? How would it affect my whole life? Discussing the situation with my husband, he had simply said, "Well, it's your decision. I certainly can't make it for you." No, he couldn't, yet I'd still hoped for a little encouragement from him to follow my heart. But my heart felt heavy as I went for my walk that morning.

Then I met my neighbor, Elsie. Her words not only encouraged me but also seemed to be an answer to my prayer. "Oh, I think it's a great idea that you're planning to care for your grandchildren," she said. "My husband Darnell's mother kept all of her grandchildren as long as she was able to."

Like the angel who spoke to Gideon, I took my neighbor Elsie's words in the same way. "The Lord is with you mighty warrior Jimmie," I told myself with a smile.

Dear Heavenly Father, I have no doubt that You can fight my battles, so I trust You with all of my life. Thank You for giving me the desire and the strength to carry out Your will for me. Continue to guide me in Your wisdom as You help me learn how to hear Your voice each day. In Christ's name I pray. Amen.

Tearing Things Down

That same night the LORD said to him, "Take the second bull from your father's herd, the one seven years old. Tear down your father's altar to Baal and cut down the Asherah pole beside it" (Judges 6:25).

Scripture: Judges 6:25-32
Song: "Is Your All on the Altar?"

"Restoration projects are all well and good in some cases," the guest speaker for a civics organization said. "But sometimes it's better to start from the ground up. You might have to tear things down first."

What a great speech, the members agreed. No one had ever put it so bluntly before. And no one had ever given these people such hope. "I had known it was time to move on," one man said. "But it was hard to convince anyone else of that. Well, now they can look at things differently. They can see the light."

The same might be said of Gideon, once he found a little courage. Following the Lord and tearing down his father's altar to Baal was no small feat for Gideon. He had the cover of night to shield him, but this didn't quell his fear.

Plus, Gideon had to face the men of the town the next day. They were angry about what had taken place. Yet their hostility also showed the futility of worshiping a false god. If Baal was really who they thought him to be, could Baal not defend the destruction of his altar?

Lord, thank You for giving me another chance to worship You in spirit and in truth. I know You are the true and living God and that You will stand by me in all situations. Whatever I need, You will supply. I thank You for it all. In Jesus' name, amen.

Answers You Can Trust

Gideon said to God, "If you will save Israel by my hand as you have promised—look, I will place a wool fleece on the threshing floor. If there is dew only on the fleece and all the ground is dry, then I will know that you will save Israel by my hand, as you said" (Judges 6:36, 37).

Scripture: Judges 6:36-40
Song: "I Found the Answer"

When it comes to receiving answers from God, we know that we can always trust them—or should. But Gideon went a step further. He asked God to show proof that He was capable of fulfilling His promise.

I wonder: Wouldn't it be a bit frightening to approach the almighty God that way and get His response? I recall the time when I stood at my kitchen window and wished for a cup of bleach. That's all I needed, one cup of bleach. And because that was all I needed, I didn't want to muster up the energy to go to the store.

I did go for my morning walk, however. And when I returned, I could hardly believe my eyes. There next to the curb was a whole bottle of bleach! Where had it come from? My walking partner, Mary Jo, suggested it had fallen off a trash truck. I never found the answer. I never used the bleach, either, because . . . I was afraid.

Gideon wasn't afraid, though. He simply took God at His word. You and I can do likewise.

Loving Father, You know my every weakness. I am thankful that You do. I am thankful that when I doubt Your answers, You understand that too! In Jesus' name, amen.

No Mismatch Too Much

The LORD said to Gideon, "You have too many men for me to deliver Midian into their hands. In order that Israel may not boast against me that her own strength has saved her, announce now to the people, 'Anyone who trembles with fear may turn back and leave Mount Gilead'" (Judges 7:2, 3).

Scripture: Judges 7:2-4, 13-15; 8:22-26a
Song: "Lead Me, Lord"

The little blue and white notecard attached to my computer says, "God is Boss." The Scripture reference on it from Proverbs 3:6 reminds me to acknowledge Him in all my ways.

God gave Gideon a similar message about his army. If that fighting force had stayed large, Israel might have boasted of her own strength in defeating the Midianites. So you know the story of how God kept downsizing the army until it was just right, going from 32,000 to 300 warriors.

What a difference in the numbers! Yet in following God's instructions, Gideon and his men accomplished the intended results.

God works similarly with us to achieve goals in the kingdom for His glory. For example, Proverbs 3:5, 6 tells us, "Trust in the LORD with all your heart and lean not on your own understanding; in all your ways acknowledge him, and he will make your paths straight." When we trust God to step out in faith, we can face even the most dismal mismatches with confidence. Gideon and his army did it. So can we.

Lord God, help me to believe and receive all that You have promised in Your word, especially Your promises of strength and victory. In the name of Christ, amen.

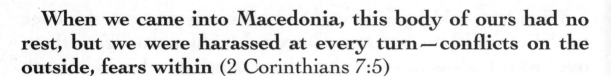

On the Battlefield Together

When we came into Macedonia, this body of ours had no rest, but we were harassed at every turn—conflicts on the outside, fears within (2 Corinthians 7:5)

Scripture: 2 Corinthians 7:5-11
Song: "Rescue"

Imagine yourself standing on a battlefield, sword in hand. From every angle, you are surrounded, and the enemy is closing in quickly. You turn to the right and to the left, looking for a route of escape. But you have nowhere to turn and no way to defeat the attackers. What do you do?

When the enemy attacks us, he comes at us from many angles, most powerfully at our very point of weakness. Apparently for the apostle Paul, his physical body was a prime target. Yet he persevered, maintaining a thankful heart for the comfort that came through fellow believers.

Usually when I go through a period of difficulty, it seems as if my whole world is caving in at once. But at the moment of my deepest struggle, I try to remind myself that God is with me. He can give me the strength to overcome any trial of faith. And He often uses others in the church to convey His encouragement.

Whatever your situation, God knows exactly what you are going through. You are not on that battlefield alone.

Lord, help me remember that no matter what battles I face, You are always there fighting for me. You give me the strength to get through anything, and You give me brothers and sisters in Christ to encourage me. Thank You, in Jesus' name, amen.

July 25–31. **Sandi Brown** and her husband, Kirk, minister in a church in Bloomfield, Indiana. They have three beautiful children and two crazy dogs.

Just Walk Away

When they sin against you—for there is no one who does not sin—and you become angry with them and give them over to the enemy, who takes them captive to his own land, far away or near (1 Kings 8:46).

Scripture: 1 Kings 8:46-50
Song: "Enemy's Camp"

I love to watch my husband and my kids playing around and wrestling together. My youngest daughter has absolutely no fear. She waits until they are all in a big pile and then flings herself onto the top! But what is most interesting is when my husband grabs one of my kids' feet. Suddenly the power they had vanishes as they hop around on one foot, struggling to stay standing. When someone else has control of one of your feet, they can control your entire body.

In a sense, the same is true of our spiritual bodies. If we give in to the temptations of sin, then the enemy begins to gain a foothold in our lives. Yes, it is true that we do all sin. But how often does this happen? The more we sin, the stronger the foothold becomes—to the point that we become desensitized to the destructive impact of our misdeeds.

The good news is that the foothold does not have to be permanent. We may be tempted by sin, but we need not give in to it. So let us ask ourselves today: What adjustments can I make to walk away from potential footholds?

Dear Father, reveal to me the footholds that may be preventing me from developing a deeper relationship with You. I pray that I can avoid falling into the traps of sin. Help me to gain a foothold in Your kingdom instead! I pray in Christ's name. Amen!

Well Done

"Therefore, O house of Israel, I will judge you, each one according to his ways, declares the Sovereign LORD. Repent! Turn away from all your offenses; then sin will not be your downfall" (Ezekiel 18:30).

Scripture: Ezekiel 18:25-32
Song: "Cleanse Me"

It's never good when you get a phone call at work from your child's teacher. I had never had that experience with any of my three children until this past school year. I received a call to inform me that my daughter had told another girl in her class that she "smelled like dead fish." That came as a shock to me, as I tried to envision my sweet daughter saying something so awful. As you can imagine, she dreaded coming home that day. She knew she would face some judgment for her actions.

Just as my daughter was judged for her actions, we will also be judged by our actions, whether good or bad. God sees everything we do, even those things hidden from others. He knows all our words and actions. He knows what our true motives are.

We know that as Christian believers, our deeds don't determine whether we receive God's gracious salvation. Instead, the Bible seems to indicate that what we do with that salvation and our spiritual gifts will determine our reward when we stand before Christ (see 1 Corinthians 3:12-15). I hope on that day He will say to me: "Well done, good and faithful servant."

Dear Father, help me to live a life You would be proud of. May I let go of any secret sins in my life, and do give me strength to make the right choices. In Christ, amen.

Reach Your Full Bloom for Him

"For three years now I've been coming to look for fruit on this fig tree and haven't found any. Cut it down! Why should it use up the soil?" (Luke 13:7).

Scripture: Luke 13:1-9
Song: "Follow On"

As far as I'm concerned, rummage sales are simply wonderful. What better way to clean the clutter from your house than by selling all that old stuff for money? That's why we have a rummage sale every year. Anything we haven't used during that past year goes out the door.

During the summer rummage sale season, I can't help being reminded of our Scripture passage today. Here Jesus tells the parable of a fig tree that wasn't producing any fruit. The man in the parable wanted to cut down this tree because it wasn't of any worth to him. A tree not producing any fruit was just a waste of space in a vineyard.

Jesus was speaking to the fruitfulness He wants to see in the lives of His followers. Are we producing fruit, or are we a bit dormant, not really growing much at all?

We know that our lives should reflect the character of Christ more and more as we walk with Him. But if we aren't growing in this way, aren't we just using up space in the church? Instead, let us strive to reach our full-bloom potential for the kingdom!

Almighty and most merciful God, I pray that You would help me to fulfill Your plan for my life. Keep me from falling to the temptation of being satisfied with where I am at the moment. I want to do more for Your kingdom and bring more people into it! In Christ's precious name, I pray. Amen.

Raising the Temperature

I know your deeds, that you are neither cold nor hot. I wish you were either one or the other! (Revelation 3:15).

Scripture: Revelation 3:14-22
Song: "Church on Fire"

Why is it that people will cheer, yell, and get all pumped up at a ball game, but as soon as they arrive at church, all the enthusiasm goes away? Often during a church service, I see folks who are ready to nod off to sleep. Others seem to have their minds in another place. Are they perhaps thinking about what to make for dinner? Yet I'm just as guilty as anyone when it comes to the occasional apathetic attitude toward the things of God.

According to the book of Revelation, the church in Laodicea was guilty of the same thing. The members there just weren't as passionate about God as they should've been. Instead of being on fire for God, they were lukewarm, doing just enough to get by.

This Scripture calls us to do an inventory of our attitudes. What kinds of things are we passionate about these days? Do we get excited for the things of God in the same way? What would it take to rekinled our desire for a deeper fellowship with our Lord?

I am going to start today to try to raise the temperature of my spiritual life. Will you join me in fanning the flames for the things of God?

Lord, how I need You in my life! Please restore a passionate, hungry attitude in me that longs for the things of Your kingdom. In Christ's awesome name I pray. Amen.

Do You Understand?

"**Everything must be fulfilled that is written about me in the Law of Moses, the Prophets and the Psalms.**" **Then he opened their minds so they could understand the Scriptures** (Luke 24:45).

Scripture: Luke 24:44-49
Song: "Tell Me the Story of Jesus"

Have you ever had trouble reading the Bible? Maybe you've read a passage and then immediately realized you retained none of it. Or perhaps after reading the text, you grasped little of the meaning. In other words, has reading the Bible sometimes felt like trying to learn a foreign language?

God has given us His Word as a guide to practical living. In a sense, it's our road map, our key to how to conduct ourselves as citizens of the heavenly kingdom. However, we can't assume we'll understand everything with just a cursory reading. As one anonymous quipster put it: "Reading the Bible without meditating on it is like trying to eat without swallowing."

I like that. I've found that I learn so much more if I pray while reading the Scriptures. Instead of just trying to interpret the words on my own, I am consulting the author!

Yes, I pray that God will reveal to me what He wants me to learn through His Word. It is amazing how the Bible makes so much more sense when I see the words through God's eyes.

O God, creator of Heaven and earth, help me to understand Your glorious Word. I pray that You would fill me with a deep desire to spend time reading the Bible. May this time be fruitful instead of just a chore that I have to do. Help me to look forward to our time everyday! In Christ's holy name I pray. Amen.

Time for a U-Turn?

Then they got rid of the foreign gods among them and served the LORD. And he could bear Israel's misery no longer (Judges 10:16).

Scripture: Judges 10:10-18; 11:32, 33
Song: "Nothing but the Blood"

How do parents react when they have to discipline their children? Do they smile and rejoice, pleased at their child's actions? No way! Instead, parents are disappointed when their kids do wrong.

I personally dread the times when I have to punish my children. I have to take some type of privilege away, and that just breaks my heart. You see, I love seeing my children happy and content.

I believe our heavenly Father's heart breaks when He sees His children doing wrong. He doesn't rejoice in reprimanding His kids! He wants more than anything to see us walk in His paths. He wants to bless us and see our lives flourish in His good and perfect will. After all, sin is a most self-destructive thing.

I love the title of the book series *"God Allows U-Turns"* by Allison Bottke. If your life has been heading down the wrong path, it is not too late to make a turn for the better. Just as he did with the ancient Israelites, he will do with us: God does allow u-turns in our lives.

Dear Heavenly Father, help me to walk down the right path with You. I want You to be proud of the person that I am and am becoming by the power of Your indwelling Holy Spirit. If I need to make a u-turn, give me the courage to do it. Show me just how destructive my sin can be, and help me change. In Jesus' name I pray. Amen.

DEVOTIONS®

August

This is my prayer: . . . that you may be able to discern what is best and may be pure and blameless until the day of Christ.

—*Philippians 1:9, 10*

Gary Allen, Editor | **Margaret Williams,** Project Editor | Photo © Liquid Library

Love at First Sight?

Or do you show contempt for the riches of his kindness, tolerance and patience, not realizing that God's kindness leads you toward repentance? (Romans 2:4).

Scripture: Romans 2:1-8
Song: "God of Grace, O Let Thy Light"

John Newton, the author of "Amazing Grace," said of himself: "I was capable of anything; I had not the least fear of God before my eyes, not the least sensibility of conscience." He said he had a "habit of swearing, which seemed to have been as deep rooted as a second nature." His last will and testament reads: "I was an apostate, a blasphemer, and an infidel."

I judge people who are like that. I take an instant dislike to someone who has a foul mouth, and treating them kindly isn't easy.

How unlike God I am. He showers the worst of sinners with blessings day after day. Each morning He gives light and breath. Every hour is a gift, and His kindness is meant to draw people unto himself. That's His plan. His idea.

Newton understood these things. He said, "Whoever . . has known, by his own experience, the need and worth of redemption, is enabled, Yea, he is constrained, to love his fellow creatures. He loves them at first sight."

Dear Father, I thank You for loving and leading me to repentance. Help me to show Your love and kindness to the people You put in my path today, especially to those who don't know You. In Jesus' name I pray. Amen.

August 1–7. **Kathy Hardee** writes full-time from her home in rural Mendota, Illinois. She hopes to glorify God with her writing.

There Goes a Christian

Throughout the period of his separation he is consecrated to the LORD (Numbers 6:8).

Scripture: Numbers 6:1-8
Song: "I'll Tell the World That I'm a Christian"

Shortly after 9/11, I began writing a column for our local newspaper. I looked at those first columns as an open door to tell people about God, and I prayed that He'd use my words for His glory.

The newspaper published my picture with each column, so before long people recognized me. It surprised me every time someone I didn't know said, "I always read your columns."

I realized I was being watched. I also knew the public confession of my faith must be accompanied by a holy lifestyle. If I acted sinfully, people would notice. What would happen to my Christian testimony then?

A Nazirite's long hair proclaimed his devotion to God. At first glance people knew that person was set apart to serve God and live a holy life. But his *actions* were the true test of his dedication. If an Israelite disobeyed his Nazirite vow, he would dishonor himself and his God.

Let's ask ourselves at the end of this day: "What did my actions prove?" May our lives demonstrate our devotion to our Lord so that others will know at first glance: There goes a Christian.

Dear Father in Heaven, I want to please You with my life. Help me put aside bad habits and attitudes that might ruin my testimony and dishonor Your name. I pray in the precious name of Jesus my Lord. Amen.

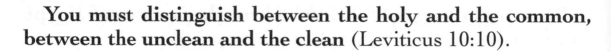

Notice the Difference?

You must distinguish between the holy and the common, between the unclean and the clean (Leviticus 10:10).

Scripture: Leviticus 10:8-11
Song: "Seek Ye First"

My mind often wanders when I'm trying my hardest to pray. One time, the notes I was taking during the Sunday sermon eventually became a grocery list. And every now and again, I sing a worship song with little thought about the one I'm supposedly worshiping. Has that ever happened to you?

There's nothing wrong with singing a song simply for fun. Writing a list before heading to the grocery store makes good sense. And a wandering mind is evidence of God's brilliant creation. However, every common act of humans pales in comparison to the privilege of worshiping almighty God.

The Lord said to Aaron, "You must distinguish between the holy and the common, between the unclean and the clean." Paul prayed that the believers at Philippi would be able to discern what is best (Philippians 1:10). Jesus told Martha, "Only one thing is needed," and, "Mary has chosen what is better" (Luke 10:41, 42). He said we should seek first the kingdom of God.

In the midst of my busy schedule, I want to take time to notice the difference between the things that will satisfy for just a short while here . . . and those other, better things. Those are the things of God, and they will remain forever.

Dear Lord, please transform my heart until I value the things You value. Help me see the importance of love, worship, humility, honor, prayer and all those things that further Your kingdom and bring You glory. In Jesus' name I pray. Amen.

Who Is Your God?

I am the LORD your God, who brought you out of Egypt, out of the land of slavery (Deuteronomy 5:6).

Scripture: Deuteronomy 5:6-10
Song: "We Now Have Met to Worship Thee"

Have you ever read a Bible verse and thought: *So what's the point?* I have. For a long time, I thought the middle part of Hebrews 11:6 didn't need to be in the Bible. It says, "Because anyone who comes to God must believe that He exists." I figured if someone prays to God, it's pretty obvious he believes God exists. If he didn't believe God existed, he wouldn't pray. Right?

Then one day, the meaning of Hebrews 11:6 became clear: If anyone comes to God, he must believe that the *God of the Bible* exists—that God. The one who spoke the world into existence and parted the Red Sea. The one who sent His only Son, Jesus, to die for sinners.

When Moses repeated the Ten Commandments to the Israelites, he reminded them that their God was the only God. Their God was the one who rescued them from slavery. Their God was the God of Abraham, the God of Isaac, and the God of Jacob.

Our God is *that* God too. Ours is the only God who acts on behalf of those who wait for Him (Isaiah 64:4). Let's wait on the God of the Bible today.

Dear God, the Father of our Lord Jesus Christ, thank You for giving me Your Word so that I can know exactly who You are—the only true God. I give my life to You, the God of the Bible, today. In the name of Jesus, who lives and reigns with You and the Holy Spirit, one God, now and forever, amen.

How Do You See God?

Fear the L ORD **your God and serve him** (Deuteronomy 10:20).

Scripture: Deuteronomy 10:12-21
Song: "Above All"

I'd like to say I obeyed my parents because I was a good kid. But that would be a lie. I obeyed my parents because they were bigger and stronger than me. I submitted to their rules, because if I didn't, I would be punished.

Obeying Dad and Mom wasn't all that difficult, though, because I knew they loved me. Their rules were for my good. Their restrictions sheltered me from the world, so I remained safe and protected in their care.

Moses knew Israel's only hope for survival depended on their view of God. They needed an awe-inspired reverence that would govern their actions. To help them think high thoughts of God, Moses said, "To the Lord your God belong the heavens, even the highest heavens, the earth and everything in it. . . . For the Lord your God is God of gods and Lord of lords, the great God, mighty and awesome" (vv. 14, 17).

The Israelites needed to know their God was the one and only Lord of all. Staying close to Him, they'd remain safe in His care. Their God, and ours, is bigger and stronger than we are—far greater in His love and mercy than we can imagine. He is worthy of our love, honor, obedience, and praise.

Dear Lord God, I long to obey You because of Your greatness and because You love me more than any other. Help me acknowledge Your power and authority over me, even as I put all of my hope in Your unfailing love. In Jesus' name, amen.

In His Service

His wife answered, "If the LORD had meant to kill us, he would not have accepted a burnt offering and grain offering from our hands, nor shown us all these things or now told us this" (Judges 13:23).

Scripture: Judges 13:15-23
Song: "Soldiers of King Jesus"

When I receive a writing assignment, I'm excited about how God might use me to glorify His name through the project. But then, after a few days, I begin to struggle. I sometimes wonder if I'm going to be able to do this work God has given me. I question whether I'm spiritual enough to write. I pray there isn't some sin interfering with my ability to properly serve a holy God. I dread the thought of saying or doing something that would ruin my testimony. I cry out, "Lord, who am I that You would use *me*?"

Manoah, I think, had similar feelings. At first he was excited about the prospect of having a son who would be set apart to God from birth. But then, after meeting with the angel of the Lord, Manoah crumbled. "'We are doomed to die!' he said to his wife. 'We have seen God!'" (v. 22).

It would be good for us to remember that God chooses the projects and He chooses the people to accomplish them. With each opportunity comes a God-given ability. We can reason, as did Manoah's wife, that if the Lord had not meant for us to serve Him, He would not have put the desire in our hearts to do so.

Lord, I thank You that the same hand that points the way also provdes the way. I can trust in You to give me all I need to accomplish Your will. In Jesus' name, amen.

God Use Me

The boy is to be a Nazirite, set apart to God from birth, and he will begin the deliverance of Israel from the hands of the Philistines (Judges 13:5).

Scripture: Judges 13:1-8, 24, 25
Song: "Just As I Am"

My parents brought our family of six to church every Sunday. I learned at a young age that God loved me. So when my mom sat me down and told me God sent His only Son to take the punishment for my sin, I gladly entered the waters of baptism. Even though I rebelled against God for a few of my teenage years, He remained faithful. I don't know why the Lord chose me to serve Him, but I'm glad He did.

Samson didn't lead a vast army. He wasn't known for making wise rulings. He never sat on a throne or led a victory march. He had a weakness for women of low character and a burning desire for vengeance. If you read his story in Judges 13–16, you'll discover he had many flaws. Yet God set Samson apart for His own purposes. I don't know why God chose Samson, but He did.

Has God been tugging on your heart? Do you sense His leading to step out in faith? Maybe you think God won't use you because you have too many flaws. Today's Scripture demonstrates that God can put into service whomever He chooses. Will you allow Him to work through you today?

Dear Lord, thank You for sending Your only Son to die for me. I'm sorry for the many times I've sinned against You. Please forgive me, and use me today in any way that pleases You. In the name of Jesus, Lord of all. Amen.

Trusting Him

As the Scripture says, "Anyone who trusts in him will never be put to shame" (Romans 10:11).

Scripture: Romans 10:5-13
Song: "'Tis So Sweet to Trust in Jesus"

When I was about 4-years-old, I lived far outside the city in an area of few homes. Our pet collie was always at my side. Often my mother let the two of us go outdoors while she made lunch.

This time, with a small child's innocence, I wandered some distance away from the house. After about 15 minutes, Mom came to the door. "Betty," she called. "Lunch is ready."

No little girl came running to her. She called my name again. Still no answer. Mom panicked, telephoning my dad, and he gathered several farm workers at a nearby nursery to help search for me. As they hunted in the neighborhood, our collie came running up. A moment later he took off down the dirt road again. The men followed and soon found me — happily splashing in lake water, perhaps a mile down the road.

Looking back, I realize my world must have been filled with great trust in Mom and Dad. I always felt safe. I was unafraid. And so it has been since I learned about the saving love of Jesus. I believe in Him. I really do trust Him.

O Lord, I thank You for saving me and giving me a life that is free from fear. May the trust You have given me shine out of my life so others will see and find that this same freedom is available to them, as well. In Christ's precious name, amen.

August 8–14. **Elizabeth Van Liere** finds joy in writing about her still-growing relationship with God. She lives in Montrose, Colorado.

You Make My Day!

So in Christ we who are many form one body, and each member belongs to all the others (Romans 12:5).

Scripture: Romans 12:3-8
Song: "We Are One Body"

Freedom flew out the window four weeks ago, the day I fell. X-rays showed I'd fractured a bone in my right foot. "I'll have to put a cast on it," the doctor said. A few weeks later he put on a fresh cast.

"Three more weeks," he said, "and then I'd like you to wear another cast for two more weeks."

The hardest part is losing my independence. I didn't realize a broken foot could cause so many restrictions. No driving—the cast is too clumsy—so a walker is my constant companion. And I'm constantly asking things like . . .

"Would you please get me a glass of water?"

"Could someone stop for dog food?"

"Has the garden been watered today?"

But I do enjoy the kindness and helpfulness of others. My grandson drove me to the store for dog food, for ink cartridges for the computer, and then to the bank. A friend picked me up for church, loading the walker in the trunk of her car. My daughter washes my hair, and friends call to see how I'm doing.

One of God's gifts to His people shines like a bright light through this experience: I am part of His family. These other members are using His gift of service to make my day.

Heavenly Father, how I thank You for my family of relatives and friends! I have a need, and they are answering it. I know You sent them. In Jesus' name, amen.

Tolerant Wisdom Needed

Accept him whose faith is weak, without passing judgment on disputable matters (Romans 14:1).

Scripture: Romans 14:1-9
Song: "More About Jesus"

One of my grandsons is blessed with a photographic memory. As a sponge soaks up water, he soaks up information. Squeeze a wet sponge—water drips out. Mention bones or planets or even what a certain Bible verse says about David, and he always adds a bit of information. However, I don't always accept his word.

His mother covers her ears when David and I disagree. It's not that the point on which we differ is so important. I guess the fun comes when I prove I'm right (even if it only happens once in awhile).

As I look at what I've just written, it strikes me as rather childish. Hmmm . . . like I'm only trying to get my own way. On the other hand, maybe I ought to remember that truth is truth. If David is right, it will stand for itself. If what he says is incorrect, instead of arguing, I could say, "What about . . . ?" Then smart young man that he is, he will investigate the matter further.

The important thing is this: I love David. I want to encourage his wide interests. I want him to continue growing mentally, physically, and spiritually. Maybe it's time that I stop arguing with him over unimportant things. It's time to smile and say, "OK. Prove it."

Father, when it comes to genuinely disputable matters, help me allow others the freedom to interpret Your word a bit differently than I do. In Jesus' name, amen.

God's Place and Mine

Joseph said to them, "Don't be afraid. Am I in the place of God?" (Genesis 50:19).

Scripture: Genesis 50:15-21
Song: "Who Is on the Lord's Side?"

Last week in Sunday school we talked about laws. Bill, our teacher, said, "Some laws can be irritating. Such as the requirement to wear a seat belt. But that law protects us, and we obey it or get fined."

"Some rules at work bug me," he continued. "Wherever I park my service truck, I must put a wedge of hard rubber behind the back wheel. When I park on a slight incline, I usually bump my front wheels up against a concrete curb. The truck can't go anywhere—but the block must still be put in place. If my supervisor sees my unblocked truck, I'm in trouble. Yet I see trucks from other companies parked without the restraint."

Bill shrugged his shoulders. "Our company made the ruling years ago. Possibly before parking brakes were improved to prevent human error."

A class member spoke up. "You've been working for this company for a long time. You should be used to the rule by now."

Bill laughed. "You're right. It shouldn't bother me. A rule is a rule. The boss is the boss. As long as I'm working for this company, I'll do as they ask." With a grin, another member added, "And stop your grumbling."

God, I live by faith, not by law. But this doesn't mean You want me to live by rules that I make for myself. Help me always to think and act according to Your will, not mine, because Your way is so much better than mine. In the name of Jesus, amen.

A Time to Stand

The midwives, however, feared God and did not do what the king of Egypt had told them to do; they let the boys live (Exodus 1:17).

Scripture: Exodus 1:8-21
Song: "The Promise"

A sad story in Voice of the Martyrs tells how 12-year-old Marcella saw Revolutionary Armed Forces of Colombia (FARC) guerrillas shoot her parents. Marcella's parents were Christian teachers. They taught children in a small farming town in the jungles of Colombia. Every day her mother, Dora, told stories about Jesus.

The FARC hated these teachers, knowing that children who hear the gospel may become Christians—and Christians do not want to fight alongside them.

A day before the shooting, a neighbor came to Dora. "The guerrillas are going to kill you and your husband tomorrow," he said. "Take your family and run."

Dora said, "We will pray. We are ready to meet the Lord." That night she told Marcella, "Mommy may be going to sleep tomorrow for a long time."

Sadly, the worst came to pass. Marcella and some of her relatives went into hiding. Later, a volunteer listened as Marcella said, "If I met the men who did this, I would forgive them. I know this would be hard, but God forgives them. So I have to as well."

Lord, I pray for those who are willing to give up their lives in Your name. Could I do the same? May I always be willing to say, "Jesus is my Lord." In His name, amen.

Onward and Upward

With her two daughters-in-law she left the place where she had been living and set out on the road that would take them back to the land of Judah (Ruth 1:7).

Scripture: Ruth 1:1-7
Song: "O for a Closer Walk with God"

Onward and *Upward*! Those words are the motto for we seniors, aged 50-years and older. Each year we take several trips in the church van. On those trips, each morning our senior minister, Ronnie, leads us in prayer for safe travel. Then in a big circle, holding hands we shout, "Onward and Upward!"

Last year a friend said, "I am so tired. My legs just don't want to go anymore." After a checkup her doctor said, "BJ, your heart isn't getting enough oxygen. You have to slow down."

It would have been easy for BJ to sit with clasped hands, head bowed, and have a huge pity party. It was harder to make her follow doctor's orders. This year, however, she is on oxygen full-time. "I'm ready to go when the Lord calls me," she says.

Meanwhile, with the help of her walker, she shuffles her way to her outdoor deck. There she plops down on a lawn chair. "I love seeing the different birds come to the feeder," she exclaims. "And look! Aren't the flowers my kids planted beautiful?"

In addition, BJ prays for those who she says are worse off than she is. As I see it, Naomi and BJ exemplify our motto of "Onward and Upward."

God, Naomi may not have always felt like it, but she kept going. I thank You for the glimpse of her positive attitude. Grant that I too may keep going forward until the day You call me home. In Jesus' name I pray. Amen.

A Time to Say Yes

When Naomi realized that Ruth was determined to go with her, she stopped urging her (Ruth 1:18).

Scripture: Ruth 1:8-18
Song: "O for a Thousand Tongues to Sing"

Fifteen years ago, four of my grandsons were in elementary school. I told their mother, "I don't need anything from the boys for my birthday. I have everything I want or need."

"Sorry," Jo Anne said with a smile. "The boys are always on the receiving end. It's time they learn to give as well as receive."

"OK, OK," I said. "I surrender."

A few days later when I came to breakfast, four boys hollered, "Surprise!" My birthday had arrived. Four small packages lay by my plate, each wrapped in comic strip paper. Each package sported a different colored bow—red, yellow, green, and blue.

The four boys stood around the table (two of them punching each other), and one smiled a big toothless grin at me. The youngest shoved his gift my way. "Open this first," he said.

A new pen, a booklet of poems, a hummingbird magnet, and a brooch came from the packages. I oohed and aahed over each gift.

"These are so nice," I said. "I'll always love them . . . and I love *you*." Four smiling boys left for school. And I understood—like Naomi—how blessed it is to receive.

Heavenly Father, You are the giver of all good gifts. Thank You for all the blessings You have poured upon me. Help me graciously to receive good things from others who love me and want to bless me too. In Jesus' name, amen.

Sharing Bread with the Poor

Rich and poor have this in common: The LORD is the Maker of them all (Proverbs 22:2).

Scripture: Proverbs 22:1-9
Song: "Morning Has Broken"

I woke early this morning. Dawn had not yet broken. So I took my time, made a cup of coffee, and sat in my favorite chair, turning to face the east window.

In just a few moments, the dawn began to creep across the eastern horizon. O, the wondrous colors! The trees are in full bud, ready to leaf out. Many of the spring flowers have begun to bloom. Spring and the newness of life come to every human being; it is up to each person to take time to enjoy the season and to give thanks to the Maker.

We used to hunt the great-tasting morel mushroom in the spring. We'd walk slowy and carefully, turning up dead fallen leaves until they revealed our tasty spring treat.

But be careful! God also created the "false morel"—very poisonous to many humans yet a perfectly good food for animals. God created both plants, and He gives them both a new life each spring. It is how we use them that makes the difference. Let us all, rich or poor, use our voices in worship and our bodies in glorifying our Maker to the best of our ability.

Lord, thank You for this wondrous new day. I eagerly look forward to what will unfold. How might I become a better, stronger witness today? In Jesus' name, amen.

August 15–21. **Judy Verberkmoes,** who lives in southern Georgia with her husband, Bob, has retired from her work in healthcare. She loves reading and studying the Bible each day.

Doing Good

Be holy because I, the LORD your God, am holy (Leviticus 19:2).

Scripture: Leviticus 19:1-10
Song: "Teach Me, Lord"

The word *holy* means, in its most basic biblical sense, to be separated or set aside—dedicated for God's service. Naturally, that means a certain goodness of character and action, a purity of lifestyle. And what a challenge that is!

Yet even very young children can do good—as a little girl did one week in late winter almost 40 years ago. One Sunday after a surprisingly short sermon, our minister told us of a new family in the area. This family's newly rented home had caught fire. The minister came upon the home before the fire trucks arrived, so he stopped to offer what assistance he could.

While watching his home burn, with all his family's possessions, the man had suffered a heart attack. Now our minister told us that the man was recovering in the ICU of the local hospital. "If any of you might be able to help this family in any way, please let me know," he said. So on the way out of church, my 6-year-old daughter blurted out to the minister: "Stop by the house later this week; we've got bunches of stuff!"

So when we got home we began cleaning and going through all our things. Soon we had gathered much "stuff" for the struggling family. It included one little girl's piggy bank —holding $3.20.

O Lord, teach me what it means today to be holy in the way You desire. In the name of the Father, the Son, and the Holy Spirit, I pray. Amen.

Just Trust!

Take your pay and go. I want to give the man who was hired last the same as I gave you. Don't I have the right to do what I want with my own money? Or are you envious because I am generous? (Matthew 20:14, 15).

Scripture: Matthew 20:1-15
Song: "Purer in Heart, O God"

Our Lord created everything in the air, on the earth, and under the earth—all things living and not living. He created humans, tall and short, in all shades of skin color. He gave us everything we need to sustain us here on earth. He also gave us *the ability to trust* our great provider to care for us.

Now let's consider the parable of the laborers in the vineyard (see Matthew 20). The first group of workers discussed and made a contract with the farmer for the payment of a denarius for the full day of work. Other workers were hired later in the day with the promise that they would be paid "whatever is right." And the workers had to choose: Would they trust the farmer to treat them right?

They did trust. Just as we can trust our Lord to do "whatever is right" in every situation of our lives, as we give ourselves into His hands. He has given us that ability.

The Lord looks at our hearts when He extends His offers of goodness and grace. Without looking around at others, without comparing our situations or blessings . . . can we just trust Him?

Father, may I seek to please You today with a full day's work, not comparing my situation with others. I long to have an open-hearted acceptance of Your goodness. For I know You always have my best in mind. Thank You, in Jesus' name, amen.

Share with Friend and Foe

The share of the man who stayed with the supplies is to be the same as that of him who went down to the battle. All will share alike (1 Samuel 30:24)

Scripture: 1 Samuel 30:21-25
Song: "Faith of Our Brothers"

When King David's men came back from battle laden with plunder, they were met by men who'd been too weak to fight. They'd stayed behind, rested, and awaited the returning warriors. Naturally, the fighting men refused to share the spoils with those who had stayed home.

But David said: "No! We'll all share alike—fighters and nonfighters." His reason was simple: All that they had won had come by the Lord's hand; it would be wrong to hoard the gifts of God. I have a feeling the fighters quickly agreed. But suppose you were asked to share with your enemies?

A friend of mine, Evelyn, was a good example of sharing God's goodness with the enemy. Her first husband was killed in World War II. A while later, several German prisoners were sent to help work her family farm, and Evelyn prepared and served meals to them. They spoke very little English. Yet they sat quietly with bowed heads, and said "Amen" at the end of Evelyn's prayers.

She was so kind and generous with those enemy prisoners. Could I have done the same?

Dear Lord, please release me from thinking only in terms of friends and enemies. Help me to remember that the blessings You give are to be shared with others—whether I like them or not. You love them, and so must I. In Jesus' name, amen.

Tell About Him

Fight the good fight of the faith. Take hold of the eternal life to which you were called when you made your good confession in the presence of many witnesses (1 Timothy 6:12).

Scripture: 1 Timothy 6:11-19
Song: "I Will Sing the Wondrous Story"

I had a close friend who for years was a Sunday school teacher for the 3–5 year olds. And how they loved her!

One year she had an adorable 4-year-old girl who was very attached to her teacher. Each Sunday when the children were instructed to go and sit with their parents, this little girl would go straight to the Sunday school teacher and wouldn't leave her side (with the parents' blessing).

One day while grocery shopping this teacher looked down, and there was little SueAnn, clinging to her grocery cart! On another occasion while the teacher was in a mall, she saw SueAnn kneeling next to a baby in its stroller. As her parents looked on the girl was holding a child's storybook, and she was telling the baby: "Let me tell you the story of baby Jesus—He *loves* you."

Now that truly warmed a Sunday school teacher's heart!

Like SueAnn, let us be ready at all times to tell about the wonderful love of Christ, to "make our good confession" of the truth, whether in person or in a crowd.

Heavenly Father, who needs to hear my confession of faith today? Bring to me the people whose hearts You've already prepared. Let Your words of mercy and peace be upon my lips. In the name of Jesus, amen.

Thanks for That Help!

Naomi had a relative on her husband's side, from the clan of Elimelech, a man of standing, whose name was Boaz (Ruth 2:1).

Scripture: Ruth 2:1-7
Song: "Blest, Blest Forever"

When my husband Bob's extended unemployment had run out and no work could be found in our area of Northern Michigan, we had no relatives to turn to as Naomi had. However, Bob did have a friend whom he'd worked for almost 20 years previously. Now he had promised Bob work, if Bob were willing to pick up and move far south, to Georgia.

"Come on down," said the friend over the phone. "I'll put you to work as soon as you get here. We make and install cabinets and countertops." So when Bob arrived, he went to work for his former coworker and old friend.

Christmas time came, and the shop always laid off the employees and closed the plant for two weeks of the year. But because they knew Bob had exhausted his unemployment benefits, they kept him on the clock to clean the shop.

We were in a "foreign land," far from family. That gift of work from a friend was a lifesaver for us. Just as it was in Ruth's life, a friendly person with some means lent a helping hand. For anyone who has been there, it is a great blessing, worthy of profuse thanks to God.

Lord, thank You for the people who took us in and helped us at such a difficult time of our lives. Look lovingly on them and grant them Your peace. I am so grateful to You for sending us to this wonderful southern community. In Christ's name, amen.

Daily Bread: It's a God Thing

Ruth gleaned in the field until evening. Then she threshed the barley she had gathered, and it amounted to about an ephah (Ruth 2:17).

Scripture: Ruth 2:8-18
Song: "Count Your Blessings"

If you lived in northern climes as a child, you're well aware of the meaning of "snow days." Children love them—those days of missed school classes due to massive snowfalls.

One year we had more than the usual snowfall in our town. And most of it fell on the weekends, making the roads impossible to drive. For three weekends in a row, it meant the children who came from school on Friday to "spend the night" with our kids couldn't get home till Tuesday! For us, it meant three extra children, along with our 18-year-old's fiancé, who worked as a baker's assistant.

When the bakery store owner realized there would be no business that next day, he kindly gave to Jeff all the pies, cakes, and breads they'd made on Friday night. We had a total of seven children and two young adults crammed into a small house, sleeping in beds, on couches, and even the floor. But the Lord provided our daily needs.

And if Ruth and Naomi were here, they'd say the same, wouldn't they? An *ephah* equals about a bushel, enough to feed the women for several days. Daily bread is God's business, then and now.

O Lord, thank You for sending the baker's kind thoughts our way. Then throughout that precious summer and fall, You gave us an abundance of fruits and vegetables for our freezer. I praise You, in Christ's name.

Relationship on the Right Track

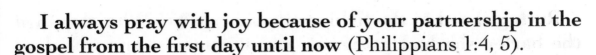

I always pray with joy because of your partnership in the gospel from the first day until now (Philippians 1:4, 5).

Scripture: Philippians 1:3-11
Song: "Be Strong in the Lord"

A good relationship with God begins and continues with joy. Of course, it isn't always easy to be joyfully grateful for some people, particularly if they are enemies. But it's not impossible when we undergird our feelings and actions with the power of God's love.

How to make it happen? Pray for people around you rather than peppering your insides with complaints about them. Pray specific prayers, pursuing the wisdom of the Lord rather than the wrangling of the devil. Seek and keep a "gratitude attitude" and thereby grow in love rather than shrink toward hate.

Make these kinds of choices that court common sense. And if it requires a spiritual magnifying glass to be able to distinguish the good in some folk, then pray for such an insightful instrument and use it well.

The apostle Paul couldn't have made it clearer: The fruits of righteousness are ripe and ready for the harvesting. The grace of God isn't parceled out in stingy proportions. It is to be shared joyfully and lavishly in a caring community.

Dear Lord, when our spirits are hungry for You, let us not digress to lesser things. Enter the classroom of our hearts and teach us each day how to live with generosity and joy. Help us to stand tall in mind and spirit. In the name of Jesus, amen.

August 22–28. **Neil Wyrick** is an ordained minister who has traveled the world as an evangelist. He has recently written a book about the hymns of John Wesley.

Definitions to Live By

LORD, who may dwell in your sanctuary? Who may live on your holy hill? He whose walk is blameless and who does what is righteous, who speaks the truth from his heart (Psalm 15:1, 2).

Scripture: Psalm 15
Song: "A Charge to Keep I Have"

The psalmist wasn't trying for subtlety when he wrote those words. He tells it like it is and seems to expect that we'll apply it in like manner. His definitions of a godly life are crystal clear: a walk through life that is blameless, righteousness properly applied, a tongue controlled, a heart and mind open to God, a good neighbor policy . . . and the list continues.

But I especially love the three words found in the second verse, "from his heart." Call it the nitty-gritty exposed. Call it remembering that there is always a danger lurking for those who hope to live holy lives. It's the threat of being legalistic to the degree that even a saintly act can almost become a sin.

In short, anyone can memorize commandments. But without "heart," rules and regulations can become as cold as ice—and just as unbending. And therein lies the grammatical lesson. Faith must be more than a noun. It must flourish because it makes these teachings verbs of action rather than merely adjectives of definition.

Almighty and most merciful God, may we think long about how we should live—but not so long that that is all we become, one elongated thinking machine! Let Your words sink into my heart, that my way of life may please You. In the name of Jesus, my Lord and Savior, I pray. Amen.

Follow and Be Blessed

When Solomon had finished building the temple of the LORD . . . and had achieved all he had desired to do . . . The LORD said to him: . . . "I will establish your royal throne over Israel forever, as I promised David your father when I said, 'You shall never fail to have a man on the throne of Israel'" (1 Kings 9:1, 3, 5).

Scripture: 1 Kings 9:1-5
Song: "Blest Are the Humble Souls That See"

When I came to Miami in 1955 to start a new church, neither I nor the other leaders were establishing a royal throne. But we sought to be obedient and that is the timeless message of our Scripture passage today—faithful faithfulness. No room for compromise. A timeless requirement to then receive the blessing of our God, the same as was promised to Solomon.

Most likely none of us will ever be a Solomon to our generation. But in our every endeavor, no matter how menial or how noble, we must ask the Lord for His continued blessing upon it. And this is the message: to consistently express our needs at Heaven's gates: to walk with God and follow His commandments. Then our efforts will be favorably blessed.

I look back over 50 years now, and the church we built still stands, a viable influence in the community. Its demographics have changed, but not its purpose. Consecrated in the name of the Lord those many decades ago, it still seeks and receives the blessings of the living Lord.

Lord, may we walk with wisdom and act with spiritual strength. May the echo of our deeds be worthy of hearing by the next generation. In Christ, amen.

Good Not Perfect

Vindicate me, O LORD, for I have led a blameless life; I have trusted in the LORD without wavering. Test me, O LORD, and try me, examine my heart and my mind (Psalm 26:1, 2).

Scripture: Psalm 26:1-11
Song: "Savior, Like a Shepherd Lead Us"

The psalmist here, on a scale of 1 through 10, seems to have given himself a 10. He is certainly making this writer nervous with his proclamation of perfection. He has obviously reached this conclusion from living an exemplary life but also from an overblown ego.

Probably not. After all David lived in a different age, and it was important under the Law to be able to test oneself by the standards of God's commands. In other places this "man after God's heart" gives the glory to the Lord.

Nevertheless, I still have the feeling that it would have done him good to sit down with Jesus, Mary, and Martha. Remember Martha? She was a woman with such a high opinion of herself it left little room for anyone to disagree with her. When it came to efficiency and effort, she gave herself an A+. Mary was wrong, and she was right. In her mind, it was that simple.

The tyranny of "I" and "me" tries to turn dross into gold. It creates a person so proud of being high and lifted up they forget to fall to their knees. It is good to work toward being blameless. It is a disaster to believe we have arrived.

O Lord God of all, save us from the tyrant named "pride." Lead us to be ruled by humility and then not be proud of the rulership. In the name of the Father, the Son, and the Holy Spirit, I pray. Amen

Hold Your Tongue!

Blessings crown the head of the righteous, but violence overwhelms the mouth of the wicked. The memory of the righteous will be a blessing, but the name of the wicked will rot (Proverbs 10:6, 7)

Scripture: Proverbs 10:6-11
Song: "Breathe on Me, Breath of God"

If one is going to win a popularity contest both in Heaven and on earth, this proverb spells out the preferred behavior. What is decent and proper comes to the forefront; what is not is given a boot from a righteous foot. Right and wrong are clearly stated.

It's as if proper moral behavior says, "You done me wrong" to the man who chooses evil over good. *Blessed* is the word applied to those who control their mouths rather than being controlled by them.

Since the day of our birth, we've been offered divergent paths. And we have chosen sometimes wisely and sometimes not wisely at all. We all know how hard it is to accept the voice of wisdom when our lesser selves seek lesser ways.

We are all remembered by the next generation and that is good—unless we have lived a life better forgotten (because it is a life overcome by "rot"). So let us choose carefully what thoughts we hold dear and what deeds become a part of us. And let our words demonstrate each blessed choice.

Lord God Almighty, help me to lengthen my commitment to You. Lead me to study what is right and practice what I learn. Help me get better control over the words that come from my mouth. In the name of Jesus, Lord and Savior of all, I pray. Amen.

Tested Strength Is Stronger

"Skin for skin!" Satan replied. "A man will give all he has for his own life. But stretch out your hand and strike his flesh and bones, and he will surely curse you to your face" (Job 2:4, 5).

Scripture: Job 2:1-9
Song: "People of the Living God"

Is it easier to flourish with integrity when the sun is shining than when the shadows have taken over? Is it easier to mind the compassionate messages of the heart when pain is greater than pleasure? Are we stronger soldiers of the Lord when we have been tested, slogging our way slowly, dejectedly forward?

It is all a matter of how we respond to the challenge. For example, consider the two ways this famous aphorism may be concluded: "What doesn't kill me . . ." What do you add?

The standard: " . . . can only make me stronger."

My frequent variation: " . . . can still make me very sick."

In Christ we are reminded that God knows what it is like to be you and me. We need not let our pain and problems win out over our prayers and determined faith.

Job stands as a giant before us. His way is to be embraced and emulated. To have a lifelong quarrel with Heaven makes no sense, for life was made for pressing on and not for pouting. Life was made for rebuilding on shattered dreams, because to do anything less is to give up on almighty God.

O God, the king of glory, may my faith be firm when all around me falter. May I praise my Lord with unrelenting fervor, even when the circumstances look bleak. Fill me with Your Spirit and carry me through! In Christ's name I pray. Amen.

Go Forth with Joy

For you who revere my name, the sun of righteousness will rise with healing in its wings. And you will go out and leap like calves released from the stall (Malachi 4:2).

Scripture: Malachi 4:1-6
Song: "The Trees of the Field"

When my cream-colored tabby was a kitten, my husband and I kept her in our large laundry room all day while we were at work. This protected our furniture and kept her safe as well. When we got home and let her out of her room, it was like releasing a racing animal out of the gate. She went wild with joy.

Likewise, don't we sometimes spend days virtually "shut out" from the blessings God has for us? Then we may become slaves to sin—it can trap us. But knowing freedom in Christ, we are like happy calves released from a stall. By the cross of Christ, we are free—free to live life to the full (see John 10:10).

The Law required sacrifices to cover sin until the Messiah would come. Calves were laid on the altar, and there is a sense in which we are like those calves; we should be on the chopping block because of our sin. God provided another way. Jesus, the spotless lamb, offered himself for our sins. Trusting in Him, we experience His healing grace. We can then go forth with joy.

Dear Father, I confess that I am sometimes captive to sin. Thank You for setting me free through Jesus Christ. Fill me with Your peace and joy. In His name, amen.

Modern-Day Tassels

You will have these tassels to look at and so you will remember all the commands of the Lord, that you may obey them and not prostitute yourselves by going after the lusts of your own hearts and eyes (Numbers 15:39).

Scripture: Numbers 15:37-41
Song: "Open the Eyes of My Heart"

August is one of the most popular months for weddings in the United States. All summer, we're bombarded with advertisements for wedding gowns, accessories, and the all-important wedding rings. Those rings are significant because of what they represent: love, commitment, and fidelity to one's spouse. Wedding rings also signify that someone is "taken." They're powerful symbols.

In the Old Testament, the Israelites wore tassels on their garments as physical reminders of spiritual requirements. While most of us don't follow strict dress codes today, reminders of God's grace are all around us. Because the new covenant is written on our hearts, the Holy Spirit infuses them into our very being. Yet God's "tassels" abound in less obvious places.

God surrounds us with reminders of Him. Whether it's the kindness of a stranger, the smile of a child, or the beauty of creation, we can't escape God's physical reminders of His presence. We need only to open our eyes to what He reveals to us, each and every day.

Dear Lord, help me to see You in the circumstances of everyday life. May I remain faithful to You because of all You have done for me. Through Christ, amen.

August 29–31. **Lisa Earl** is a technical and freelance writer based in wester Pennsylvania. She also teaches an online writing course and enjoys figure skating as a hobby.

Worthy of Worship?

Those who make them will be like them, and so will all who trust in them (Psalm 115:8).

Scripture: Psalm 115:3-11
Song: "Turn Your Eyes upon Jesus"

In the summer of 2009, people around the world were bombarded with nonstop media coverage of the death of Michael Jackson. The "King of Pop" had become a cultural icon in the 1980s and continued to fascinate fans in the first decade of the new millennium. Even though his personal struggles were evident in his physical appearance and through well-publicized controversies, fans still idolized the performer.

But humans are not meant to be worshiped. We are made to worship God. As much as we like to admire celebrities for their good looks and talent, when we elevate them to a place where they don't belong, they often can't handle it.

We can't handle this "celebrity worship" either. Today's passage reminds us that we are also lost if we don't follow God and elevate Him to the position that belongs only to Him. When we create cultural idols, we lose. They will always make mistakes, always disappoint us and eventually die.

Jesus Christ is the only one worthy of our praise. He can handle not only our praise but also carry every sin we've ever committed or will ever commit. Now that's someone truly worth worshiping!

Living Lord, You alone are worthy of praise. You deserve my absolute devotion, reverence, and worship because of who You are and what You've done for me. Forgive me for revering others over You. In Jesus' name I pray. Amen.

A Lesson for Our Society

Today you are witnesses that I have bought from Naomi all the property of Elimelech, Kilion and Mahlon. I have also acquired Ruth the Moabitess, Mahlon's widow, as my wife, in order to maintain the name of the dead (Ruth 4:9, 10).

Scripture: Ruth 4:1-10
Song: "The Family of God"

Ruth and Boaz were brought together at the right place, at the right time. The rightness of responsible action—of doing one's duty—comes through clearly. Here the sanctity of obligation is alive and well.

The biblical custom of levirate marriage required that a brother-in-law must marry his brother's widow. She was then protected from poverty and favored with companionship. The family line would continue, for any children born of this union would be considered the same as the children of the deceased brother.

There's enough goodness in all of this to bring a smile to the face of anyone who is pleased by virtue and mercy. This was a community whose laws evoked the will of God and where compassion spread wide and far.

It is a story steeped in unselfish human behavior as a rule. It says that civilized behavior is blessed by blossoming into a civilized society. Isn't it a great lesson for our own place and time?

Almighty and gracious Father, may we live in a compassionate community because we have helped to make it so. May our hands reach out to help rather than hurt and to heal rather than wound. In the name of the Father, the Son, and the Holy Spirit, I pray. Amen.

DEVOTIONS®

September

Let the wise listen and add to their learning, and let the discerning get guidance.

—Proverbs 1:5

Gary Allen, Editor   **Margaret Williams,** Project Editor   Photo © i Stockphoto

DEVOTIONS® is published quarterly by Standard Publishing, Cincinnati, Ohio, www.standardpub.com. © 2010 by Standard Publishing. All rights reserved. Topics based on the Home Daily Bible Readings, International Sunday School Lessons. © 2008 by the Committee on the Uniform Series. Printed in the U.S.A. All Scripture quotations, unless otherwise indicated, are taken from the HOLY BIBLE, *NEW INTERNATIONAL VERSION®. NIV®.* Copyright © 1973, 1978, 1984 by Biblica, Inc.™. Used by permission of Zondervan. All rights reserved. *The New King James Version (NKJV)* Copyright © 1982 by Thomas Nelson, Inc. *New American Standard Bible (NASB),* © The Lockman Foundation, 1960, 1962, 1963, 1968, 1971, 1972, 1973, 1975, 1977, 1995.

They Give with Joy

Each man should give what he has decided in his heart to give, not reluctantly or under compulsion, for God loves a cheerful giver (2 Corinthians 9:7).

Scripture: 2 Corinthians 9:6-12
Song: "Jesus Paid It All"

I got into my car carrying a glitter pencil and a paper cup full of water. What would compel an almost 30-year-old woman to have these items? My nieces. Those two little girls won't let anyone leave their house empty-handed. They sent me home with the water for my cat and the pencil for me. I felt bad taking the pencil from my 2-year-old niece, but my sister was adamant: "You have to take what they give. If you don't, they'll cry!"

These girls epitomize cheerful giving—to the point where *not* giving makes them sad. It reminded me of my grandmother. I couldn't leave her house empty-handed either. Then it hit me: Cheerful giving runs in the family. It was passed down from Grandma, to my mother, to my sister, to them.

I think maybe this gift skipped over me. If only I could be so generous! After all, God's Word encourages us to give from the heart, and He even helps us do so. All we need remember is this: Selfless giving comes from loving the source of every good and perfect gift. May His generosity fill us and flow out to those around us.

Heavenly Father, thank You for everything You have provided. You have given me so much. Help me to share even a portion of it with others. In Jesus' name. Amen.

September 1–4. **Lisa M. Earl** is a technical writer based in western Pennsylvania who also teaches an online writing course. Lisa enjoys figure skating and spending time with her husband, Josh.

Trustfully Near

Do not plot harm against your neighbor, who lives trust-fully near you (Proverbs 3:29).

Scripture: Proverbs 3:27-35
Song: "Let Us Break Bread Together"

Whether we know it or not, we exercise trust on a daily basis. We trust that our lights will come on when we flip the switch in the morning, that water will come out of the faucet, that others will drive on the correct side of the highway, and that our car will get us to work. In fact, we're surprised when these things don't happen. We even exercise trust in our neighbors; many of us believe that our neighborhoods are safe, for the most part.

Today's Bible passage uses the phrase "trustfully near." We live trustfully near to those around us, but God is so much nearer than even our neighbors. He lives in our hearts through the Holy Spirit.

Yet how much do I trust God on a daily basis? Do I trust more that things will "work like they should" than I trust that God is taking care of me? You see, I tend to be shocked when I receive a blessing from God. It's the reverse of how I feel about my faucet. I'm shocked when the faucet *doesn't* respond, and I'm shocked when God *does*.

God is infinitely more trustworthy than anything in this world. Let us focus on heavenly realities and the nearness of our God, to whom we can live trustfully near.

Dear Lord, help me to trust You above all else. Help me to see Your heavenly realities as more real than earthly things. May I rest in the certitude of Your promises as I walk close to You today. In Jesus' name I pray. Amen.

Remember the Source

By his knowledge the deeps were divided, and the clouds let drop the dew (Proverbs 3:20).

Scripture: Proverbs 3:13-26
Song: "Thou Art Worthy"

I was valedictorian of my college class. You'd think I would have gotten over that by now. Really—it's going on 10 years now. I'm a little stuck in the past, but what does it matter at this point in my life? College was a lot of hard work, a lot of effort. I earned the honor, right?

Hard work does pay off. In fact, it's wise. But wisdom is not something that I can possess on my own.

Today's passage reminds me that even the clouds have to be allowed to drop dew. In a sense they don't just drop it on their own—for every process of creation has been set in motion by its original Creator. Why should I be any different?

True wisdom comes by acknowledging the source of all wisdom: God himself. In other words, "the fear of the Lord is the beginning of wisdom" (Psalm 111:10). When we take credit for our accomplishments—when we self promote, when we consider ourselves better than others—we are not wise. The Bible specifically commands us to consider others better than ourselves (see Philippians 2:3). Any personal achievement, then, is truly God's Spirit living in us and working through us. Today, let us remember the one who is worthy of all praise.

Father, You are the fount of all wisdom, knowledge, talent, and ability. Everything I have comes from You. Humble me; help me to give You the glory. Through Christ, amen.

No Longer on Stone

Let love and faithfulness never leave you; bind them around your neck, write them on the tablet of your heart (Proverbs 3:3).

Scripture: Proverbs 3:1-12
Song: "How Gentle God's Commands"

I'm a stickler for rules. I work full time as a technical writer, and I value accuracy and precision. I'm one of those people who refuses to throw away instructions for anything—from microwaves to makeup to computer software. After all, some poor technical writer did all that work.

Did you know God has done some technical writing? He wrote the Ten Commandments on stone tablets—an ancient instructional manual of sorts. But even while Moses was on Mt. Sinai getting those ethical "specs" from God, the people became impatient and made a golden calf to worship. They abandoned God's commands and separated themselves from His law.

Through Jesus Christ the law is now written on our hearts, and we cannot be separated from it. He is the one who fulfilled that law, and He lives within us. Thus, God's love and faithfulness will never leave us.

When I was a teen, I wore a cross necklace. Although that piece of pretty jewelry didn't make me a Christian, it was a symbol, a reminder hanging around my neck. The cross represents the new, everlasting covenant between the Father and the Son: because of Christ's obedience, I'm accepted into God's family.

Father God, thank You for Your covenant of grace written upon my heart. May I give unceasing praise to Your Son, who won my salvation. In His name, amen.

Oops!

Hear, my son, and be wise; And guide your heart in the way (Proverbs 23:19, *New King James Version*).

Scripture: Proverbs 23:15-19
Song: "Lead, Kindly Light"

"I will follow you," my mom shouted across the parking lot. She was in town for a wedding and was coming to my house afterwards. She followed me for a while . . . but never made it home. After several hours, she showed up with a story that made our family's blooper reels. Here's the story:

Apparently, after stopping at a light, she began following a vehicle similar to mine. She followed this lady clear across town to her garage. The frightened woman jumped out of her car and demanded to know why my mother was following her. All Mom could say was, "Oops!"

We too can get on the wrong road by chasing after things. We can become consumed with getting more money, bigger houses, and finer cars. It may seem right at the time—but purely mindless consumption can lead to the wrong address.

You see, in order to keep our priorities right, we need a proper guidance system. That's where God's Word is so important. He clearly shows us the way, helping us avoid that horrible "oops" when we get to the end of the trail.

Lord, thank You for Your Word. It led me to Jesus, and now it directs my steps, showing me how You want me to live. Thank You for not leaving me on my own—and, Lord, please help me obey You today. In Jesus' name I pray. Amen.

September 5–11. **Diana Stewart** is a retired insurance agent residing in Oklahoma City. Her passion is writing and serving in women's ministry at her church.

Splinters Are God's Specialty

O LORD of hosts, Blessed is the man who trusts in You! (Psalm 84:12, *New King James Version*).

Scripture: Psalm 84:8-12
Song: "Do Not Be Surprised"

"Nooo!" . . . screamed my youngest granddaughter, Kate. She had a splinter in her finger and didn't want me to remove it, certain I'd cause her great pain. I gently coaxed her to trust me: "I'll be very careful, Honey." Soon I'd accomplished a fairly pain-free extraction, and Kate was a happy girl.

A few weeks later, when Kate was with her parents, she got another splinter in her finger. Her dad prepared to remove the stinging barb, but Kate refused. She told her dad that only her grandma could remove splinters, and she needed to go to my house.

Why? Because she had trusted me in the past, and I had come through. Therefore, she knew she could trust me again.

How many times has God taken care of us in the past? When life brings us splinters, maybe we should be more like Kate. What if we stopped and reminded ourselves of our long history with God's care for us? Remembering will give us the confidence to trust Him with today's wounds. How blessed would our lives be if we could just let go and trust Him to remove those pesky splinters along the way.

Father, I thank You for loving me and for taking care of me when I am hurt. You alone are trustworthy, and You have said that You are an ever-present help in time of trouble. And for that I praise You this day, and always. In the name of the Father, the Son, and the Holy Spirit, I pray. Amen.

Danger . . . Peace Ahead!

Be very courageous to keep and to do all that is written in the Book of the Law of Moses, lest you turn aside from it to the right hand or to the left (Joshua 23:6, *New King James Version*).

Scripture: Joshua 23:1-8
Song: "How Firm a Foundation"

When the bottom falls out and trouble comes, I have no problem falling on my face before God. I know where to go in tough times. However, when things are good and everything is coming up roses, I think God needs to post a "Danger Ahead" sign for me. Why? Because I can become complacent.

Can you relate to that? Instead of pouring my heart out to the Lord, as I do amid the trying circumstances, I spend less time with Him, and my prayers can become sort of rote. And isn't that a recipe for disaster?

Peace is good, but it needs a warning label: "If an overdose occurs, you may lose consciousness." During those wonderful times of peace, we can easily lose our awareness of God's upholding presence. It may seem as if we aren't "needing" Him as much. Then, the next thing we know, our hearts become cold.

How can we stay close to God during the peaceful good times? For one thing, we can feed on His Word daily, like a famished person, and then seek to obey the principles we discover. If we can do that, we will avoid getting derailed, even by peace.

Lord God of my life, please help me to recollect Your abiding presence, in good times and bad. Keep me in the center of Your will that I might glorify You in all I may encounter today. In Christ's name I pray. Amen.

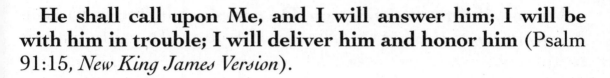

Storm Safety Instructions

He shall call upon Me, and I will answer him; I will be with him in trouble; I will deliver him and honor him (Psalm 91:15, *New King James Version*).

Scripture: Psalm 91:9-16
Song: "Flee as a Bird"

The thunderclap was deafening. When my eldest grandchild, Emily, was 2-years-old, my husband and I took her to lunch. As we were leaving the restaurant in pouring rain, I had her in my arms. My husband had pulled around, opened the passenger side door from inside the car, and was still sitting behind the wheel. *Boom!* More thunder. In an instant Emily leaped from my arms and launched into her grandfather's lap, holding onto him for dear life. She knew where her safety was, and she was fleeing to it.

Sometimes I wonder: Do I really know where to flee for safety? Life brings terrible storms sometimes. Whose lap can I leap into?

God says He is an ever-present help in times of trouble. He is close. It stands to reason, then, when the storm rages and our hearts begin to race, we need to flee to the Lord. He is our deliverer, our safety in the storm.

The reality is this: No one loves us as God does. He can be counted upon in ways that no grandfather could ever match. Therefore, His lap is the place to be. Leap . . . He is waiting.

Thank You, **Lord,** for loving me as You do. I know that Your thoughts and Your ways are higher than mine, and You always do what is best for me. Help me to trust You more and more and not be afraid when the storms come. In Jesus' name, amen.

You Have the Right to Choose

My son, if sinners entice you, Do not consent (Proverbs 1:10, *New King James Version*).

Scripture: Proverbs 1:8-15
Song: "Choose Ye Today"

Trapped! That's the way my Christian friend described his sin problem. He would feel so sorry for what he had done and would plead for forgiveness. Then, before he knew it, he would be right back repeating his mistakes. Hopelessness would set in. Where was the escape?

Then one night, in great sorrow, he cried out to the Lord, asking Him for the way out. Later, my friend described how he heard the Lord's voice in his spirit as clearly as if it had been audible: "It is a choice. Being sorry is not enough to free you from the trap of sin. You must choose to reject the sin and follow me."

Our lives abound with choices, don't they? What shall we eat? Where should we live? Who should we marry? Yet, sometimes, the simple choice to reject sin evades us. Why? Maybe it's this: even though we feel sorry about our behavior, we love our sin even more. Until we reach that point of surrender—giving up actions that are pleasurable (though we may regret them later)—our lives will flounder in misery. Maybe you needed to read this today. Maybe today is the day that the light of choosing has come on for you. Escape is right in front of you.

Lord, You know my frame and what makes me tick. Please help me to choose right over wrong. I know that You never tell me to do anything unless You provide a way for me to do it. So, thank You for the strength to obey. In Jesus' name, amen.

Learn and Live

He also taught me, and said to me: "Let your heart retain my words; Keep my commands, and live" (Proverbs 4:4, *New King James Version*).

Scripture: Proverbs 4:1-9
Song: "I Remember When My Burdens Rolled Away"

The old saying goes: "We live and learn." But wouldn't it be better if we could "learn and live" instead? (In other words, don't you just hate to mess up in life?)

Thirty years ago I took a wrong turn. Apart from prayer or seeking much discernment, I decided that I wanted to buy a house. The timing of my obsession wasn't good, and God kept closing the door. I refused to be deterred, however, and forced every closed door open.

You guessed it. Owning that house was an absolute disaster! Immediately upon closing, the real estate market crashed. The flat roof leaked like a sieve, and there was no way out for me and my family. We were stuck.

God has shown me over the years that He loves me and wants the best for me. When He shuts a door, He wants me to trust Him—and leave the door shut. His ways are the best ways.

He has graciously given us His Word and indwelt us with His Spirit. He has provided all the godly wisdom we need for living. Our job is to accept His words, to simply learn (from Him) and live.

Father, thank You for loving me and helping me live this life in Your will. You said that if I lack wisdom, I can ask, and You will give it generously. Please give me the ears to hear Your wisdom and the strength to obey it today. In Jesus' name, amen.

Shhh . . . Don't Tell!

Let your eyes look straight ahead, and your eyelids look right before you (Proverbs 4:25, *New King James Version*).

Scripture: Proverbs 4:10-15, 20-27
Song: "Thy Mercy and Thy Truth, O Lord"

"You have to act like you don't know!" my friend shouted as she was leaving. She had just revealed, in advance, a secret that would soon become common knowledge. But in the meantime, I had to act as if I didn't know about it.

The whole event made me feel rather paranoid—as if I were always looking over my shoulder. When I was around other people, I became guarded, just in case I slipped up and said something about the secret I was supposed to keep at all costs. *Why did she have to dump this in my lap?*

Do you have secrets weighing you down? Are you constantly looking in the rearview mirror and tiptoeing around, on guard all the time? God gives us help here. He tells us to immerse ourselves in His Word, and then obey what we learn. This will fill our lives with godly wisdom and give us clean hearts. We won't be looking to the right or left, because we will have nothing to hide.

The fact is, honesty and straightforwardness will bring health to our spirit and spring to our step. (Then we can run the other way when we spot those friends who just can't keep secrets.)

Heavenly Father, thank You for showing me the way to live and for freeing me from the lies that permeate my world. You have given me the freshness of a clean heart and the confidence of knowing You will direct my paths. I love You, Lord. In the holy name of Jesus, my Savior, I pray. Amen.

The Right Connection

He who gathers crops in summer is a wise son, but he who sleeps during harvest is a disgraceful son (Proverbs 10:5).

Scripture: Proverbs 10:1-5
Song: "Be Thou My Vision"

A sleepwalking teenager stepped out of her second story bedroom window one night and plunged 25 feet to the ground. She landed feet first, creating six-inch deep holes in the ground. Before collapsing she cried for help, and her parents took her to the hospital. To the astonishment of the doctors, she hadn't broken or sprained anything. Equally amazing was the fact that she didn't wake up until well into the next day.

Today's verse states that someone who sleeps "during harvest" is a disgrace. But it's really more about someone who sleeps *through* a harvest, presumably to avoid working. Oversleeping doesn't just avoid work, it also bypasses communicating and interacting with people and God—disconnecting from life.

Someone I know says, "You do the connecting, and God does the perfecting." That is, if we make the effort to reach out to God through study and prayer (or simply sit and soak in the silence), God will meet us where we are and gradually transform our lives.

Perfecting God, You are the creator of the universe and the author of life, and You daily speak words of truth, light, and life. Please create in me ears that are willing to hear Your wisdom and truth. Give me a heart that is willing to respond in obedience as I connect with You each day. In the name of Jesus, amen.

September 12–18. **Greg Johnson** is a technical writer for a software corporation in Southern California. He and his wife have two adult children and enjoy world travel.

Speak the Truths That Heal

The lips of the righteous nourish many, but fools die for lack of judgment (Proverbs 10:21).

Scripture: Proverbs 10:18-22
Song: "Hungry"

The Nathan company's July 4th hot dog eating contest is a well-known annual competition held at Coney Island. It was recently viewed by 30,000 spectators and an additional 1.5 million TV-viewing households. During the event, more than 20 contestants consume as many hot dogs and buns as possible in 10 minutes. In 2009 the winner ate 68 hot dogs and buns in 10 minutes and set a new American and world record.

Each "athlete" has his or her own strategy. Some break the dogs in half and eat them together; others soak and squeeze the buns to make them easier to swallow. Bottom line: lots of volume, little nutrition.

Today's verse suggests that righteous words nourish the soul — words saturated with wisdom, truth, and love spoken to encourage others. Elsewhere in Proverbs we read that our words have the power to heal or destroy. Thus we are challenged to choose words that bring life and healing.

The apostle Paul encouraged us to be "speaking the truth in love" (Ephesians 4:15), with the idea of helping the other person. So instead of just thinking kind thoughts about someone, why not speak the words?

Healing Lord, because the words I speak have immense power, help me to guard my speech and test every word that comes from my lips. May I speak words of loving truth to my family, friends, and neighbors today. In Jesus' name, amen.

Never a Doubt

When the storm has swept by, the wicked are gone, but the righteous stand firm forever (Proverbs 10:25).

Scripture: Proverbs 10:23-28
Song: "How Great Is Our God"

I still can remember lying on the hospital bed, wondering whether I'd live or die. It had been two weeks, and the doctors were no closer to an explanation for why the tumor-like growth in my neck was doubling in size every few days. Nor did they know what they could do about it. My wife was pregnant with our first child and, frankly, I didn't want to die.

However, after struggling with anger, doubt, resentment, and fear, I raised the white flag of surrender and told God that my life was His to deal with as He pleased (as if He didn't know that already). And whether I lived or died, I would trust Him for the outcome. A week later the surgeon removed a golf-ball sized nonmalignant growth from my neck, and I recovered in time to celebrate the birth of my son.

When life throws seeming tragedies at us, it is often difficult to believe He is truly our good shepherd. We may wonder whether all things do indeed work together for the good. But I've come to believe this: We can depend on the rock-solid fact that our Creator loves us with an unconditional and everlasting love that will never let us go.

Loving Lord, You are infinitely immense and beyond my understanding; yet You are present and personal, seeing my every need. Please help me to begin and end each day by putting my life in Your hands. Let me trust You the whole way, down every road You lead me. In the name of Jesus, my Savior, I pray. Amen.

Look It Over

A fool shows his annoyance at once, but a prudent man overlooks an insult (Proverbs 12:16).

Scripture: Proverbs 12:12-16
Song: "A Shield About Me"

We sometimes hear in the news that a police officer's body armor saved his life. And, surprisingly, in many cities K-9 police dogs are even being issued their own body armor. When a low-caliber bullet strikes the armor, it gets caught in a web of exceptionally strong fibers. The fibers absorb and spread the impact energy throughout the vest until the bullet is stopped.

Today's verse says that a prudent person "overlooks an insult." In other words, they "look over" the insult and consider it without letting it hit home. It reminds me of science fiction movies where bullets gradually slow down and hover harmlessly in front of the intended victim. Why not handle insults the same way? We can let them hover harmlessly out in front of us while we look them over.

Over the years I have found two questions helpful in diagnosing an insult: What does the comment say about the *speaker*? And what does it say about *me*? That is, does this person regularly make stinging comments, or is this out of the ordinary? Is there some sliver of truth in the comment that might actually help me? It doesn't hurt to look it over. And it might just help.

Sustaining Lord, Your Word proclaims that You are a shield about me and that I am constantly held in the palm of Your hand. What a safe place to be! Please grant me the wisdom to look over and evaluate the negative comments that come my way. I know that I can always cast my cares on You. In Christ's holy name I pray. Amen.

The Fountain of Life

The fear of the LORD is a fountain of life, turning a man from the snares of death (Proverbs 14:27).

Scripture: Proverbs 14:27-34
Song: "Have Thine Own Way, Lord"

We usually notice them in the shadows, watching to see if we come to a complete stop before continuing on our way. Sometimes even an *empty* highway patrol car parked along the side of an interstate is enough to slow the flow of traffic. (I've quickly hit the brakes, for just that reason, plenty of times.)

California Traffic Court records indicate that over 15 million traffic citations are written each year in the state, most for speeding or failing to stop. That's an incredible number—over 40,000 tickets per day—and those represent just the folks who got caught.

I would certainly do a better job of driving if a police officer were sitting beside me 24/7. Yet I sometimes forget: the Creator of the universe has every facet of my life constantly in view. And that fact should result in "fear"—that is, reverent, profound respect—for the Lord.

Instead of being intimidating, this profound respect is described as a "fountain of life" to us. It releases us to walk alongside God as the hands and feet of Jesus in our world, serving and loving others on His behalf.

Lord, Your purposes run as true as the purest mountain stream. You have told me that my sins are cast away from me as far as the east is from the west. Please grant me the freedom to thrive in the midst of Your supportive presence. Help me to know and feel that I am Your forgiven and cherished child. In Jesus' name, amen.

Life's Best Condiment: Love

Better a meal of vegetables where there is love than a fattened calf with hatred (Proverbs 15:17).

Scripture: Proverbs 15:15-19
Song: "Love Divine, All Love Excelling"

The food we eat every day can't immediately be used by our bodies. There's a process: digestion starts with the saliva in our mouths as we start chewing. Next the food gets mixed up with digestive juices in the stomach before being emptied into the small intestine. Liver and pancreatic chemicals further break it down. Finally, the digested micronutrients are absorbed through intestinal walls and transported throughout the body. When the process works properly, we've got a good start on radiant health and vitality.

Today's verse suggests that a loving home is perhaps the healthiest condiment in the world. The most exotic and delicious cuisine goes sour when consumed amidst relational chaos and strife. Thus the apostle Paul wrote, "'In your anger do not sin': Do not let the sun go down while you are still angry" (Ephesians 4:26).

Untreated anger, like raw food, is a harsh shock to our system (of relationships). Once anger takes root, bitterness is not far behind. It can poison our words, looks, thoughts, and decisions. With anger it's best to get it out—give it to the Lord—and then let it go for good.

Reconciling Lord, may the words of my mouth and the meditations of my heart be acceptable in Your sight. May Your peace rule in my heart, in my home, and everywhere I go from this day forward. In Christ I pray. Amen.

Stop, Look, and Listen

Folly delights a man who lacks judgment, but a man of understanding keeps a straight course (Proverbs 15:21).

Scripture: Proverbs 15:21-33
Song: "Change My Heart, O God"

"If something sounds too good to be true, it probably is." This idea usually prompts us to perform due diligence before making a decision, especially when it involves our money.

Eve, in the Garden of Eden, typically gets a bad rap for single-handedly plunging all of humankind into sin. In her defense we can remember that she had no experience with deception. (Though you'd think red flags might have gone up the second she started trading theological insights with a talking snake!)

The most surprising thing in Eve's case? When the serpent completely contradicted God's commands with a bold-faced lie, she never stopped to consider that he might not be telling the truth.

That wily serpent is still on the hunt for victims, using the same subtle approach: "You deserve this . . . No one will get hurt . . . It's good for you." And sooner or later we may just give in.

Thankfully, we can consciously choose to stop this process before it carries us away into sheer folly. Let us determine to take every thought, motive, and desire before the throne of grace and test it there through the filter of God's truth. We can expose tempting deceptions for what they really are—bold-faced lies.

Purifying Lord, You are the source of truth and life. Please help me to hear Your voice through all of the distractions and temptations of daily life. May your truth lock me onto Your straight course and holy path. Through Christ, amen.

You—the Work of His Hands

Ask Me about the things to come concerning My sons, And you shall commit to Me the work of My hands (Isaiah 45:11, *New American Standard Bible*).

Scripture: Isaiah 45:9-17
Song: "Where He Leads I'll Follow"

"What do you want to be when you grow up?" an elderly man once asked my 5-year-old daughter. She looked skyward and pulled on a lock of hair as she considered how to answer. She finally murmured, "I want to be a ballerina," but then added quickly, "or a truck driver."

When I worked as a high school counselor, the students who entered my office door had rarely thought past the level of my daughter's early musings. However, even after they completed some tests designed to help give them direction in life, neither they nor I could say with certainty what their future might hold. How could we?

We don't know what path lies before us. But God does. Further, when critics question the future of His people, His answer is His commitment to lead each of us along a blessed pathway with Him. Whether we work as a ballerina or a truck driver, He abides daily with us who love Him.

My Lord, why do I contrive plans for my future when I cannot predict the events of the next hour? Please quiet my heart, and help me to remember that Your will for me is to be filled with Your Spirit each moment of each day. May I simply see Your face and trust Your leading. In the precious name of Jesus I pray. Amen.

September 19–25. **Shelley L. Houston,** of Eugene, Oregon, has served as a high school teacher and counselor and as executive director of a Christian college in Bend, Oregon.

Asking with Wisdom

Ask what you wish me to give you (1 Kings 3:5, *New American Standard Bible*).

Scripture: 1 Kings 3:5-14
Song: "I Do Not Ask, O Lord"

When I first heard the story of Solomon asking for wisdom, my child's heart filled with desire. Following the king's example, I prayed for wisdom. But I suspect my motives included a longing for the accompanying fame and riches God gave Solomon.

None of us is pure of heart—but I know that God honored my prayer. Not that I have always made the wisest decisions. However, His Spirit has often given me the wisdom to do right in my life. And even though I've yet to acquire fame or wealth, my life has been rich in real blessings.

Recently, I suffered a serious wrong from others. The pain and financial cost severely reduced my health and my family's resources. I swung between stunned rage and fearful worry. With such intense emotions clouding my wisdom, I sought counsel from a godly friend.

He urged me to let God "reimburse" me for my true losses and seek only actual costs. I recognized this as wisdom, but you know what? Those tainted motives of my childhood are still with me. I wondered, if I let God handle my situation, will He restore everything exactly the way I want it to be? (Or, as His child, can I just be grateful for the wisdom and strength to do the right thing?)

O God, forgive my grasping at the apparent stabilities of this world. Instead, open the eyes of my heart to the great provider, Jesus Christ, my Savior. In His name, amen.

Seeking Humility

[If] My people who are called by My name humble themselves and pray, and seek My face and turn from their wicked ways, then I will hear from heaven, will forgive their sin, and will heal their land (2 Chronicles 7:14, *New American Standard Bible*).

Scripture: 2 Chronicles 7:12-18
Song: "Regard My Grief and Rescue Me"

Do you ever feel that you could be reading a Greek tragedy when God gives these kinds of warnings to His people? It's as if the people are doomed to failure. Why would people who belong to such a great king ever consider crossing Him?

Sometimes I wonder what kind of mental gymnastics David had to do before he could sleep with Bathsheba—and then kill her husband to cover up the child she carried. But then I remember . . .

Have you ever broken the law? repeatedly? unashamed and blatantly? I have . . . and I do. And because "everyone does it," I convince myself that I'd be foolish to refrain. That's true even though I am only writing about my habit of speeding five or so miles an hour on the highway.

The mind-set that allows me at times to avoid guilty feelings about speeding is the same trick David's mind must have played on him as he spied a beautiful bather. We are no different, are we? We're the same Greek tragedy guaranteed to end in a heap—except for the saving, healing hand of God.

Lord, I surrender my foolish mind and self-loving ways. I pray You would forgive my arrogance and restore in me a humble and obedient heart. Through Christ, amen.

A Timely Word

Like apples of gold in settings of silver Is a word spoken in right circumstances (Proverbs 25:11, *New American Standard Bible*).

Scripture: Proverbs 25:11-15
Song: "Speak for Jesus"

"You know that God killed his own Son, don't you?" my professor said. The class gaped. "Ha!" he continued. "Nice god!" I wasn't afraid to defend my faith, but his cynical rant came in a continuous stream, leaving no room for comments.

Why do I have to be in this class? I thought. But I knew there was a reason. I sighed and prayed, *God, give me the wisdom, the opportunity, and the words to speak to this man in love.* That night, while doing my homework, I wrote a careful criticism of my professor's harangue against Christianity.

In the next class he handed back our assignments and paused to give me a brooding look. "Class," he said. "This woman says I have been misrepresenting what Christians think."

I stared helplessly at him. "So, what about it, Shelley? Why don't you take the podium and tell us what it's all about?" I rose and walked slowly to the front, facing hundreds of students.

Now, God! Give me the right words . . . now!

I had 10 minutes to explain the gospel from creation to the day of the Lord. I don't remember exactly what I said. But when I sat down, I knew His words hung precious in eternity.

O God, help me to remember that finding the right time to speak is as important as finding the right words. Cause me always to be willing and able to speak, but sensitive to Your leading. And may every word of witness be wrapped in true compassion for the hearers—that I may love them as You love them. Through Christ, amen.

Ministry at Home

Let your foot rarely be in your neighbor's house, Or he will become weary of you and hate you (Proverbs 25:17, *New American Standard Bible*).

Scripture: Proverbs 25:16-20
Song: "O Master, Let Me Walk with Thee"

My grandparents lived with my husband and me for a few years before they passed away. This arrangement was a great blessing to them—and to us and our children—but we all sacrificed some favorite habits to make it work.

My husband and I gave up our den and an attached bedroom, which could be closed off from our rowdy preschoolers. This allowed my grandparents some quiet, but we all worried that they might need something and we would not hear them. Therefore, we placed a baby monitor in their rooms so they could call out for help if needed. Not being accustomed to such technology, they sometimes forgot that I could hear them.

One day, as I was working in the kitchen, I heard my grandmother say, "If her husband could keep her home, he could make half a woman out of her!"

This gave me a good laugh, but it also hurt a little. Weren't all of my activities outside of the home important?

Slowly I learned that being home and taking care of my own family was an important part of a life lived for Christ. And the blessed outcome? I'm sure certain people were glad to have my nose out of their business!

God, why am I so drawn to activities that take me away from home with little purpose? Forgive my wandering feet and heal any harm I've done. In Jesus' name, amen.

Am I Open to Plunder?

Like a city that is broken into and without walls Is a man who has no control over his spirit (Proverbs 25:28, *New American Standard Bible*).

Scripture: Proverbs 25:21-28
Song: "Search Me, O God"

"Joe has no filter," my son said, referring to a troubled friend in his church. "What comes to his mind, comes out his mouth. He scares off girls . . . and guys just want to rearrange his face!"

This may have been a bit of an exaggeration, but certainly Joe had some social challenges. My son explained that people in the church often avoided Joe since he was so aggressive, opinionated, and often just plain inappropriate.

I felt badly for Joe and was grateful that my son had made him a friend. Joe needed a friend. But even more he needed the Spirit—he needed self-control.

In a follow-up conversation with my son, I heard that Joe was looking for a new church. He felt that no one cared about his needs.

My son was crushed when he told me about this. He blinked back tears as he said, "It makes me wonder whether this church is where I'm supposed to be."

"I can't answer that," I said. "But don't you think that many of Joe's troubles come from his lack of self-control?"

My son nodded and said, "But the people of the church didn't care enough about him to work with him and help him grow."

O, **God**, my heart goes out to Joe—and to my son. It's true that a person with no self-control opens himself up for ruin. But help us to help them! Through Christ, amen.

Hide and Seek

It is the glory of God to conceal a matter, But the glory of kings is to search out a matter (Proverbs 25:2, *New American Standard Bible*).

Scripture: Proverbs 25:1-10
Song: "An Awe Full Mystery Is Here"

My main occupation is searching out the mysteries of God. Other ventures also occupy my time—like nurturing my family, serving the church, and, oh yes, freelance writing. But nothing has more eternal significance than contemplating and delving into the mysteries of God. It's just so fascinating!

Once my 10-year-old son questioned me about why a rule in sports seemed so unfair. I began my explanation with something like, "I was just reading in the Bible today . . . "

"Mom!" he interrupted in exasperation. "Not everything is about Jesus!"

I laughed. I understood his frustration. But really—everything *does* revolve around God! I only need open my eyes to it.

Think of one element of God, His awesome grandeur as Creator. I see this in a mighty mountain, a lightening storm, a thunderous waterfall, a raging fire, the sun rolling triumphantly across the sky. Nature, with God's Word and Spirit to guide me, clearly reveals this aspect of God—and that is just one part of His mystery. His secrets unfold on the stage of life when I seek Him. I've only to watch each act to determine the romance, adventure, and drama before me.

God, reveal yourself to me today. Alert me to Your truth and purposes in all creation, secreted in the circumstances, rules, and rhythms of life. In Jesus' name, amen.

Balance

Choose some wise, understanding and respected men from each of your tribes, and I will set them over you (Deuteronomy 1:13).

Scripture: Deuteronomy 1:9-17
Song: "May the Mind of Christ, My Savior"

"I can do it myself" was the first full sentence my daughter learned. She wasn't even 2 years old, but she was determined. As a parent I found it difficult to sit back and watch her struggle as she tried to prove that she could indeed do it herself. But, of course, I find myself struggling to do it all myself quite often. And I wonder why the burden is so heavy.

Moses realized his people had grown to such a number that he could no longer govern them by himself. And this great leader asked for help.

When I am feeling overwhelmed, I need to evaluate my schedule and prayerfully ask God how to increase my effectiveness. Often others are waiting for opportunities to help. Recognizing my limitations means placing greater faith in God and His people. We can serve the Lord together. And that's when balance returns to each of our lives—leading to effectiveness, too, in all our kingdom work.

Lord, at times I am that 2-year-old child. I think I can do it all myself. Help me to hold on to the responsibilities that are mine and release the others to You. I will trust You to find the right persons to handle all the other things that I can't do on my own. In the precious name of Jesus my Lord I pray. Amen.

September 26–30. **Rhonda Thorson,** of Oklahoma City, has been freelance writing for 20 years. She is the mother of two and the wife of a minister.

His Protective Hand

The LORD saved Hezekiah and the people of Jerusalem from the hand of Sennacherib king of Assyria and from the hand of all others. He took care of them on every side (2 Chronicles 32:22).

Scripture: 2 Chronicles 32:20-26
Song: "Protect and Save Me, O My God"

Traveling at 70 mph on the interstate, the car flipped four times before coming to rest back on its wheels. The fate of the passengers unknown, my husband, daughter, and I stopped our car and jumped out. Our horror turned to relief and praise when we realized our son and his fiancée were OK.

We'd been traveling back from vacation in two separate cars. When another car pulled out in front of my son, he swerved to miss it. As his car flipped, we cried out to God, watching helplessly from our own vehicle. As we arrived at the scene, though, we found our beloved ones shaken and bruised, but fine. God had protected them "on every side."

We have an enemy who will attack us from every side. He knows our blind spots and weak areas. He comes against us because he is the enemy of our souls. When King Hezekiah and the prophet Isaiah cried out to God, He saved them from the hand of all their enemies. He took care of them on every side. Can we trust Him to do the same for us today?

Heavenly Father, what do I have to fear, knowing You protect me from every attack? You provide a watchful care that sees on every side, protecting me and guarding me from the fiery darts of the enemy. Thank You for the peace this brings to my heart today. In the name of Christ I pray. Amen.

Bold as a Lion

The wicked man flees though no one pursues, but the righteous are as bold as a lion (Proverbs 28:1).

Scripture: Proverbs 28:1-5
Song: "Our God Reigns"

He watches through blades of deep grass and waits for the perfect opportunity. Suddenly, he takes off at speeds of up to 50 miles per hour. The chase is on.

Lions are among the most daring and ferocious of animals. Thus they appear as symbols of power, courage, and nobility on family crests, coats of arms, or flags. Kings of the jungle, they boldly face their prey and the challenges of the jungle.

Andy is a Christian whom I consider as bold as a lion. In 2008, while serving in Afghanistan, Andy was hit in the neck by sniper fire. The bullet severed his spine, leaving him paralyzed from the waist down. He has suffered surgery, hours of intense physical therapy, and the difficulty of learning a whole new way of life. He boldly faced the enemy he fought in Afghanistan, and he faces the challenges at home with similar courage. Furthermore, Andy is the first to tell you that his boldness and strength come from the Lord.

Whether we face enemies on foreign soil, physical challenges, or the enemy of our souls, we can meet them with lionhearted boldness. Yes, through the Spirit of Christ living within us, we can do it.

Lord, I don't always understand why things happen. Yet You have given me a boldness to face the challenges and climb the mountains placed before me. Thank You for a courage that comes from knowing You are near. In Jesus' name, amen.

The Cookie Confession

He who conceals his sins does not prosper, but whoever confesses and renounces them finds mercy (Proverbs 28:13).

Scripture: Proverbs 28:8-16
Song: "The Mercy of God Is an Ocean Divine"

Dinner is on the stove. A jar sits on the counter, full of his favorite cookies. But Mom had said, "No cookies before dinner."

Slowly he sneaks up on that jar. He carefully picks up the lid, reaches in with his tiny hand, and pulls out the delicious prize. He carefully replaces the lid. He opens his mouth to take the first bite . . . just as he hears Mom walking into the kitchen!

He shoves the whole cookie in his mouth and stands straight with wide-eyed innocence. But moms know. "Did you take a cookie after you were told not to?" As he opens his mouth to say no, bits of cookie fall down his shirt and onto the kitchen floor.

Why did he lie when the evidence was clear? Why didn't he confess his wrongdoing?

We, like this little boy, have done plenty wrong—mostly *not* involving cookies. Yet with the figurative cookies still in our mouths, we are reluctant to confess our wrongdoing. Are we afraid of consequences? Do we think He doesn't know? The Scripture tells us that whoever confesses and renounces sin finds mercy. When we bring our sins to God, His response is forgiveness and mercy. He already knows what we've done; He's just waiting to extend His grace.

Merciful Lord, I want to do Your will. I find joy in obedience. But Father, when I do sin, I thank You that I can find forgiveness when I confess to You. Thank You for Your measureless grace given to me through Christ and His cross. In His name, amen.

Faith in Action

A faithful man will be richly blessed, but one eager to get rich will not go unpunished (Proverbs 28:20).

Scripture: Proverbs 28:20-28
Song: "Faith Means We're Sure"

How will we pay for groceries? we wondered. Early on in our youth ministry, we served at a small church in Arkansas. Our children were both young, and we were paid very little. Still, we loved the people, and they cared for us in many ways.

One Saturday we were traveling the 20 miles it took to get to a grocery store. We'd often write a check for groceries on Saturday, knowing my husband would get paid on Sunday, and we could have the check in the bank by Monday morning.

But on this day we felt guilty about it. Were we trusting the Lord to provide for us or taking matters into our own hands? We began shopping, but our hearts grew heavier. In a declaration of trust in God, we returned a cart full of groceries and went out to the car. When our then 4-year-old son asked why we left our food, we replied: "God is going to provide for us this week." After a silent trip home, we arrived wondering what to do when dinner time came.

We both began to cry and praise the Lord as we opened the door to the house: covering the entire kitchen floor were large bags of groceries!

Thank You, **dear Lord**, for Your provisions in my life. My faithfulness to You results in riches far beyond compare and a life lived in the secure promises of Your Word. O Lord, I believe—but help me in my unbelief! In the name of the Father, the Son, and the Holy Spirit, I pray. Amen.

My Prayer Notes
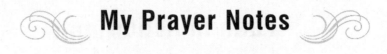

_____

_____

_____

_____

_____

_____

_____

_____

_____

_____

_____

_____

_____

_____

_____

_____

_____

_____

_____

_____

_____

DEVOTIONS®

OCTOBER

 May your unfailing love rest upon us, O LORD,
even as we put our hope in you.

—Psalm 33:22

Gary Allen, Editor | **Margaret Williams,** Project Editor | Photo © Futuredigitaldesign | Dreamstime.com

DEVOTIONS® is published quarterly by Standard Publishing, Cincinnati, Ohio, www.standardpub.com. © 2010 by Standard Publishing. All rights reserved. Topics based on the Home Daily Bible Readings, International Sunday School Lessons. © 2008 by the Committee on the Uniform Series. Printed in the U.S.A. All Scripture quotations, unless otherwise indicated, are taken from the *HOLY BIBLE, NEW INTERNATIONAL VERSION*®. *NIV*®. Copyright © 1973, 1978, 1984 by Biblica, Inc. ™. Used by permission of Zondervan. All rights reserved. Holy Bible, *New Living Translation* (NLT), © 1996. Tyndale House Publishers. *Contemporary English Version* (CEV), © 1991, 1992, 1995 American Bible Society. *New American Standard Bible* (NASB), © The Lockman Foundation, 1960, 1962, 1963, 1968, 1971, 1972, 1973, 1975, 1977, 1995. *King James Version* (KJV), public domain.

A Very Bad Day

A fool gives full vent to his anger, but a wise man keeps himself under control (Proverbs 29:11).

Scripture: Proverbs 29:2-11
Song: "Now Let Every Tongue Adore Thee"

It is going to be a very bad day . . . I wake up late for work. The car will not start. I am late for an important meeting. I miss lunch. I get stuck in heavy traffic. I burn dinner. I go outside to mow the lawn, in response to a chastising letter from the neighborhood association complaining about our tall grass. You guessed it: The lawn mower won't start.

By this time, I am not happy. In fact, I'm quite angry. I want to kick the trash cans, yell at the children, set fire to the lawn mower, and scream at the top of my lungs.

But wisdom says the neighbors are watching. They want to know if the joy I claim will sustain me through a tough day. My children are watching. They want to know if it's OK to be angry without losing control. My coworkers are watching. They're wondering whether I serve a God who gives me peace in the storms of life.

We chose to eat out that night and talk and laugh as a family. At bedtime, I held the kids close as we prayed, and I thanked God for the wisdom to keep anger from hurting my witness.

Heavenly Father, I realize things will happen to me that can stir anger. I also know that others are watching my response. Give me the wisdom to control my anger and allow You to bring laughter and joy to a frustrating day. In Jesus' name, amen.

October 1, 2. **Rhonda Thorson,** of Oklahoma City, has been freelance writing for 20 years. She is the mother of two and the wife of a pastor.

Freedom or Fear?

Fear of man will prove to be a snare, but whoever trusts in the LORD is kept safe (Proverbs 29:25).

Scripture: Proverbs 29:16-27
Song: "Stand Up, Stand Up for Jesus"

The first high school football game of the season was ready to begin. The stands swarmed with eager fans. It would be a beautiful night for a game, but prayer was recently prohibited.

The announcer welcomed the fans. After we sang the national anthem, he asked that we share a moment of silence. The first few seconds were quiet, except for the September breeze blowing and the clanging of a chain against the flagpole.

Then, softly, it began. It started at one end of the bleachers and quickly spread. "Our Father which art in heaven . . ." (Matthew 6:9, *KJV*) grew louder and louder. Soon everyone had joined in the model prayer in perfect unison.

Though I've said the model prayer many times in my life, I'd never heard it recited more beautifully than on that warm and starry night. It was unplanned and unrehearsed, springing from the hearts of believers who weren't afraid to stand and pray.

The game began, the fans cheered, and time moved on. But we all knew we had been part of a divine moment that night, as we chose obedience over fear, and prayed.

Almighty and everlasting God, thank You that I can pray, regardless of my surroundings. Thank You that I need not fear others, but can trust You to protect me. I will carry that night of prayer in my heart and remember the beauty of Your faithful children honoring You in unity under a shadow of oppression. I pray this prayer in the name of Jesus, my Savior and Lord. Amen.

Understanding It All

He made their hearts, so he understands everything they do (Psalm 33:15, *New Living Translation*).

Scripture: Psalm 33:13-22
Song: "Wait, O My Soul, Thy Maker's Will"

Have you ever done something and then later wondered why you did it? Human reasoning can be faulty, even in the best of situations. When I was much younger, I remember my mother scolding me for something I had done. When she asked me why I did it, my only response was, "I don't know." Those who deal with children hear that excuse a lot.

While we are wonderfully made (Psalm 139:14), we often choose our own way or will over God's wise leading. Sometimes we may think we know the circumstances better than our Lord, but we really don't. Not only does God know what we will do; He knows why we're going to do it. (Sometimes, I still don't know why I do what I do!)

So for today, let us purpose to do what God would have us do. Let us reach the lost with encouraging words and deeds. Let's minister to one another with tasks that are worthy of "well done" (Matthew 25:21) by our Savior. God knows the reason we do everything. Nothing we do, think, say, or feel will escape God's attention. Let's honor Him today in all we do.

Lord, I don't always understand why I do things, but I know that You know me intimately. Help me to live by the leading of Your Spirit today and to please You in all I do and say. In Jesus' name, amen.

October 3–9. **Pete Anderson** lives in Florida with his wife and younger son. When not teaching the fourth grade, he enjoys going on mission trips and leading worship.

Meaningless

I saw that all labor and all achievement spring from man's envy of his neighbor. This too is meaningless, a chasing after the wind (Ecclesiastes 4:4).

Scripture: Ecclesiastes 4:4-12
Song: "We'll Work Till Jesus Comes"

Yes, I work hard for my money. I feel that I earn every dollar of my paycheck. I'm not claiming to be one hundred percent efficient, but I do work hard, and I usually enjoy my teaching profession. Yet I am required to stay up-to-date with trends and programs that are offered to make me a better teacher. (Did I already tell you that I work hard?)

You no doubt work hard at your vocation also. Maybe you are already retired and have completed your life's work. Whatever your situation, work either is, or was, a major part of your life. Is that bad?

If we are doing our work for the approval of others—other than God, then our work is meaningless. Yes, I want to please my principal, but more than that I want my Savior to be pleased with what I do. I work not because I envy my neighbor's house or possessions, but because I know God gave me certain talents to use for His glory.

Working so I can have a better car than my neighbor is like chasing after the wind. I'll never catch the wind, and I'll never be better than my neighbor.

Savior God, when I am pleasing You, doing Your will, I'm building treasures in Heaven. May all I do today count for You and have eternal value in Your kingdom. Through Christ my Lord, amen.

Ears Open, Mouth Shut!

As you enter the house of God, keep your ears open and your mouth shut! Don't be a fool who doesn't realize that mindless offerings to God are evil (Ecclesiastes 5:1, *New Living Translation*).

Scripture: Ecclesiastes 5:1-7
Song: "Open Our Eyes, Lord"

Sometimes it's hard to discern what the Word of God is trying to communicate. That's not the case with this verse. As we enter the house of God, we are to keep our ears open and our mouths shut. That doesn't mean we aren't to speak with each other. But our focus is to be on the Lord: to listen and learn what God is saying to each of us. We learn by listening, so our mouths have to be closed.

In fact, it's just common sense, a good rule of thumb, to listen first and speak second. But when it comes to the Word of God to us, it's more than just good sense; it's a matter of spiritual life and death. There is always something life-giving and death-defying to learn from hearing and heeding Scripture.

I ask my 4th-grade students to enter my classroom each morning silently as they begin their work. That is the way we are to enter the house of God. We should attend expecting God to speak to our hearts and minds. Whether or not we've been a Christian for months or years, our Savior has something to say to each of us.

Father in Heaven, help me to be quick to listen and slow to speak. As I open my Bible today, open my ears and my heart to the truths of Your Word. In the name of Jesus, who lives and reigns with You and the Holy Spirit, now and forever, amen.

Good Times and Bad Times

Enjoy prosperity while you can. But when hard times strike, realize that both come from God. That way you will realize that nothing is certain in this life (Ecclesiastes 7:14, *New Living Translation*).

Scripture: Ecclesiastes 7:1-14
Song: "Trust, Try, and Prove Me"

"My wife and I have had 17 wonderful years together . . . We've been married for 27 years!" I hope you can laugh with me at that statement. You see, what the speaker was trying to communicate was that for 17 of the 27 years of their marriage, it was nice to be living in prosperity. The other years were difficult and challenging. Those years were harder to manage.

While the statement above was supposed to be funny, it isn't funny when hard times come crashing in. But hard times and prosperity both arise only with the sovereign Lord's permission. The same God who was Lord over the prosperous days is the Lord over the challenging days.

Looking back on our 27 years of marriage, my wife and I can remember times of plenty and times of want. Both are precious when we recall who has been in charge all along the way. When we realize that God is always watching, always nearby, we can go through difficult times with confidence. When we sit with our family albums and think of the blessings of serving Him in each time and place, we simply say: "The Lord is good!"

I know, **Lord,** that times are difficult and challenging for many. Help me to encourage and to help others in Your name. When times are difficult for me, help me to remember that You know my situation. In Jesus' name, amen.

Common Sense

If the ax is dull and its edge unsharpened, more strength is needed but skill will bring success (Ecclesiastes 10:10).

Scripture: Ecclesiastes 10:5-11
Song: "Come, Let Us Reason"

Ever used an ax? That tool can be quite handy for chopping wood or cutting down trees. I used an ax once. I borrowed it from my neighbor and used it to chop down a tree that was close to my house. I was trying to save money, so instead of hiring someone to do it, I decided it looked easy enough to do on my own. Wrong!

First, my ax wasn't all that sharp—but that didn't stop me from using it. Second, I didn't exactly know what I was doing. That didn't stop me from using it either. I swung the ax with all of my might and, eventually, the tree next to my house fell. Yes, it fell . . . on the house!

I learned two things that day. You need a *sharp* ax, and you need someone with *skill* to use it.

That is exactly what King Solomon tells us. We can apply these words, generally, to the choices we make in life. Common sense, the sense God gives us through wisdom, should permeate our lives so that we make good choices. Part of what that means is to know our strengths and weaknesses, to know what we ourselves can accomplish and what we may need to ask others to do for us.

Almighty and most merciful God, help me to make the choice to follow You in the most practical ways. Especially, today, give me the wisdom to appreciate the skills of others and to benefit from them. In the name of Jesus, amen.

What's Gonna Happen Next?

Foolish people claim to know all about the future and tell everyone the details! But who can really know what is going to happen? (Ecclesiastes 10:14, *New Living Translation*).

Scripture: Ecclesiastes 10:12-20
Song: "Only Trust Him"

I enjoy watching college football. I am very definitely a fan. Every summer, before the season begins, I start to wonder who will be the national champion for the next season. The football magazines are published, and I must peruse them to see who they predict will win. It's a lot of fun and fantasy.

Fantasy? That's right. You don't really think they know who's going to win, do you? Sure, they analyze the teams and coaches. The magazines interview everyone from the coach to the quarterback to the janitor. They probably spend hours upon hours coming up with their national championship picks. Still, no one knows.

Our Scripture today asks a simple question: "Who can really know what is going to happen?" Well, besides God himself, no one can. I like the way the famous baseball quipster Yogi Berra put it: "It's tough to make predictions, especially about the future."

So, what do we do? Take one step at a time into our future, asking God to provide the courage and wisdom to meet every challenge with grace.

O God, help me to discern Your way and will for me as I go through this day. Help me keep my focus on what You would have me be today, rather than worrying about what will happen tomorrow. What happens tomorrow is in Your hands. In Jesus' name, amen.

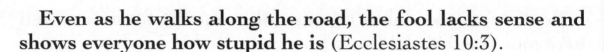

Anticipate the Consequences

Even as he walks along the road, the fool lacks sense and shows everyone how stupid he is (Ecclesiastes 10:3).

Scripture: Ecclesiastes 9:13–10:4
Song: "Praise to the Heavenly Wisdom"

I know there are some wise, godly children. However, many children are foolish in their choices, simply due to a lack of experience. That's why we expect children to make mistakes. But do you know any adults who demonstrate constant foolishness? Adults should know better.

A foolish person cannot act wisely. He cannot be something that he isn't. But there's hope for such a person. The Bible says, "If any of you lacks wisdom, he should ask God, who gives generously to all without finding fault, and it will be given to him," (James 1:5). We are to ask God for wisdom, and God will generously grant it.

Perhaps you have heard of the expression "a fool and his money are soon parted." Simply put, a foolish person spends money without planning. If the foolish man wants something, he buys it without thinking that he needs to eat. A wise person plans when the appropriate time is, so he can buy the wanted item.

If you have done some foolish things, ask God to forgive you. Ask God for wisdom, and He will respond generously. And look down the road to see what mistakes to avoid in the future. As someone once said: "Wisdom is simply the anticipation of consequences."

O Lord, help me to be wise in all of my dealings with everyone I meet. Help me to honor You, Lord, in the way I live my life. In Jesus' name, amen.

Rescued Once Again

Be not far from me, O God; come quickly, O my God, to help me (Psalm 71:12).

Scripture: Psalm 71:1-12
Song: "Draw Me Nearer"

The toddler wobbled unsteadily as his mother let go of his hands, and he took his first steps. His father knelt only a few feet in front of him, heartily cheering his son's attempt at walking. After only a couple seconds of delight, the child lost his balance. The father swiftly extended his arms and snatched the child from any possible injury. He hugged his son and praised his efforts. The boy never realized that he was spared from danger only because his father was so close to him.

Often we fail to step out because of fear of failure or disappointment. But the great men and women of Christian history overcame their own doubts and fears by simply trusting God. They knew that He was always close by to rescue them if needed. David went against a giant. Moses confronted the Pharaoh. Paul stood tall before Caesar. Knowing God was with them gave them the courage to accomplish great things.

We may never face such large challenges. But in our daily life, we can put aside the fears that hold us back from reaching our full potential in Christ. Even if we fall, God will safely rescue us with His loving embrace.

Father, thank You for always being close to me and ready to help me when I stumble. You always come to my rescue when I call on Your name. Through Christ, amen.

October 10–16. **Jeff Friend**, big fan of the Baltimore Orioles, is also an award-winning writer and speaker who lives in Florida with his wife, Nancy.

Mommy, I'm Bored!

All of life is far more boring than words could ever say. Our eyes and our ears are never satisfied with what we see and hear (Ecclesiastes 1:8, *Contemporary English Version*).

Scripture: Ecclesiastes 1:1-11
Song: "Jesus, Savior, Come to Me"

Timmy's plans for a fun day playing outside with his friends had been washed away by the steadily pouring rain. In his bedroom, he briefly pushed around a few of his toy trucks, dabbled with a puzzle, and even played a video game. Although he had many toys, nothing held his attention for more than a moment as he grumped lazily around his room. He found his mother and sadly announced, "Mommy, I'm bored. I don't have anything to play with!"

We've all been like Timmy at times. God has blessed us in a great variety of ways, and we see His gifts all around us—friends and family, a home, the beauty of nature, and so much more. Yet when our plans fail or we face disappointment, we focus on our own misery, forgetting the good things in our lives. We become bored with all that we have, and nothing seems to satisfy us.

But when we turn our attention to our Father's great love for us, we understand that our days can be exciting. We can stop and simply enjoy His presence. We can serve and worship Him in gratitude. In other words, living for Christ is a wonderful adventure every day.

Dear Lord, thank You for giving my life purpose. You shower blessings on me daily. Help me to be thankful and keep my eyes focused on You. Show me more ways that I can serve You joyfully with a grateful heart. In Christ's name, amen.

Good Workers Needed

Most of all, I enjoyed my work (Ecclesiastes 2:10, *Contemporary English Version*).

Scripture: Ecclesiastes 2:1-11
Song: "Work Is Sweet, for God Has Blest"

My friend had just retired after working 35 years for a large company. It had been a successful career as he advanced from a low-level position to management. His family and coworkers gave him a festive retirement party on his last day. When I saw him a few days later, I said, "I guess you're really going to miss working there." But his answer surprised me. "I hated every minute of every day at that place," he said.

I suppose most of us have been dissatisfied with a job at some time or another. But I couldn't imagine being totally miserable at work for over 35 years.

Work can take many forms, and being productive on behalf of God's creation is beneficial for everyone. Jesus was a carpenter, for example. And the apostle Paul's craft was tent making. They knew the value of doing a job well to earn their way in the world.

Whether young or old, each of us has a special gift or talent given by God. We may be called to use it in the workplace, at home, or in a ministry of the church. So whatever we do, we can do it as unto the Lord for His glory.

My Father, thank You for the talents You have given me. Let my work glorify You. May I do everything with thankfulness to my best ability. May I never give a half-hearted effort, whether in the workplace or in service to You. I pray in the name of Jesus, my precious Lord and Savior. Amen.

If You're Happy and You Know It

God will keep you so happy that you won't have time to worry about each day (Ecclesiastes 5:20, *Contemporary English Version*).

Scripture: Ecclesiastes 5:10-20
Song: "Happy the Man Who Feareth God"

Sue and Tom eagerly planned for their approaching wedding. After three years of romance, they were more in love now than ever. Each moment together held loving gazes, passionate words, and tender touches. Every thought and dream centered on their lives together and their hopes for the future. They were so happy together that nothing else seemed to matter. Although they knew there would be tough times ahead, for now their complete happiness kept any negative thoughts far from their minds. Their love would be their strength.

Yet this young couple would eventually find that it is very easy to let the troubles we encounter in life become overwhelming. There are bills to pay, illnesses to endure, various family issues to confront, and the list goes on.

But we do not have to face these challenges alone. God promises to bear our burdens and to give us His joy. We can be assured that He knows every detail of our difficult circumstances, and His love will be strong enough to see us through them. Yes, we have a loving relationship with our Father, and His joy will keep us happy and hopeful now and forever.

Father, Your love for me makes my heart joyful. May I always remember You are with me, every moment of my life, and I can rest in Your presence. Thank You for Your guidance and comfort through this life. I pray in the holy name of Jesus. Amen.

Always Right on Time

There is an appointed time for everything. And there is a time for every event under heaven (Ecclesiastes 3:1, *New American Standard Bible*).

Scripture: Ecclesiastes 3:1-8
Song: "Trusting Jesus"

Our corporate meeting planner frantically looked over his detailed agenda. In a few hours thousands of people would be arriving for a three-day conference, and he was responsible for everything running smoothly. His lengthy list charted every aspect of the event to the smallest detail: arrival of the caterers, room check-in times, podium setup, multimedia hookups.

Nothing was left to chance. Each event had a designated time, and everything had to go exactly as scheduled. If not, one problem would lead to another, and the whole conference would become a nightmare. So every detail was of extreme importance.

Schedules are often very necessary. Complex events must be well-planned to be successful. In an even greater sense, consider the precise timing of God's creation. What if the sun was off schedule by several hours once in a while? or if winter lasted three months too long? Can you imagine the serious situation that would create?

God's timing is perfect. He maintains order, not just in nature, but in our lives also, as we surrender to His will. So let us trust our lives to Him completely.

Loving God, I see Your majesty and divinity all around me. Everything You do is perfect and according to Your plans. Thank You for watching over me and being my source of help in all things. I submit to Your will for my life. In Christ's name, amen.

Nature's Shining Beacon

Light is sweet, and it pleases the eyes to see the sun (Ecclesiastes 11:7).

Scripture: Ecclesiastes 11:1-8
Song: "Sunshine on the Hill"

There are many beautiful things to admire in nature, but few compare to the splendor of the sun. People walk along a beach to see the uncountable colors of a setting sun. Watching the sun rise over a mountain range is breathtaking. The sun peeking through clouds after a storm lights up the sky. The beauty and power of the sun can be taken for granted in the rush of daily life, but simply considering them for just a moment can be awe inspiring.

But the sun is also a symbol of hope. It brings encouragement to those who have suffered through a long night. Its warmth gives life to the earth and health to our bodies. Its light dispels the fears and loneliness of the darkness. Merely by its presence we are assured that God is in control of all things.

It's no wonder God placed the sun as the center of our solar system. It is essential to our survival. Likewise, the light of the world, Jesus Christ, should be the center of our life. Without Him, what a dark existence we would know! He is our hope, and He supplies everything we need. Like the sun He created, He is certainly a being of awe, power, and beauty.

Dear Father in Heaven, Your creation rejoices in You. You are the warmth, light, and power I need in my life every day. I praise You for being the source of my hope. May I be a light to others as Your love shines through me. In the name of Jesus, Lord and Savior of all, I pray. Amen.

What's the Point?

Now all has been heard; here is the conclusion of the matter: Fear God and keep his commandments, for this is the whole duty of man (Ecclesiastes 12:13).

Scripture: Ecclesiastes 11:9–12:7, 13
Song: "Master, Speak! Thy Servant Heareth"

Have you ever listened to a speaker ramble on and on—and then, when he mercifully reached his conclusion, you wondered what his point was supposed to be? Using fancy phrases and fluffy words may impress an audience, but the purpose of a speech is to leave listeners with at least one key point they can apply in their lives. I've heard speakers whose main goal seemed to be simply to hear their own voices. All those words, and not a single point I could remember. How frustrating!

But do we read the Bible and listen to sermons the same way? Reading exciting Bible stories about great men and women can be enjoyable. Hearing an interesting sermon can be quite motivational. But do we really seek to understand what we've read or heard so that we can grasp the most important point and apply it to our way of life?

The Bible abounds with profound topics and concepts. Dig deep and cherish every word. But when "all has been heard," the main point remains—"Fear God and keep his commandments." As we read His Word, let's remember: When God speaks, He always has a point worth remembering.

Dear Lord, reveal yourself to me through Your Word. May I listen to Your voice and follow Your guidance. Your Word speaks life to me. Help me remember the basic truths of the Scripture as its light shines on my path. In Jesus' name, amen.

God's Goodness

I give you every seed-bearing plant on the face of the whole earth and every tree that has fruit with seed in it. They will be yours for food (Genesis 1:29).

Scripture: Genesis 1:26-31
Song: "This Is My Father's World"

In 1921, African-American botanist George Washington Carver appeared before a senate committee in Washington, D.C. As some Southern congressmen pelted him with racial slurs, Carver opened his briefcase and showed the senators products he had made from the lowly goober pea—the peanut.

Carver hoped the committee would favor a tariff on peanuts imported from China. That would enable Southern farmers to sell more of their crop. A senator asked Carver, "How did you discover all these products could be made from peanuts?" Carver answered, "From the Bible. Genesis tells us God gave all plants for food."

All of God's creation was made to benefit humankind. Plants of every description produce food. Trees absorb carbon dioxide from the atmosphere and release oxygen into it. We couldn't survive without such a delicate balance of these elements.

When you hold an apple or peach in your hand, thank God for food. As you take a deep breath, whisper a word of praise to God for the perfect composition of air. God is good!

O Father, when I think of the multitude of blessings that come from Your hand, a simple thank You seems inadequate. Praise to You, through Christ my Lord! Amen.

October 17–23. **Jewell Johnson** lives in Arizona with her husband, LeRoy. The couple has six adult children and nine grandchildren. Besides writing, Jewell enjoys walking, reading, and quilting.

One Plus One Equals One

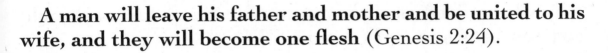

A man will leave his father and mother and be united to his wife, and they will become one flesh (Genesis 2:24).

Scripture: Genesis 2:18-24
Song: "Bind Us Together"

After I married and moved to another state, I became more appreciative of my parental home. At Christmas our family traveled back home. When each of our children was born, I'd spend a few days under my mother's watchful care. Yet I recognized I was only visiting my parents; my husband and I had established our own home.

When a man and woman unite in marriage, the Bible admonishes them to break the closest earthly tie they have known and to create a new family. The newlyweds are to cleave—stick, adhere, and weld—to each other.

The wife consults with her husband, not her mother, when she makes decisions. The husband talks things over with his wife, not his father. The new couple love each other above anyone else and take responsibility for the care of each other.

Of course, many adjustments are required to achieve oneness. To be "one flesh" is more than a physical union; the couple is joined emotionally, psychologically, and spiritually—a union of hearts and lives. As a husband and wife work hard on their marriage, over time they grow so close that they are truly one in spirit.

Lord, my marriage and home seem to be under attack by cultural forces these days. Help members of my household to join hands with You and determine that nothing will separate us from each other in Your love. In Jesus' name, amen.

Come Home to God

You have lived as a prostitute with many lovers—would you now return to me? (Jeremiah 3:1).

Scripture: Jeremiah 3:1-5
Song: "I Will Sing of the Mercies of the Lord"

One Sunday afternoon a teenage girl appeared at our door. After an argument with her parents, she had run away. Now, hundreds of miles from home, she had second thoughts and contacted my minister-husband.

She wanted to return home, but she also wondered whether her parents would *want* her back. When her concern was posed to her mother and father, they answered, "Return. By all means, come home."

The nation of Judah had left the one true God to worship and serve idols. Jeremiah's entire book is a plea for Judah to return to God. Yet he too posed the question: If the people returned to Jehovah, would He reject them? God had every right to disown the wayward, idol worshiping people—to divorce himself from them. But the merciful God willingly took them back.

We shouldn't play games with God or minimize the seriousness of sin. Yet should we stray from Him, there is a way back. People can be unmerciful at times. But God, like the parents of a beloved runaway child, with arms open wide, welcomes anyone who returns to Him.

Almighty and gracious Father, I am so thankful that a thousand mercies await me when I return to You. Thank You for this gift. I am sorry for my sin, and I depend upon Your mercy to draw me back to Your ways. Let me never break our fellowship again. In the holy name of Jesus, my Lord and Savior, I pray. Amen.

God Loves the Unfaithful

"In that day," declares the Lord, **"you will call me 'my husband'; you will no longer call me 'my master'"** (Hosea 2:16).

Scripture: Hosea 2:16-23
Song: "God of Grace and God of Glory"

Linda and George had been married several years when George had an affair. Naturally, Linda was angry, deeply hurt, and wanted to file for divorce. Through counseling, however, she found grace to forgive her repentant husband and work at making their marriage strong enough to survive the infidelity. In some ways Linda and George's experience was similar to Hosea and Gomer's.

God asked Hosea to do a strange thing: he was to marry a known prostitute. Although Hosea was a faithful husband, Gomer wasn't faithful to him. She ran off to become a slave prostitute. Hosea rescued her, and again she spurned him.

The entire event was intended as an object lesson to the nation of Judah. God had favored them, answered their cries for help, and sent them godly leaders. Yet they didn't acknowledge Him or His laws; instead, they turned to other "lovers." Through Hosea's actions, God reminded the nation of His steadfast patience and love for them.

One day when Jesus rules, God will no longer be as a master to Israel. No, they will then have a loving relationship with God as their husband. See God today as your faithful husband. Draw near to the one who loves you unconditionally.

Dear God, as a wife depends on a loving husband to care for her, I look to You for all my needs. You are enough for now and all eternity. In Jesus' name, amen.

Plenty of Love to Share

Dear friends, since God so loved us, we also ought to love one another (1 John 4:11).

Scripture: 1 John 4:7-12
Song: "Love Lifted Me"

When Joyce had a disagreement with her minister (my husband), she took her young child out of my Sunday school class and placed him with another teacher. Hurt and sad, I struggled to love Joyce. In fact, I mentally rehearsed angry speeches in which I told her a thing or two.

Reading Bible verses on forgiveness, I knew I needed to forgive Joyce and show her love. Yet waves of resentment washed over me whenever I saw her at church. Finally, I told God I couldn't do it on my own: I needed His help.

One day when I walked into church and saw Joyce, I heard a whisper in my heart, "I have plenty of love to share." My mind immediately went to Calvary, and I saw His cross. Right there, I asked Jesus' love to transform all the resentful feelings.

Now when my feelings get injured and I think I have every reason to be angry with a family member or friend, I again hear the words, "I have plenty of love to share."

There's really no need to harbor bitterness or hold grudges. When Jesus has love to give—the same love He displayed for us at Calvary—there is plenty to spread around.

Almighty and most merciful God, I can't love people on my own, especially those who disagree or contend with me. I accept Your love in my heart, the love that made it possible for You to love me—and those who spit on Your precious Son, Jesus. I pray this prayer in His name, my Savior and Lord. Amen.

An Unfaltering Love

Love never fails (1 Corinthians 13:8).

Scripture: 1 Corinthians 13
Song: "Lord, Lay Some Soul upon My Heart"

One day in 1817, Elizabeth Fry, a Quaker mother of 10 children, visited the women's section of London's Newgate prison. Nothing prepared Elizabeth for what she encountered. Hundreds of lice-infected women and their children were crowded into four rooms where they slept on straw. Each prisoner received one small loaf of bread a day. Bullies served as guards and, with cruel treatment, ruled over the women. They received no medicine, and deaths from typhus were common.

Elizabeth determined to do something for the prisoners, but what could she, a housewife, do? Women of that time had little influence or power, but that didn't stop Elizabeth. She returned to the prison armed with her Bible, needles, thread, and cloth.

She read the Bible to the inmates and organized sewing and knitting classes. Meanwhile, she pled with authorities for improved conditions. Soon her efforts brought change, and she eventually was recognized as an authority on prison reform.

It all began when one woman reached out with unfailing love. We may have few talents, but we can love. Intelligence or financial status has no bearing on our ability to show kindness and mercy. Love is never defeated, is never brought to the ground. Quite simply, it never fails.

Dear Father, someone needs a lift today that only I can give. Make my heart sensitive to people's needs, so I will be a loving friend to those fettered with confusion and feelings of hopelessness. I pray in Jesus' name. Amen.

A Refreshing Stream

You are a garden fountain, a well of flowing water streaming down from Lebanon (Song of Solomon 4:15).

Scripture: Song of Solomon 4:8–5:1a
Song: "Source from Whence the Stream of Mercy"

In the middle of the desert community where I live there is a fountain that every hour shoots water 330 feet into the air. People come from miles around to stand in awe of the sight.

Why all the interest in a water fountain? Because water refreshes us. When we drink a glass of cool water, we say a satisfied *ah*. If we see a gently flowing brook, we experience serene feelings.

The Song of Solomon describes the husband and wife relationship as a garden fountain—pleasant and refreshing. If the wife becomes upset, like a gentle stream the husband strives to calm her spirit. When a husband comes home after working a long day, the wife engages him in uplifting conversation, thus refreshing her mate.

We all need refreshing at times. God has provided many "streams" where believers can be refreshed. His Word revives us in discouraging times. Words from Christian friends, as a bubbling brook, can serve to encourage. Prayer, like a cool drink on a hot day, always renews lagging spirits.

Avail yourself of God's fountain. In relationships with family and friends, be to them a delightful, refreshing well of flowing water.

Dear Lord, often life lacks zest. I need refreshing. Refresh me, and may I be as a pleasant stream to those I meet today. In the name of Jesus, amen.

Listen to Your Mama

Whoever gives heed to instruction prospers (Proverbs 16:20).

Scripture: Proverbs 16:16-20
Song: "Teach Me, My God and King"

Yes, there is a generation gap, and it seems to be widening. In most cultures, people honor their elders and teach children to heed their parents. Our culture, by and large, does not. Now that I have reached the far side of the generation gap, I hear myself saying again and again, "If only I had listened!"

We watch teens rushing toward destruction. We see marriages unraveling. Young ministers—sometimes older ones—pursue programs that leave their people behind. Dads and moms allow hobbies and personal interests to rob them of time with their children. (I could introduce you to a man who would gladly trade every fishing trip he ever took for the memory of one afternoon on a small lake catching bluegills with his boys.)

In this culture wise elders don't attempt to bridge the gap unbidden or wave a scolding finger. But they can't help longing for an occasional open heart, someone willing to draw on the wisdom that years offer. They hear youth say, "Mother just doesn't understand the world we live in." Maybe so, but Mother was once young, and she knows things youth cannot know. Listen to your Mama!

Heavenly Father, help me search out the wisdom of those who have walked before me. Help me to heed every instance of wise advice. In Jesus' name, amen.

October 24–30. **Lloyd Mattson** is a retired minister and author living in Duluth, Minnesota. He has been a regular contributor to devotional publications over the years.

Be a Heart-Mender

The Spirit of the Sovereign LORD is on me, because the LORD has anointed me to preach good news to the poor. He has sent me to bind up the brokenhearted, to proclaim freedom for the captives and release from darkness for the prisoners (Isaiah 61:1).

Scripture: Isaiah 61:1-7
Song: "Burdens Are Lifted at Calvary"

A young man sat alone, his face buried in his hands. The caskets were gone, one large and two small. The young man had been the live-in boyfriend of the mother and two young sons who had died in a terrible accident. Scorned by grieving family and friends, he sat alone. Yes, the young man's life was a mess, but his heart was breaking. No one cared, not even me—a professional clergyman.

I didn't know him; I did not approve of the life he led. He was about the age of my middle son. Had he been my son, I would have wished for him a shoulder to cry on.

Jesus mingled with sinners. He ate with them and healed their broken hearts. He said, "As the Father has sent me, I am sending you" (John 20:21). These words carry awesome weight. He was sent to mend broken hearts; He sends us to do the same.

That sad moment was not the time to scold or evangelize the young man, but to comfort him. His memory haunts me. I have wondered what might have happened had I paused to bind up his wounded heart.

O God, king of glory, give me a heart for the hurting, that I might share Your love and compassion, no matter their circumstance. In the name of Jesus, amen.

All These Things

Better the little the righteous have than the wealth of many wicked (Psalm 37:16).

Scripture: Psalm 37:10-17
Song: "A Child of the King"

I grew weary of a widow friend's repeated complaints about the clutter in her home. She lived alone after a long and happy marriage. Knickknacks and mementos from years of travel filled walls and shelves throughout the house. Stacked in an upstairs room were boxes of essays, poems, notes, and memorabilia from a long teaching career. "Whatever am I going to do with all this stuff!" she said.

One day I told her, "Go through your home. Place a red sticker on what you really need. Then go away and employ a friend to get rid of the rest."

"Oh, I couldn't do that!" she said. "What if they threw away something I need?"

How we cling to our stuff! I do it too. But recently I followed my own advice. My bride of 66 years went home to Heaven, leaving me with memories in every closet and drawer. Disposing of her things was too painful; I assigned the task to my family.

Now her closet is as empty as my heart, but my dear partner in a long ministry lives on in acts of kindness that her memory leads me to perform. The only thing of worth in all the world is a person. The rest is junk.

O Lord of all, give me the grace to clear my life of clutter, so I can live richly for You, until I see You, face to face. In the name of Jesus, I pray. Amen.

Hold On Here!

Yes, LORD, walking in the way of your laws, we wait for you (Isaiah 26:8).

Scripture: Isaiah 26:7-11
Song: "Blessed Quietness"

Wait a minute! One morning I was driving through the usual heavy traffic toward my office, my mind on many things. On my desk lay countless tasks, some with near deadlines, made the more urgent by an impending trip. This high level of stress had gone on for months.

Suddenly, I could drive no more. I struggled to move out of traffic. I pulled to the curb to wait for my head to clear. Slowly my thoughts and emotions stopped swirling, but I knew I was on dangerous ground.

Whenever we are caught in the illusion that busyness is next to godliness, trouble looms. Sitting there with cars streaming by, something in me said, *Wait a minute!* "Be still before the Lord and wait patiently for him; do not fret" (Psalm 37:7). I made it to the office, cleared my desk, and took a few days off. I did not wait to call in sick; I called a halt *before* I got sick.

When we get worn-out doing God's work, we need to remember whose work it is. God and the world got along quite well before we came along. He never lays on anyone burdens greater than they can bear; it is we who assume more than God expects.

Heavenly Father, I need to heed the call to stillness and learn to say no. When the gale blows, grant me a quiet island where I can revel in the Holy Spirit's constant presence. Through Christ I pray. Amen.

It's Hard to Die

Be merciful, just as your Father is merciful (Luke 6:36).

Scripture: Luke 6:32-36
Song: "Must Jesus Bear the Cross Alone?"

Jesus spoke many hard sayings. Is it really possible to show mercy in the same way God shows mercy? Do we really want the Father to forgive us as we forgive others? And that hardest saying of all: Are we ready to die for Him?

Jesus spoke that hard saying to those closest to Him: "If anyone would come after me, he must deny himself and take up his cross and follow me" (Matthew 16:24). Denying self runs contrary to our times; surely I have rights! But Jesus didn't stop with a simple moral decision. Those who would follow Him must take up their cross daily. The cross meant one thing: death.

Dealing with this theme, the speaker at a men's retreat handed out small metal crosses. He told the men, "Carry the cross in your pocket to remind you of Jesus' command. When tempted to be selfish, finger the cross; when tempted to sin, finger the cross. Let it remind you that you died with Christ so you can live unto Him, not only in eternity, but right now."

The speaker had it right: We can never know joy until we learn to die to self and give ourselves to others. But self doesn't die easily. That is the meaning in Jesus' words following this hard saying: If you live for self, you lose your life; die to self, you come alive.

O Eternal Lord God, give me the grace to surrender self so I may come alive to You. Then show me how to bring others to Your glorious cross. In the name of the Father, the Son, and the Holy Spirit, I pray. Amen.

Hard Choices

As for me, it is good to be near God (Psalm 73:28).

Scripture: Psalm 73:10-26
Song: "Near to the Heart of God"

By definition, a Christian is a follower of Christ Jesus. Faith includes following. It is folly to suggest that a person can accept Jesus as Savior but not as Lord. A follower may stumble, for learning to walk takes time. But following Jesus is what marks us as Christians. The Great Commission makes this clear.

Four components make up the commission: going, discipling, baptizing, and teaching. We might paraphrase the commission this way: As you go through life, make disciples (learners). Identify new disciples with Jesus' earthly body, the church, through baptism. Then teach them to obey all He commanded. Obeying and following mean the same.

Yet Jesus' teachings reach far beyond evangelism and church life, vital as those are. We have not fulfilled Jesus' commission until we have taught, and that is an ongoing process. That teaching must not overlook a fifth component of the great commission: "And surely I am with you always, to the very end of the age" (Matthew 28:20).

That is the wonder of the gospel. Jesus' presence inhabits every moment of life equally, for each individual. He walks with us as guide, counselor, and companion. Who would not want to follow a master like that?

Thank you, **Lord of glory,** for your constant presence in my life. Help me to keep you ever in my thoughts today. I pray this prayer in the name of Jesus, my merciful Savior and Lord. Amen.

On the Mountain with Jesus

When he saw the crowds, he went up on a mountainside and sat down (Matthew 5:1).

Scripture: Matthew 5:1-12
Song: "Lord, Speak to Me"

Jesus had a different take on ministry than most of us have. With crowds pressing and His popularity rising, He took to the hillside and sat down. When we find a crowd, we plunge in and scurry about; the bigger the crowd, the more we scurry, lest someone get ahead of us. When we hustle too hard and too long, we wear out, and then we sit down. Jesus never hurried; He knew His priorities.

Sitting was the normal teaching posture for a rabbi, and Jesus spent most of His time with an inner circle, 12 men. They came to Him on the hillside, and He taught them. As the story continues, we learn that at least some from the crowd joined the disciples, but the Master did not accommodate the crowd. He taught the few the fundamentals of His kingdom—that they someday might teach others.

We can learn from both Jesus' method and His message. Christians make up His inner circle today. If we are to carry His purpose forward, we need first to spend time on the mountain. When God's truth fills our hearts, He may send us to many or few. But whichever the case, all we have to share is what we learn on the hillside from Jesus.

Almighty and everlasting God, take me often to the hillside with Your Son to be refreshed so that I might refresh those around me. Remind me always that all I have to give is what You have freely given to me. In Jesus' name, amen.

Perfect Forever!

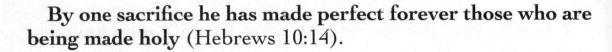

By one sacrifice he has made perfect forever those who are being made holy (Hebrews 10:14).

Scripture: Hebrews 10:11-18
Song: "Rock of Ages"

Most sports have some standard of perfection. It's the hole in one in golf, the 300 game in bowling, a baseball pitcher who retires 27 batters in order. But no matter how skillful one may be, perfection in the world of sports is fleeting. We soon fail again.

Perhaps the sports world could serve as a reminder of how often we fail to live up to God's standard of perfection. Jesus has accomplished for us what we could never do on our own. By His sacrifice He has imparted to us His righteousness, His perfection. But the Scriptures also affirm our need for continued growth, since we are made perfect even while we are in the process of being made holy.

An old familiar hymn says, "Be of sin the double cure, cleanse me of its guilt and power." In faith we trust we have been relieved of guilt (made holy), and in faith we trust God for continued strength as our journey toward holiness progresses.

The challenge, therefore, is to live up to that which has already been accomplished. We are to live as one already cleansed. We have been adopted as children of the king; let us live like it!

Lord God Almighty, increase my faith. May I never take for granted the precious cleansing I received at Calvary. May I live as one cleansed and called to holiness this very day. I pray this prayer in the name of Jesus, my Savior and Lord. Amen.

October 31. **Dan Nicksich** is a minister serving in Somerset, Pennsylvania. He has written for numerous Christian publishers over the years.

DEVOTIONS®

November

Sing to the LORD, for he has done glorious things;
let this be known to all the world.

—*Isaiah 12:5*

Gary Allen, Editor   **Margaret Williams,** Project Editor   Photo © iStockphoto

DEVOTIONS® is published quarterly by Standard Publishing, Cincinnati, Ohio, www.standardpub.com. © 2010 by Standard Publishing. All rights reserved. Topics based on the Home Daily Bible Readings, International Sunday School Lessons. © 2008 by the Committee on the Uniform Series. Printed in the U.S.A. All Scripture quotations, unless otherwise indicated, are taken from the *HOLY BIBLE, NEW INTERNATIONAL VERSION*®. *NIV*®. Copyright © 1973, 1978, 1984 by Biblica, Inc. ™. Used by permission of Zondervan. All rights reserved. *King James Version* (*KJV*), public domain.

Sin and Sickness

When I kept silent, my bones wasted away through my groaning all day long (Psalm 32:3).

Scripture: Psalm 32:1-5
Song: "Heal Us, Emmanuel, Hear Our Prayer"

Within days of her husband's death, Doris was rushed to the hospital with a suspected heart attack. Tests failed to reveal anything that could explain her condition. In the meantime, battling episodes of violent sickness, Doris grew weaker and settled into a deep depression. She was eventually treated for various stress disorders, and when she still did not improve, she was committed to the psychiatric ward.

A minister was visiting another patient when he struck up a conversation with Doris. They formed a relationship, and he continued to visit her. Eventually Doris admitted to feelings of intense guilt; her husband had died before she could confess an affair she'd engaged in years ago. The wise minister led her to the forgiveness found only in Christ. Within days her symptoms began to disappear, and she was soon able to return home.

The medical community has often demonstrated the truth of David's words, especially when it recognizes the connection between guilt, stress, and sickness. So often, only in acknowledging hidden guilt do we find deep healing.

Lord, I cannot hide my sins from You. May I freely acknowledge my failures that I may experience Your mercy and Your healing power. In Jesus' name, amen.

November 1–6. **Dan Nicksich** is a minister serving in Somerset, Pennsylvania. He has written for numerous Christian publishers over the years.

The Prayers of the Righteous

Is any one of you sick? He should call the elders of the church to pray over him and anoint him with oil in the name of the Lord (James 5:14).

Scripture: James 5:13-18
Song: "Lord, Listen to Your Children Praying"

Luke was only a few weeks old when the episodes started. At first they were thought to be epileptic seizures, but this was eventually ruled out. After extensive tests he was diagnosed with a rare, mitochondrial disorder. These disorders impair the body's ability to digest food and absorb protein. Unfortunately, the medical community has yet to find a cure.

In keeping with the Scriptures, Luke's parents requested the elders in their church to come and pray over Luke. It was an emotional scene in a crowded hospital setting.

Four months have gone by, and Luke has gained strength. He finally returned home after a lengthy hospital stay. Each day brings its own challenges, but also proves to be a blessing to family, friends, and a caring church community. Luke has given us the unique opportunity to be the loving community of faith we are called to be. And you would not guess the doctor's long-term prognosis by looking at Luke.

Are you experiencing times of trouble? times of joy? sickness? God's Word promises that the prayers of His righteous people can bring hope and healing.

Lord God Almighty, I know how special children are to you. Be with those parents who suffer because of the suffering of their children. Give them hope and comfort in the promises of Your Word. In the name of Jesus, the great physician. Amen.

A Plank in the Eye!

Can a blind man lead a blind man? Will they not both fall into a pit? (Luke 6:39).

Scripture: Luke 6:37-42
Song: "Open My Eyes, That I May See"

Our youngest son was an intern at the local drama theater. He loved being part of the behind-the-scenes action for the stage plays. There were sets to build, costume and scene changes to perform, and technical equipment to run. He even got to be on stage as an extra in one scene of *The Pajama Game*.

Here's one of the best parts of all, in his opinion: The theater opens the doors during its final dress rehearsal to a local service group for a free viewing. The lucky recipients? The Blind Center. It's not that all of their constituents are totally blind. Many are only partially impaired. But there's still something poignant about the Blind Center taking in a play.

You wouldn't trust a blind man to lead someone who was also blind. Jesus states the painfully obvious to impress upon us a deeper lesson. Those who stand in need of forgiveness should not presume to stand in judgment of other sinners.

We are often blind to our own faults—which to others are as obvious as a plank sticking out of our eye. Only those who have been humbled before God are truly fit to help others deal with their sins.

Most merciful God, I don't want to be blind to my own sins and failures, and mistakes. It's easy to see the faults of others while overlooking my own. Please help me to see clearly the way to my own repentance before I dare to speak to another. And then may I speak only in the love of Christ. In His name, amen.

Better Than What We Expect

This is how my heavenly Father will treat each of you unless you forgive your brother from your heart (Matthew 18:35).

Scripture: Matthew 18:21-35
Song: "Grace Greater Than Our Sin"

Susan Boyle shocked the world with her first appearance on *Britain's Got Talent*, the television show. As this middle-aged lady walked on stage, it seemed that the audience and judges had already dismissed the frumpy looking spinster as being out of place on a theatrical stage. Within seconds of opening her mouth to sing, however, attitudes changed. Susan Boyle's performance went far beyond what anyone would expect.

God's grace is like that. It's beyond what we expect, beyond what we deserve. And that's the point; it is precisely forgiveness that we don't deserve. As one of my teachers defined *grace*: "Favor bestowed when wrath is owed."

A man asked for time to pay his debt. Study his words carefully. He asked not to be forgiven but simply for time to repay the debt. He seems to be deluding himself, since it is a multimillion dollar debt in a culture where work brings pennies a day. But the master totally forgives the debt.

Now that's a picture of grace. For in similar fashion, God forgives our sin. You and I have been forgiven a debt we could never repay. Dare we refuse to forgive another's sin against us?

O Lord of Heaven and earth, may we extend to others the same gift we have received from You. Forgive us our debts, as we forgive our debtors. In the holy name of Jesus, my Lord and Savior, I pray. Amen.

When Jesus Comes to Dinner

Therefore, I tell you, her many sins have been forgiven—for she loved much. But he who has been forgiven little loves little (Luke 7:47).

Scripture: Luke 7:40-47
Song: "Let Jesus Come into Your Heart"

We spend some extra time straightening up the house whenever guests are coming for dinner. My wife goes out of her way to cook a special meal. Upon their arrival, our guests' comfort becomes our focus.

What if Jesus were coming to your house for dinner? What kind of welcome would you extend? How important would His comfort be to you?

Simon the Pharisee neglected the accepted social norms of the day when he hosted Jesus. Rather, it fell to a woman of sinful reputation to welcome Him with tears of repentance and perfume for His feet.

The woman saw Jesus as Savior, as one who offered forgiveness. The Pharisee watched Jesus, though, looking for an opportunity to criticize Him. The woman saw Jesus as worthy of respect and honor. Simon showed disrespect and contempt.

He who has been forgiven little loves little. I've often wondered if there's not something a bit ironic in the words. Simon needed forgiveness. He just wasn't aware of it. Perhaps it's not that some are forgiven little, but rather, that they remain unaware of their need.

Father, may my life reflect a deep awareness of the forgiveness I've received. May I live each day as if Christ were to be my honored guest. In His name, amen.

Reconciliation Before Death

First go and be reconciled to your brother; then come and offer your gift (Matthew 5:24).

Scripture: Matthew 5:17-26
Song: "Brothers, Joining Hand to Hand"

A family gathered to bury their brother. The parents had already passed on, so the four adult siblings (two sisters, two brothers) bore the responsibility.

I was told the family had been at odds with each other for years. One of the sisters acknowledged the sad truth. "It's too bad it took this to bring us together. Some of us haven't seen each other in years, and this is the best we ever got along. It's too bad Johnny had to miss it."

How sad when family members don't get along with one another. Jesus wanted to be sure it would not be that way in His family. He teaches us that reconciliation must precede worship. One cannot sincerely praise God with a heart harboring ill will toward others.

Are you angry at someone? Have you spoken abusively? It's time to seek reconciliation.

Even our acts of worship take second place when disunity exists. Someday, perhaps sooner than we think, the opportunity for reconciliation will have passed. Perhaps this is another reason for the urgency Jesus attaches to matters such as these. Let us go and be reconciled before it's too late.

Father, how sad when family members fail to love. How sad when we allow discord instead of seeking peace at all costs. As we seek your favor, may we realize that our relationship with you addresses how we treat others. In Jesus' name, amen.

Simple Love

All the Law and the Prophets hang on these two commandments (Matthew 22:40).

Scripture: Matthew 22:34-40
Song: "I Love the Lord"

Sunday morning church was a part of my routine before my first birthday. Soon after, Sunday nights joined Sunday mornings, followed by Wednesday night youth group in my teens, Tuesday night Bible study in my 20s, and Saturday night services in my 30s. Committees, conferences, and couples groups were added to my schedule as was any mentoring and discipleship I could squeeze into snippets of free time.

It seemed most days were consumed with something laudable: church work. Yet the weight of my bulging schedule spread my emotions and energy thin. Though service for God was good, I also knew that the chaos of my life wasn't of Him. How could I begin to change?

It occurred to me that I'd made the expression of my faith more complicated than it ought to be. In my need to feel significant, I'd equated "doing for God" with "loving God." Driven and overscheduled, I realized that my faith no longer resembled the simple trust I'd learned from childhood.

I needed to get back to the basics—love God; love others. According to Jesus, that pretty much sums it up.

Dear Father, I easily complicate what You created to be simple. Teach me to simply love You and love others with everything that's in me. In Christ's name, amen.

November 7–13. **Michele Cushatt,** of Highlands Ranch, Colorado, is an international traveler and passionate communicator who has written for numerous periodicals.

A Difficult Road

Impress them on your children. Talk about them when you sit at home and when you walk along the road, when you lie down and when you get up (Deuteronomy 6:7).

Scripture: Deuteronomy 6:1-9
Song: "Jesus Loves the Little Children"

Driving down the roads of Port-au-Prince, Haiti, I wondered if I'd made a mistake bringing my two youngest boys on a mission trip. Rotting garbage littered the streets, the 100-degree heat creating an oven and filling the air with it's baked stench. Poverty dripped off of every dilapidated building. So many poorly fed and shoeless children! I glanced at my 12-year-old and noticed his innocent eyes, round and appalled at what he saw. *What was I thinking, God? I'm not sure he's ready. What if I've made a mistake?*

For a moment doubts assailed me, and my heart sank. And then I remembered Isaiah 58:10 — "If you spend yourself in behalf of the hungry and satisfy the needs of the oppressed, then your light will rise in the darkness." God's Word is as much for my son as it is for me.

I'm to talk about the Word of God to my children when I sit and lie down and get up. Sometimes that means brainstorming about how our family can reach out to the poor from the comfort of our kitchen table. Other times it means taking a walk down garbage-strewn streets in Haiti — and living the Word.

I am so quick to doubt, **Father,** when You know best what my children need. Give me the courage and wisdom to be a parent who boldly leads my children down even the difficult roads in following You. Through Christ I pray. Amen.

A Short To-Do List

Do not go about spreading slander among your people. Do not do anything that endangers your neighbor's life. I am the LORD (Leviticus 19:16).

Scripture: Leviticus 19:13-18
Song: "Lord, Be Glorified"

My to-do list was a mile long, and I didn't have time for a break. Resenting the interruption, I picked up the ringing phone with a halfhearted "hello." The tearful voice on the other end needed a few minutes of my time, but all I could think about was what I needed to get done.

It's easy to look at the Bible as nothing but an extended to-do list (with a heavy dose of "to-don'ts" thrown in). I can grow overwhelmed by its many different instructions while missing the heart of the message. What if I can't keep everything straight?

Jesus effectively calms our fears when He boils down the do's and don'ts into two easy-to-remember themes: love God and love people (Matthew 22:34-40). If those two themes govern our lives, then spreading slanderous gossip or treating a neighbor with disregard won't be an option. Debts will be paid and time will be made for a hurting friend who needs a few minutes on the phone.

In other words, love will dictate how we behave. It will be a love that flows from God's boundless love for us.

You have always shown me love, **Father,** generous and unending. Help me to see ways that I can show the same kind of love to the people in my life—whether it's an old friend on the phone or a stranger at the store. In Jesus' name, amen.

From Foreigner to Family

The alien living with you must be treated as one of your native-born. Love him as yourself, for you were aliens in Egypt (Leviticus 19:34).

Scripture: Leviticus 19:33-37
Song: "I Am a Poor Wayfaring Stranger"

One step from the cold door and I froze. I was late, and this was my first time with such a group. On the other side of the door sat a roomful of at least 20 experienced writers, already comfortably in their chairs (and more than comfortable with each other). I was neither. Invited by a friend, I took weeks to muster the courage to visit—though now I doubted whether I'd take that final step into their presence. Anticipating their stares, I took a deep breath and grabbed hold of my determination.

My fears were put immediately at ease by smiles and warm introductions. Though years have passed and I now proudly call this precious group of writers my dear friends, I'll never forget those first few moments with them. I stood just beyond the door feeling very much like a foreigner.

It might be the Spanish-speaking person in my neighborhood or the ragged man hovering in the back of our church. Or maybe it's the first-time visitor to our group of writers. Whenever I encounter an "alien" face, I must never forget that I too know what it's like to feel out of place and alone. Will I be the first to lay down the welcome mat?

Father, who needs the warmth of my welcome today? Who stands on the fringes in my neighborhood or at my workplace? Show me the faces You see, and deepen my heart's capacity to love them the way You do. Through Christ I pray. Amen.

Joint Agenda Needed

In this same way, husbands ought to love their wives as their own bodies. He who loves his wife loves himself (Ephesians 5:28).

Scripture: Ephesians 5:25-33
Song: "I Could Sing of Your Love Forever"

For years the Army challenged recruits with "Be All That You Can Be." The theme encouraged hard work and personal excellence, which effectively inspired patriotism and loyalty. However, the same slogan in a marriage could wreak havoc.

Our culture seems to encourage husbands and wives to demand their rights and do whatever it takes to get ahead. Selfishness can mask itself as the pursuit of individual dreams. In a desire to "be all he can be," a husband may work long hours to get that next promotion, neglecting his home life. Or a wife might show her independence by forming questionable relationships.

Through the voice of Paul, God addresses the beauty of maintaining a joint agenda—the marriage partnership. Like Christ's covenant with the church, marriages are built and sustained when both individuals mutually esteem the relationship as much as their individual pursuits. Are we aware of and involved in helping our wives achieve their dreams? Do we creatively try to find ways to invest in our husbands' endeavors? Bottomline: Are we committed to the covenant of marriage above our own personal agendas? In a marriage, a joint agenda is the only way for us to truly "be all that we can be."

Too often, **Lord,** I only see my needs in my marriage. Open my eyes and heart to Your agenda for our relationship. In Christ's name I pray. Amen.

Leaving a Legacy

Teach the older men to be temperate, worthy of respect, self-controlled, and sound in faith, in love and in endurance. Likewise, teach the older women to be reverent in the way they live, not to be slanderers or addicted to much wine, but to teach what is good (Titus 2:2, 3).

Scripture: Titus 2:1-5
Song: "I Offer My Life"

She's 15 years old, and her only example of womanhood is a mother who spends more time with her current boyfriend than she does with her daughter. He's 17 and has never heard either of his parents say the words, "I believe in you." She's been a cheerleader for three years and uses her body as if it's her only asset. He skips church to hang out at the skate park, because it's the only place he doesn't feel like an outcast.

These are real kids living a tough reality. Each one loves God and is trying to figure out how to live for Him. I don't always agree with their choices. In fact, there are times when I want to pull my hair out with frustration. How can I possibly make a difference?

But then I hear Jesus' voice: "Let the little children come to me . . . for the kingdom of heaven belongs to such as these" (Matthew 19:14). Jesus wasn't annoyed with the interruptions of those young in their faith who needed His guidance. In fact He came for them, just as He came for you and me. Are your arms and schedule open to those who need a more mature voice to teach them of God's love?

Lord, You have brought me far and rescued me from much. Teach me to teach others in the way I live and speak, with wisdom and respect. Through Christ, amen.

Loving the Critics

If you love those who love you, what reward will you get? (Matthew 5:46).

Scripture: Matthew 5:38-48
Song: "Amazing Love"

I'd never been so hurt. The fact we'd been friends for over 20 years only deepened the wound. The way I'd been treated stood out in stark contrast to the years of life and loyalty shared for decades. Then one incident decisively eroded our history.

Perhaps the hurt was understandable, but it quickly morphed into something more sinister. Our paths crossed often, and soon I found it hard to share the same room without a desire to either act out or run. Anger complicated the hurt, eating away at my core and sapping my enjoyment of other relationships.

I'd always thought of myself as loving, gracious, and quick to forgive. But the longer my anger continued, the more I challenged my assumptions. Why couldn't I let it go? What was keeping the hurt from healing? Revisiting Jesus' teaching on relationships, I realized that I had no problem loving those who loved me in return; my struggle lay in loving someone who didn't return the favor.

Jesus spoke plainly to those who prided themselves on "easy" love. Pulling from an abundance of experience, He reminds us all: Loving your fan club comes naturally; loving your critics requires determination and prayer (Matthew 5:44).

Lord, You know I'm still in process, and there are moments I'd rather use my strength to hang on to my grudges than to nurture love. You have loved me with an everlasting love. Let that be my inspiration. In Jesus' name, amen.

Strike First

Deliver me, I pray thee, from the hand of my brother, from the hand of Esau: for I fear him, lest he will come and smite me, and the mother with the children (Genesis 32:11, *King James Version*).

Scripture: Genesis 32:6-12
Song: "I Must Tell Jesus"

On a walk a minister recognized a man breaking stones along the side of the road. The hard work required that he kneel down to strike the blows. The minister saw that he was quite effective, which got him thinking. "John, I wish I could break the stony hearts of my hearers as easily as that."

"Perhaps," he said, "you don't work on your knees."

We should always do our hardest work on our knees. Certainly hard hearts can't be broken otherwise. Jacob learned this on the eve of meeting Esau, his angry brother. Bringing an armed force, Esau was undoubtedly ready to exact revenge. And he would have done so, if Jacob had not wrestled in prayer.

Who smote whom on that occasion? Jacob feared Esau would smite his family. But since Jacob struck first in prayer, Esau had a change of heart. When it comes to prayer, timing is crucial. Strike hard and often—and always first! As poet William Cowper declared: "Satan trembles when he sees the weakest saint upon his knees."

Almighty and gracious Father, give me the wisdom to quickly survey my trouble that I may be first to come before You in prayer. In the mighty name of Jesus, amen.

November 14–20. **Richard Robinson** is a senior pastor in Denver, Colorado. He enjoys singing in a gospel quartet, writing, and doing computer graphic design.

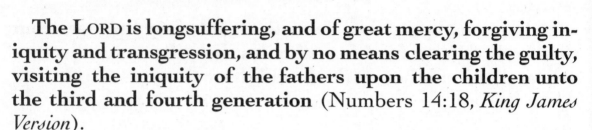

Living with Dynamic Tension

The LORD is longsuffering, and of great mercy, forgiving iniquity and transgression, and by no means clearing the guilty, visiting the iniquity of the fathers upon the children unto the third and fourth generation (Numbers 14:18, *King James Version*).

Scripture: Numbers 14:13-19
Song: "King of the Universe"

Jerry Bridges, in his book, *The Joy of Fearing God*, draws a fascinating analogy that illustrates spiritual tension. He describes how centrifugal and centripetal forces pull in opposite directions from each other at the center of rotation. He likened it to a stone being whirled about on the end of a string. The stone exerts outward (centrifugal) force on the string while the string exerts inward (centripetal) force on the stone. When one is removed, the other immediately disappears.

Bridges then makes the connection between fearing and loving God. The Lord's perfect holiness forces us to pull away from Him in fear. Yet His amazing love draws us back to Him. If we deny one of these divine attributes, we immediately lose the impression of the other.

We always need a dynamic tension between reverencing and loving God. Like Moses, we can favor God's compassion, but we should never forget His correction. In this life, love and fear work together to keep us from flying apart.

O God, Creator of Heaven and earth, thank You for keeping me in check by inspiring me to both revere and love You. I need this double emphasis in a one-sided world. In the name of the Father, the Son, and the Holy Spirit, I pray. Amen.

Who Are You?

Who am I, O Lord God? and what is my house, that thou hast brought me hitherto? (2 Samuel 7:18, *King James Version*).

Scripture: 2 Samuel 7:18-29
Song: "I Surrender All"

J. Hudson Taylor is considered one of the greatest missionaries in history. However, he thought otherwise of himself. "It seemed to me that God had looked over the whole world to find a man who was weak enough to do His work, and when He at last found me, He said, 'He is weak enough—He'll do.'"

And then to show that this was not an exception but the rule, Hudson added, "All God's giants have been weak men who did great things for God, because they reckoned on His being with them." King David surely had the same conviction.

God answered the king's request to build the temple with a gracious but firm "No." Instead, Solomon, his son, who was next in line to the throne, would have that architectural honor. To his surprise David was promised something much greater—an indestructible royal line (see vv. 25-29).

After receiving this far-reaching promise, David's attitude revealed how insignificant he knew himself to be. The first words out of his mouth sum up his sense of unworthiness before God: "Who am I, O Lord God?" David was finally weak enough to receive a special promise. And if you are weaker than you've ever been before—take heart. God has been looking for you.

Dear Lord, help me to confess my weakness so that I can claim Your strength. Let me glory in my weakness through the mighty grace of God. In Jesus' name, amen.

Dare to Believe!

He stretched himself upon the child three times, and cried unto the LORD, and said, O LORD my God, I pray thee, let this child's soul come into him again (1 Kings 17:21, *King James Version*).

Scripture: 1 Kings 17:17-23
Song: "Tell It to Jesus"

A woman once told the great preacher G. Campbell Morgan, "Oh, I could never take my little problems to God. I wouldn't want to bother him with those. I take only the big problems to God." He answered, "Are any problems big to God?"

To an infinite God, all problems to us are no problem to Him. Even raising the widow's dead son wasn't any bigger to God than healing him of an ordinary sniffle. But a resurrection is the greatest miracle to mere mortals.

But maybe it takes a big prayer to a big God to get a big answer. In the widow's case, only Elijah, a prophet of renowned prayer power, would have faith to believe God to this extreme.

It's easy to understand the widow's reaction. The shock of losing her son pushed her over the edge. In her grief she even indirectly blamed the prophet. But when this sad tragedy perplexed the widow to doubt, it provoked the prophet to dare.

To my way of thinking, the raising of the widow's son clearly demonstrates a profound truth. Faith does the most when it dares the most.

Almighty and everlasting God, give me the courage of my convictions. When others doubt, let my prayer dare to do the impossible. In the name of Jesus, who lives and reigns with You and the Holy Spirit, one God, now and forever, amen.

Heralds of the Golden Age

Sing unto the LORD; for he hath done excellent things: this is known in all the earth (Isaiah 12:5, *King James Version*).

Scripture: Isaiah 12
Song: "We've a Story to Tell to the Nations"

When still young, the deaf, mute, and blind Helen Keller was taken to Phillips Brooks for spiritual instruction. Using the simplest terms, the great preacher told the girl about Jesus.

As she heard the gospel message, her face lit up, and she spelled out in the hand of Brooks this reply: "I knew all the time there must be one like that, but I didn't know his name." Her hunch was right. In an imperfect world with an imperfect existence, she found the perfect Savior.

At this time in history there is great ignorance about the Lord Jesus. But someday, when He sits on His throne in Jerusalem, His fame will sweep over the world. He will dominate the news in inverse proportion as He is ignored today.

Now that we know the Lord, let us make Him known to others. The need to know the Lord will still exist in that future day, but even more so in this present day. Right now we can praise, call, declare, mention, sing, cry out, and shout!

In our day we sing the Lord's praises from our little perches around the world before the great dawn. "In that day," which Isaiah foresaw, we shall be viewed as the early heralds of the world's true golden age.

Thank You, Lord, for letting me proclaim the good news to a sad world. Give me the courage to boldly proclaim Your praises to those seeking hope and help. In Jesus' precious name I pray. Amen.

A Private Line

Ye shall seek me, and find me, when ye shall search for me with all your heart (Jeremiah 29:13, *King James Version*).

Scripture: Jeremiah 29:10-14
Song: "Teach Me to Pray"

H. G. Wells, the celebrated science fiction writer, became a religious agnostic. Why? For one thing, he saw his prayers apparently failing. While taking an accounting exam for which he was not prepared, he pleaded in desperation for God to "balance his books." When the figures didn't add up properly, he angrily said, "All right, Mr. God, You won't ever catch me praying again!" So ended his interest in prayer.

Wells is an example of one "playing by his own rules." And that is just what he did—he played at prayer. However, he could have looked into the Bible to study prayer on God's terms. There we are called to pray with all our heart. In other words, if prayer were a telephone, it would be a private line.

Prayer was Israel's direct hotline to God. However, they turned it into a polytheistic connection where Jehovah shared a party line with other gods. Of course, such an arrangement only shut prayer down. God hung up and took no more calls until the nation wanted a private line again. After 70 years in captivity, Israel was ready to reconnect.

I'm learning that God set up prayer to link my heart to His. It won't work when modern idols share the connection.

God, my Father, forgive me for the uninvited chatter on my prayer line with You. When the Spirit calls, help me to listen only to Your voice in my heart. In the name of Your Son, my Savior, I pray. Amen.

Sharpen Your Axe

When ye pray, use not vain repetitions, as the heathen do: for they think that they shall be heard for their much speaking (Matthew 6:7, *King James Version*).

Scripture: Matthew 6:5-15
Song: "Nearer, My God, to Thee"

A sweating woodchopper was hacking away at a tree. But he wasn't making much progress for all his effort. Finally, an observant man suggested he sharpen his axe. With a look of astonishment, the woodsman replied, "It's already tough enough getting this job done without taking time to grind an axe!"

But time spent sharpening is time saved chopping. This is even more applicable to prayer. If you sharpen your prayer on the wheel of the Lord's teaching, you will chop down more answers. A dull understanding of prayer will still work, but barely. A sharp understanding will work wonders in less time.

Don't pray harder until you first pray smarter. "Vain repetitions" are just so many swings of a dull axe head: whack away, but no chips will fly on impact. Repeating even the Lord's model prayer can become a mindless ritual, getting duller with every recitation. "Be not ye therefore like unto them" (v. 8, *KJV*).

By all means, form your prayer into an axe head of steel. Truth is the metal of prayer. Also, get a handle on your prayer. Don't make it hard to hold onto because you carry it to an extreme. But above all, keep it as sharp as a sword to cut through the thickest need.

Dear Lord, forgive my zeal for prayer without knowledge. Show me where I'm getting dull before I wear myself out. In Jesus' name, amen.

Growing in Trust

Be still before the LORD and wait patiently for him; do not fret when men succeed in their ways, when they carry out their wicked schemes (Psalm 37:7).

Scripture: Psalm 37: 1-8
Song: "Behold the Lamb of God"

"It isn't fair!" I squealed. As a youngster I was quick to notice any extra privileges my older sister enjoyed. She could stay up later at night and hang out with our parents, while I dragged myself up to bed. On weekends my sister was allowed trips to the roller skating rink with her friends. When our family took vacations, she had more money to buy souvenirs. Oh, the injustice of it all! My childish protests were frequently met with my father's no-nonsense reminder: "Life isn't fair."

Dad wisely knew that learning to accept disappointments is an important part of growing up. As Christians, when we face situations that just don't seem fair, we can look to Jesus to see how He responded when evil men plotted against Him. Surely, at His crucifixion, our Lord endured the greatest unfairness of all. Yet patiently He endured the agony of the cross, trusting His heavenly Father completely. What an example for all of us!

Dear heavenly Father, help me to be still and wait patiently before You in my trials. Teach me to follow the example of my Savior and to walk in His humility and trust. I want to surrender my will to Yours, O Lord! I pray this prayer in the name of Jesus, my merciful Savior and Lord. Amen.

November 21–27. **Barbara Tuttle** and her husband live in Lansing, Michigan. They recently celebrated the births of their seventh, eighth, and ninth grandchildren.

No Matter What!

Since he has no root, he lasts only a short time. When trouble or persecution comes because of the word, he quickly falls away (Matthew 13:21).

Scripture: Matthew 13:18-23
Song: "At All Times God is Calling"

We bought a "fixer-up" house, and we're knee-deep in problems right now. We face major issues with wiring, plumbing, mice, and spiders. We need to paint everywhere and put down lots of carpeting. Plus, there are no kitchen cabinets, and we get to assemble and install them ourselves. Did I mention that we have to move into this house in two weeks?

It seems as though we have 10 million things to do before moving in. The pressures are mounting. We haven't been to church in the past few weeks—that is weighing heavily on us.

It's tempting to keep moving down our to-do list and to skip church again tomorrow. But my husband and I decided today that we will be back in church tomorrow, no matter what.

We don't want to allow our current struggles to keep us from worship and fellowship with other Christians. Our troubles are temporary, and in the light of eternity, not important at all. In fact, we know in our hearts that we need to walk closely with Jesus in the midst of our troubles. If we ever needed to hear God's Word and receive encouragement from His people, it is now.

Father, I don't want to be driven by my list or my fears of not getting everything done. I want to be a Christ follower, driven by His love. Help me to stay faithful in worship, fellowship, and outreach to others. In Jesus' name, amen.

Now, Lord?

Be always on the watch, and pray that you may be able to escape all that is about to happen, and that you may be able to stand before the Son of Man (Luke 21:36).

Scripture: Luke 21:29-36
Song: "Open My Eyes, Lord"

Planes and helicopters have blind spots, just as cars do. These blind spots interfere with the ability to see an approaching aircraft. So pilots must learn to compensate by swiveling their heads around and scanning all parts of the sky.

Jesus says that He will come like a thief in the night — unexpectedly. That means He's as likely to come during a moment when we are lying, as when we are telling the truth. He might come while we are praying, or while we are gossiping about our neighbor. Maybe He comes when we're treating our spouses with love and respect. But He might come when we're arguing, in a spirit of unforgiveness.

If we aren't attentive to our lives, we will develop spiritual blindspots, and then our faith will surely suffer. As the ordinary days roll on, we may lose perspective and not see the meaning in them. We might even begin to make moral compromises and then attempt to justify them.

I want to become more alert, this very day, to my Lord's abiding presence with me. I just don't know when I'll see Him, face to face.

Dear Lord, open my eyes to my spiritual blindspots. Help me not to worry and fret about things that won't even matter 10 years from now. Instead, may I devote myself to those things that will matter for eternity. In the precious name of Jesus, amen.

One Moment at a Time

When they arrest you, do not worry about what to say or how to say it. At that time you will be given what to say, for it will not be you speaking, but the Spirit of your Father speaking through you (Matthew 10:19, 20).

Scripture: Matthew 10:16-20
Song: "All That I Need"

Corrie ten Boom rescued Jews from Nazi persecution in Germany during WWII. I am humbled by her family's courage, faithfulness, and surrender to Christ. When the Nazis discovered that Corrie and her sister were housing Jews, they were sent along with the Jews to the Ravensbruck concentration camp. In her book, *The Hiding Place*, Corrie reveals that the grace of God was present with her during her imprisonment.

Corrie remembered a childhood conversation with her father, which took place years before she was imprisoned. In the conversation she asked her father how she would be able to bear it if she were ever to be persecuted for her faith or have to die. Her father responded by asking Corrie to think about the time that she received her train ticket when taking a trip. Was it before the trip? No. The conductor gave Corrie her boarding ticket just as she stepped onto the train.

We need not worry. Whatever may come in our future, Jesus is already there with our ticket. He will give us what we need, just when we need it.

Gracious heavenly Father, how I need You! Help me to completely trust You with my life, moment by moment. Teach me to worry less and to know and believe that You have everything ready that I will ever need. In the name of Jesus. Amen.

Beauty and Value

Are not two sparrows sold for a penny? Yet not one of them will fall to the ground apart from the will of your father (Matthew 10:29).

Scripture: Matthew 10:24-31
Song: "His Eye Is on the Sparrow"

My husband and I are moving into a small home. It only has one closet, so we've been searching for a bed frame that has drawers built into it for storage. After much searching, I finally met a woman who has this type of bed frame. She thinks it's an "ugly old thing" and can't wait to get it out of her house. But I need those drawers, and I can't wait to get them into mine!

Both beauty and value are in the eye of the beholder. An auctioneer with a keen eye can look at people's discarded castoffs and know where to start the bidding. The auctioneer knows that some old things are a rarity because they just aren't made anymore. He can spot the "junk" that will command a high price on the auction block.

We are rather like the sparrow, aren't we? The Savior looks at us, plain as we are, and He sees beauty. He looks through our ugly sin and brokenness to see who we were created to be. Jesus valued us so much that He paid the ultimate price for us with His blood on Calvary. This is what it means to be ransomed, rescued, saved, and redeemed. I am so thankful for the loving care of my great Savior!

Thank You, **Lord,** for transformed lives. Teach me to see others the way You do—that I might be keenly aware of the worth and value of everyone You bring into my life. In the precious name of my Lord Christ I pray. Amen.

Staring Down the Lion

Be self-controlled and alert. Your enemy the devil prowls around like a roaring lion looking for someone to devour (1 Peter 5:8).

Scripture: 1 Peter 5:6-11
Song: "I Will Overcome"

"I didn't know if I even wanted to resist it. It held tremendous power over me." Driving in my car, I heard a man on Christian radio telling about his struggle with pornography. He went on to explain that the first big hurdle for him was deciding that he really did want to fight his compulsion. Mostly, he feared he had no power within himself to overcome.

One night, filled with disgust and remorse, he cried out to God: "Help me!" What happened is a really exciting story. The power of God's love was unleashed when he partnered with God to break his addiction. The Savior walked beside him, giving him courage and strength day by day.

Today, this man walks in victory, living in freedom and full of faith. He helps others with the grace he received. In his voice I hear the joy and passion he feels in this new life of freedom.

He pays close attention to what he reads, listens to, and watches on television. He is alert to the call of temptation and guards his heart by staying away from the things he knows could "trigger" a relapse. Bottomline: The enemy is now banging on closed doors.

Dear God, You know my deepest struggles. Help me! I pray that You will give me the courage to resist my own temptations and not look back. Through Christ, amen.

Forget About It!

Who of you by worrying can add a single hour to his life? (Matthew 6:27).

Scripture: Matthew 6:25-34
Song: "Peace Be Still"

Psychologists sometimes employ reverse psychology to treat resistant anxiety. For instance, they may encourage their anxious patient to designate a time period each day to sit and think about his worries. Now that's an interesting appointment to put on our calendars—"Worry time!"

The idea is that making a deliberate effort to worry at, say, 2:00 on Tuesdays, frees the mind to focus on more important things for the rest of the day. Sound like a good idea?

Excessive worry can truly drain our energies. We can get so distracted by our anxieties that we create new problems for ourselves, being unable to focus on the tasks in front of us. More importantly, focusing on our worries and anxieties can blind us to to important issues in our relationships. Our children, spouses, family, and friends need our attention too.

Worry can also rob us of our joy. Worried people are tense and unhappy. Often, too, they are sleep deprived. A worried mind is apt to develop poor coping skills or addictive behaviors. Maybe we would do well to release all this negative energy at once. Sit and worry for 10 minutes. Then forget about it!

Gracious Father, help me not to be consumed with worries. Life is too short! I want to fully live the life before me. So help me to grab hold of Your promises when I am worried. Grant me insight into my own poor coping skills, and teach me to cast all my cares on You. In the name of Jesus, I pray. Amen.

No Best Time to Witness

Then the high priest asked him, "Are these charges true?" (Acts 7:1).

Scripture: Acts 7:1-8
Song: "Be Bold, Be Strong"

It's tough to be falsely accused, thoroughly misunderstood. In most cases it means a bit of embarrassment or perhaps some damage to our reputation. But for Stephen the cost was much higher. As a result of the accusation that he spoke "words of blasphemy against Moses and against God" (Acts 6:11), Stephen would face execution.

Stephen knew this could happen. Nevertheless, he gave a full and inspiring account of himself before the high priest. He went into detail about the scriptural witness and the part that the righteous one played in the whole history of Israel.

In other words, Stephen used a tough circumstance in his life as a great opportunity to witness to the truths of the gospel. Can we do the same?

Most of us pray for the chance to witness to a seeking friend or an unbelieving neighbor. We envision that day when everything will be just right and a prime opportunity will open so that we can speak of our faith in Christ. But God may answer our prayer a little differently. He may allow a significant trial in our lives to be the launching pad for another person's first step toward Him.

Holy God, thank You for Stephen's bold example. When the time is right, give me the courage I need to speak out for You. In Jesus' name, amen.

November 28–30. **Gary Wilde** is the editor of *Devotions*®. He and his wife, Carol, enjoy walking along the beaches of Florida's gulf coast.

Chosen to Serve

Observe [these laws] carefully, for this will show your wisdom and understanding to the nations, who will hear about all these decrees and say, "Surely this great nation is a wise and understanding people" (Deuteronomy 4:6)

Scripture: Deuteronomy 4:5-9
Song: "Let Me Be a Light"

I remember playing games of football on the school playground as a kid. Back then, at recess we'd quickly choose up teams and play our hearts out until it was time to go back to our classroom. I don't know if they still use our method anymore: two captains were designated. Then those two alternately picked the players they wanted, from the most desired to the less skilled.

I know, it could be brutal, especially if you were the last kid standing. But it was great to be chosen first or to be chosen at all!

Let's think about the concept of being chosen. Is it only a privilege? only a matter of pride (and perhaps childish boasting)?

In the Bible to *be chosen* means primarily to be called by God to a particular responsibility. That is what defined the people of Israel in their status as God's chosen people. They were to be a witness for Him among the nations. They were to be "a light for revelation to the Gentiles" (Luke 2:32). Having been chosen meant having been given a divine task of witnessing. Similarly, when we live lives of peace and good works among our neighbors, they surely see something of our Lord shining through.

Father, help me to live in a way that honors You. May the light of Jesus shine into my heart so that I might share His light with others. In Your Son's name. Amen.

Remember Your Roots

Then you shall declare before the LORD your God: "My father was a wandering Aramean, and he went down into Egypt with a few people and lived there and became a great nation, powerful and numerous (Deuteronomy 26:5).

Scripture: Deuteronomy 26:1-11
Song: "Faith of Our Fathers"

I am reading a new book written by a friend of mine. It is mostly an autobiography, filled with stories of his family—beginning with his grandparents. He was one of nine children, and his genealogical history is important to him. As he puts it: "You can't really know who you are until you know where you came from."

I see that concept coming through clearly in our Scripture today. Notice how important it was for the people to remember where they came from as they entered a new land. They must recall, in specific terms, that their father was Abraham and that he was a simple "wandering Aramean," who chose to obey God. Then the whole history is recited, giving credit to God for all the great things He did on behalf of the family of Israel.

What a great example for us to follow—to remember that we were born again from a kingdom of darkness into a kingdom of light! We were adopted as God's children and now serve Him out of gratitude (Ephesians 1:5). No matter our earthly history—whether it brings us a rush of pride or a twinge of shame—if we are in Christ, we have a glorious genealogy, an awesome family, and a very bright future.

Dear Father, whatever our spiritual heritage, we are now part of your eternal family. Thank You for delivering us out of darkness into Your glorious light. Thank You for allowing us to be Your children. In the name of Your Son who made it possible, amen.

My Prayer Notes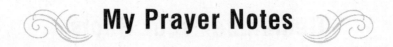

DEVOTIONS®

December

Looking forward to the city with foundations, whose architect and builder is God.

—Hebrews 11:10

Gary Allen, Editor   **Margaret Williams,** Project Editor   Photo © Liquid Library

DEVOTIONS® is published quarterly by Standard Publishing, Cincinnati, Ohio, www.standardpub.com. © 2010 by Standard Publishing. All rights reserved. Topics based on the Home Daily Bible Readings, International Sunday School Lessons. © 2008 by the Committee on the Uniform Series. Printed in the U.S.A. All Scripture quotations, unless otherwise indicated, are taken from the HOLY BIBLE, *NEW INTERNATIONAL VERSION*®. *NIV*®. Copyright © 1973, 1978, 1984 by Biblica, Inc.™. Used by permission of Zondervan. All rights reserved. *King James Version* (*KJV*), public domain.

Shine the Light

Listen to me, my people; hear me, my nation: The law will go out from me; my justice will become a light to the nations (Isaiah 51:4).

Scripture: Isaiah 51:1-6
Song: "Let the Light Stream In"

As I enjoyed a watercolor painting, I marveled at how narrow lines of white space defined people and objects. I've dabbled in watercolor, so I know how hard it is to leave such margins. The paint may run. And then the painting may look amateurish if the white spaces aren't properly blended into the whole. Yet this particular painter used white to make glorious light shine down upon the scene, truly the mark of a talented artist.

Just as the "white" of a painting brings light to a scene, and defines objects, so God's Word brings light to our society in a way that defines morality and justice. Do governments wonder what is right or wrong in a human rights issue? Check God's Word. Do communities wonder what is fair or unfair to residents? Consider God's Word. Do individuals wonder how to treat those with whom they disagree? Consult God's Word.

As I read God's Word each morning, I try to apply His principles to the situations of my life. We need never think any issue is too complicated. God's light shines brightest in the darkest places.

Dear Lord, thank You for revealing Your character to me through Your Word. May those who govern us look to Your wisdom in all things. In Jesus' name, amen.

December 1–4. **Shirley Brosius** lives in Millersburg, Pennsylvania, and is the author of a devotional book. She enjoys reading, walking, and playing games with her five grandchildren.

Is Your Fruit Ripening?

Every tree that does not produce good fruit will be cut down and thrown into the fire (Matthew 3:10).

Scripture: Matthew 3:1-10
Song: "I Long to Glorify Thee"

During my college years, I worked on a fruit farm. Each spring we climbed ladders to cull developing peaches, pears, apples, and plums from heavily laden branches. Picking off some of the young fruit helped the remaining fruit to develop into nice-sized produce. Customers who visited the farm's market wanted mature fruit that had received plenty of sunshine and nutrients.

The goal of a fruit farmer is to produce good fruit. The goal of a Christian is also to produce good fruit—spiritual sons and daughters. That is, we want to influence others for Christ so that they turn to Him as Lord. That may happen as we speak of Him. But since actions often speak louder than words, we can also grow spiritual fruit by living lives laced with love, joy, peace, patience, kindness, goodness, faithfulness, gentleness, and self-control (see these fruit of the Spirit in Galatians 5:22, 23). Such qualities attract people hungry for fruit.

In the natural world, good fruit provides the vitamins and minerals we need to develop healthy bodies. On our spiritual journey, good fruit—the effect of our works done in the power of the Spirit—inspires others to come to Christ.

Dear Lord, fill me with the fruit of Your Spirit so that I may pass it on to others in word and in deed. May my life be transformed by Your presence so that others may come to know You. In Jesus' name, amen.

Drop That Anchor!

We have this hope as an anchor for the soul, firm and secure (Hebrews 6:19).

Scripture: Hebrews 6:13-20
Song: "I Would Be True"

Early martyrs amaze me. Vibia Perpetua nursed an infant when arrested after Roman emperor Septimius Severus declared it illegal to speak of Christianity. Her father begged her to recant her faith, but she stood firm. Her pregnant slave, Felicitas, was also arrested. The women prayed that she would have her baby early so that she might have the privilege of suffering for her faith along with Perpetua in a Roman arena.

To them, Heaven was so real that they considered it a privilege to give their lives for Christ.

Would I do the same? I honestly don't know. I do know that God offers me daily opportunities to strengthen my faith so that it remains firm and secure. By reading Scripture, I learn how God has worked in this world down through history. By praying, I connect with someone who loves me more than I can imagine.

By reading about early Christians and fellowshiping with Christians today, I hear of their faith in trying circumstances and how God ministered to them. I don't want to miss any opportunity for God to strengthen my faith. You see, I want to be ready—no matter what.

Dear Lord, thank You for promising to be with me, no matter what the circumstances. I trust that as trying times come into my life I will have a wonderful sense of Your presence . . . and hold firm to the faith. In Jesus' name, amen.

What's Your Name?

The LORD had said to Abram, "Leave your country, your people and your father's household and go to the land I will show you" (Genesis 12:1).

Scripture: Genesis 12:1-9
Song: "Where He Leads Me"

Given the name Isabella at birth, Sojourner Truth, a former slave, changed her name to reflect her calling to ministry. "Sojourner" represented her itinerant lifestyle, and "Truth" described the message of God that she declared. We can imagine the opposition a black woman faced in the mid-1800s as she advocated abolition and women's suffrage across New York, Connecticut, and Massachusetts. Sojourner even took a trip west in response to God's call.

We read in Genesis how another person experienced a name change in response to God's call. Born Abram, which means "exalted father," his name was changed by God to Abraham, which means "father of many." Abraham left his homeland to settle in a foreign country—and became a great nation—simply because God asked him to go.

These individuals offer sterling examples of obedience to the Lord. By prayer, study, and consultation with other Christians, I have also tried to discern God's will for my life. I'm not sure how He might change my name. But I am sure that God is able to use me, and any other person, who says "yes" in response to His call.

Dear Lord, thank You for the promise to go with me wherever You call me to go. Please show me the path You have for my life, step by step. In Jesus' name, amen.

Contentment in a Tent

By faith he [Abraham] made his home in the promised land . . . he lived in tents, as did Isaac and Jacob, who were heirs with him of the same promise (Hebrews 11:9).

Scripture: Hebrews 11:8-16
Song: "I've Got a Mansion over the Hilltop"

In a grainy black-and-white photo sit three young men warming their hands over a fire. Snow is piled high around them, and a tent sits in the background. Mark and his friends decided to go tent camping one wintry weekend. They toughed it out in freezing temperatures and had a great time. When they followed up that winter adventure with a warmer one in spring, water and mud seeped slowly into their tent. They had little faith they'd be well protected this time. So . . . they headed to a hotel with a solid foundation—and dry bedding.

Contentment in a tent doesn't come easy. But Abraham and his immediate descendants couldn't escape to a hotel when sand storms blew in or thieves approached. Yet Abraham had the faith and foresight to look forward to "the city with foundations, whose architect and builder is God" (v. 10).

God may not call us to pack up and move into a tent as He called Abraham. Yet like Abraham, we too are called to live by faith, to do His bidding, and to content ourselves in His promise of Heaven.

Lord, give me the faith of my spiritual father, Abraham. Teach me to be content wherever You direct me, knowing that You are always with me. Through Christ, amen.

December 5–11. **Katherine Douglas** lives in Swanton, Ohio, where she enjoys writing devotionals for several publications. She's also written a number of devotional books for people with pets.

By Faith, Abraham . . .

By faith Abraham, when God tested him, offered Isaac as a sacrifice (Hebrews 11:17).

Scripture: Hebrews 11:17-22
Song: "Find Us Faithful"

Lloyd Ogilvie, chaplain of the US Senate from 1995 to 2008, once made this observation: "Far too many of us are not attempting anything bold, adventuresome, and courageous enough to need the Spirit's wisdom and power, much less His fire." What an indictment of my own paltry faith.

Over a dozen times in Hebrews 11, we find the phrase "by faith." In today's verses we're told of the faith of the patriarchs and others. By faith these men and women acted on what they believed and in whom they trusted. What they did, what they said, how they conducted their lives, challenges us to step outside our own daily routines.

What is God calling you to do? Take in an ailing loved one? Work at a soup kitchen? Man a polling place? Help in the church nursery? Participate in a short-term missions trip? Go back to school? Start a Bible study in your neighborhood?

Not everything God calls us to do is big—except, perhaps, to us. We've never done it before, or we don't think we're up to the challenge? That's why we are called to do the best things—not necessarily the biggest things—"by faith."

What will you do by faith today?

Lord, I want to put my faith to work. Make me willing to stretch myself beyond what I think I can do and trust what You can indeed do through me. In the powerful name of Jesus I pray, amen.

Good Credit

So then, he is the father of all who believe but have not been circumcised, in order that righteousness might be credited to them (Romans 4:11).

Scripture: Romans 4:9-15
Song: "Father Abraham"

"Credit debt? Bad credit? No credit at all? We can help!"

Have you heard that advertisement on the radio? If by default, identity theft, or poor money management we've gotten into debt, a number of companies stand ready to help . . . for a price.

When it comes to our debt of sin before a holy God, there's no self-induced bailout plan. No religious ceremony or accomplishment of good works can reverse our bad credit before God. For biblical Abraham and his people, neither could circumcision transform the heart. The only way to have a clear and clean record before God is through faith. In faith we trust God to do what we are powerless to do.

What makes this God-given righteousness even more special is that it's called "blessedness" (v. 9). Blessedness touches all of life. It brings peace, joy, and assurance. Not even a good credit rating can bring all of that into our lives. Just as we sang the chorus as children in Sunday school, so too again we can declare: "Father Abraham has many sons . . . I am one of them and so are you. So let's all praise the Lord!"

Father, I'm humbled by the righteousness of Christ that You give me through faith. I know that everything that I have is a gift from You. Thank You for the blessedness You bring into my life. Through Christ I pray. Amen.

Alien Righteousness

Also for us, to whom God will credit righteousness — for us who believe in him who raised Jesus our Lord from the dead (Romans 4:24).

Scripture: Romans 4:16-25
Song: "Heaven Came Down and Glory Filled My Soul"

I've sat in the captain's chair. When the Star Trek tour came to Detroit, Michigan, in 2009, I plopped myself down in the captain's chair (wearing my official Star Trek insignia T-shirt), and I looked around the reconstructed *Enterprise* "bridge" from the set of the 1960s television series. What a heady moment! I didn't see, nor did I expect to see, any aliens. I may be a rabid "Trekker," but I don't for a minute believe in Klingons, or Romulans, or even UFOs. I do, however, believe in an alien righteousness.

"Alien righteousness." I first heard that term used by a Sunday school teacher. He was teaching on the passage we read today in Romans 4. Righteousness, provided for us by God himself through the atoning work of Jesus Christ, is imputed — *credited* to our account — by the grace of God.

God's righteousness is alien in that it is something outside us. It comes from beyond us. We can't manufacture it, work ourselves into it, or obtain it by any means. We are incapable of righteousness apart from its gift by the Creator of time and space.

Righteous God, I know I have no righteousness in myself, though I want to live righteously. Live in and through me, Lord Jesus, by the power of Your Holy Spirit. I pray in Your precious name. Amen.

A Covenant Remembered

He remembers his covenant forever, the word he commanded, for a thousand generations, the covenant he made with Abraham, the oath he swore to Isaac (Psalm 105:8, 9).

Scripture: Psalm 105:4-11
Song: "Fear Not, Thou Faithful Christian Flock"

When the League of Nations formed after World War I, its Covenant included a five-point pledge. Number one on the list stated that member nations would protect "the territorial integrity of other member states." Even though U.S. President Woodrow Wilson spearheaded the formation of the League of Nations and its Covenant, the U.S. as a whole wanted nothing to do with it. The United States adopted an isolationist policy. In less than a generation, the League quickly unraveled. Its Covenant was of no effect when World War II erupted.

The Bible abounds with covenants. God's covenant with humankind through Noah (Genesis 9:8-17), God's covenant with Israel through Abraham (numerous texts, including today's), God's covenant through the Law, and finally, God's "better covenant" with us through Christ Jesus (see Hebrews 7–13).

When God makes a covenant, He can and will fulfill it. What He promised to Abraham, He reiterated to Isaac and repeated to Jacob. And, indeed, the Israelites eventually returned to their covenant land. Yes, when He establishes a covenant, God sees it through—everlastingly.

I thank You, **Lord,** that Your covenants are true and eternally binding. Thank You that what You promise You see through to completion. I praise You, Lord, my covenant-keeping God. In the name of Jesus I pray. Amen.

No Surprises Here

May the God of peace, who through the blood of the eternal covenant brought back from the dead our Lord Jesus, that great Shepherd of the sheep, equip you with everything good for doing his will (Hebrews 13:20, 21).

Scripture: Hebrews 13:17-21
Song: "Worthy the Lamb"

For her 40th birthday, Lois's husband hosted a surprise birthday party. Amazingly, she never even suspected it. Her husband didn't let their kids in on the secret—not even the collegian, who undoubtedly could have kept the surprise a secret. What made it extra special for Lois was the presence of her mom and dad. They made the 600-mile round trip just for her.

No one likes a bad surprise. There's nothing like a good surprise, however, to bring simultaneous laughter, excitement, and tears. To pull off a good surprise brings its challenges, but what a treat for everyone when it happens.

God has never been, nor will He ever be surprised. Before He established time, He knew from eternity that the crown of His creation, mankind, would sin. And He knew what He would do. He planned accordingly and made provision for our salvation "before the foundation of the world" (1 Peter 1:20, *KJV*).

I suspect we may have more than a few surprises awaiting us in Heaven. But as for our God, He is never surprised.

Dear Father, it humbles me to think that You planned for my salvation from eternity. Help me to live thankfully and honorably before You, in my thought life and in everything I do and say. Thank You for the shed blood of Jesus on my behalf. In the name of the Father, the Son, and the Holy Spirit, I pray. Amen.

Cutting Covenant

When the sun had set and darkness had fallen, a smoking firepot with a blazing torch appeared and passed between the pieces (Genesis 15:17).

Scripture: Genesis 15:1-6, 12-18
Song: "Nothing but the Blood"

The year was 1960, and two preteen girls took a break from their play. Linda pulled a safety pin out of her pocket. "We can seal our friendship forever by becoming blood sisters."

Susan regarded her friend warily. "How do we become 'blood sisters'?"

"We just prick our fingers with this pin, then put them together to mix our blood. Ta-da! Blood sisters! Want to?"

Squeamish Susan opted out. "Nah. We'll always be best friends anyway."

This (thankfully, no-longer popular) childhood ritual probably came from the practice of "cutting covenant." In the classic work, *The Blood Covenant,* by H. Clay Trumbull, the author describes variations of blood covenant in ancient cultures the world over.

God, the initiator of covenant, established His covenant with Abraham by and through blood. Today's lesson takes us to the covenantal event we've studied all week. Pointing to the stars, God tells Abraham that His covenant with him reaches much further than the patriarch can imagine. Yet, through faith like Abraham's, we're blessed by the new covenant made in Christ.

I praise You, **Father.** You keep every covenant and every promise You make. I pray that I never make a promise I can't or don't intend to keep. In Christ's name, amen.

Abundant Provisions

My God will meet all your needs according to His glorious riches in Christ Jesus (Philippians 4:19).

Scripture: Philippians 4:15-20
Song: "God Will Take Care of You"

We were strangers in a strange land. Twenty of us arrived in palm tree–dotted Costa Rica for a few adventures—and to do volunteer work in small highland villages. Half our group spoke Spanish, and the other half relied on crinkled cheat sheets.

But our three guides set us at ease instantly when they introduced themselves in English and helped load our luggage onto the bus. Within minutes, they gave each of us a personalized handbook, outlining each day's itinerary. The book also contained useful Spanish phrases, local expressions, food recommendations, currency conversion charts, and a set of Costa Rican–themed crossword puzzles to play while traveling.

Our guides not only met our needs, but also exceeded our expectations. They anticipated our uneasiness in a new culture and addressed that anxiety. On the fourth day of our stay, a squirrel monkey bit one of our students. Our guides called the home office and then drove us to a hospital.

On a much larger scale, God does something similar. From the wealth of His riches and His knowledge of eternity, He amply provides for our every need.

Father, thank You for demonstrating Your loving care by often providing for me before I even realize my needs exist. In Jesus' name, amen.

December 12–18. **Vicki Hodges** lives in the mountains of western Colorado, where she's a Spanish teacher at one of the local high schools.

Extraordinary Living

His son by the slave woman was born in the ordinary way; but his son by the free woman was born as the result of a promise (Galatians 4:23).

Scripture: Galatians 4:21-28
Song: "Rejoice in the Lord"

Food? Check. Sleeping bags? Check. Matches? Check. Our family intended to camp in a remote mountain range of western Colorado. We wouldn't see other people for several days.

Autumn rainstorms saturated the ground, and nighttime temperatures hovered around freezing. When we finally located a campsite and pulled in, our pickup and trailer were mired in the mud. We unhitched the trailer, shoveled, pried, pushed, and pulled, but we were hopelessly stuck. As angry storm clouds gathered overhead, we asked God for help.

Nothing happened: no superhuman strength, no bursts of extreme adrenaline, no helicopter. Finally, we decided to ride the four-wheel ATV off the mountain and travel toward the nearest town to contact a towing company. But after driving five miles, we met two guys in a heavy-duty pickup. Within an hour, they had winched us free of the swampy muck.

Abraham and Sarah had asked God to give them a child and expected Him to fulfill their request in the normal way. When He didn't do it, they abandoned the idea. However, God's plan was to operate through the modality of impossibility. He chose to delight them with the extraordinary.

Lord, remind me that whether You answer my prayers in an astonishing manner or without flair, Your ways are always good. Through Christ, amen.

Amazing Faith

I will surely bless you and make your descendants as numerous as the stars in the sky and as the sand on the seashore. Your descendants will take possession of the cities of their enemies (Genesis 22:17).

Scripture: Genesis 22:15-19
Song: "Faith Is the Victory!"

"I was really nervous because I've never done this before. And I think Indy was nervous too. She kept shaking because there were flies, so I held on really tight—I didn't want to fall off. But I believed that Indy wouldn't let me fall. I just knew she wouldn't because I know she believes in me as much as I believe in her." These were William Sylvester's thoughts, as quoted in the *Tribune & Georgian* newspaper in Camden County, Georgia. William is a 12-year-old with autism. At the Special Olympics state horse show, he and Indy, his favorite quarter horse, made a great team. And this young boy's faith in his horse was rewarded with a first place medal.

God honored Abraham's amazing faith and obedience by promising to multiply his descendants beyond numbering. Astronomers believe there are more stars in the universe than grains of sand on the earth. God has most assuredly fulfilled His promise to Abraham; his descendants are countless down through the ages.

Lord, thank You that through faith I can become more than a medal-winning conqueror through Christ. When I'm nervous and uncertain about situations in life, help me have the confidence to approach You with solid faith. I trust You to be faithful to Your promises to provide for me and to protect me. In Jesus' name, amen.

A Remarkable Gift

If one of you says to him, "Go, I wish you well; keep warm and well fed," but does nothing about his physical needs, what good is it? (James 2:16).

Scripture: James 2:14-24
Song: "My Life Is in You, Lord"

"I cleaned out my closet and found some black dress shoes for you, Aimee. You can try them on at church tonight." Linda arrived with three trash bags of shoes for our daughter. Annoyed that she had to rummage through 31 pairs of unwanted castoffs, Aimee searched for the ebony shoes and jammed the bags into the trunk of our car. As she entered church more than slightly frustrated, she observed that one of the usually hyperactive teenage girls was barefoot and uncharacteristically solemn.

"Krista, why aren't you wearing shoes on such a freezing, snowy night?" Krista explained that because they had left home in a hurry she forgot her shoes and her dad refused to return home in order to retrieve them. Aimee immediately felt remorse for being aggravated and asked Krista to select a pair of shoes from the "shoe closet" in our crowded trunk. God had answered Krista's unsolicited request before she even voiced a need.

Aimee could have chosen to scold or tease Krista for forgetting her shoes. Or she could have told Krista she hoped she would be warm enough in bare feet. Yet the truth of one of our favorite quotes rang clear. "Your walk talks, and your talk talks, but your walk talks louder than your talk talks."

Lord, remind me to live the gospel and not just talk about it. Help me turn personal frustration into blessings for others. In Christ's name, amen.

Talking Rocks

If they ever say this to us, or to our descendants, we will answer: Look at the replica of the LORD's altar, which our fathers built, not for burnt offerings and sacrifices, but as a witness between us and you (Joshua 22:28).

Scripture: Joshua 22:21-29
Song: "When I Look into Your Holiness"

"How much farther? We've been driving forever. There's nothing to do, and we're hungry." The highway between Rock Springs and Jackson Hole, Wyoming, consists of beautiful scenery, but also stretches of dry barrenness. My husband invented the car game, "Who can find the most antelope along the side of the road while we're driving to Yellowstone National Park?" The kids entertained themselves for at least an hour by scouring the hillsides in order to locate antelope. Steve promised to award the winner with a candy bar.

Somewhere between the 13th and 17th antelope, our daughter, Marci, began noticing waist-high stacks of rocks on the hillsides. She asked Steve if he could explain them. He said that sometimes sheepherders built monuments from rocks in order to mark the location of nearby water holes. Sometimes the monuments commemorated a notable grave site.

People saw the altar that the children of Reuben and Gad had built. They, like Marci, wondered about stacked stones. They eventually realized it was never used for sacrifice. The memorial spoke of a close association with each other and with the Lord.

Father, thank You for making Christ the great altar, bridging the way of communion between You and me. In Your holy name I pray, amen.

Heed the Warnings!

Every way of a man is right in his own eyes: but the LORD pondereth the hearts. An high look, and a proud heart, and the plowing of the wicked, is sin (Proverbs 21:2, *King James Version*).

Scripture: Proverbs 21:1-5
Song: "Be Still for the Presence"

"Warning: Vaporizer produces hot steam and could cause injuries." Similar warning signs infiltrate our society. Toy labels warn of the choking hazard of small pieces, road signs warn of dangerous curves, and weather channels warn of upcoming storms. Sleeping pills even warn of the possibility . . . that they may cause drowsiness!

With such warnings so common, it's curious that we would ever choose to do wrong. Our friend, Tom, recently made poor choices in his relationship with his girlfriend. Several people advised him to end the relationship and warned him about her behavior. Nevertheless, he ignored us all and did what he thought was right. Months later, he learned his girlfriend had deceived him, dated other guys while they were engaged, and plunged him into significant debt.

How often do I ignore warnings and consequently yield to sin? God's Word abounds in gentle (and not-so-gentle) warnings. Any of us would be wise to pay careful attention. Every one of those warnings is for our own good.

Father, You will never lead me in the wrong direction. Your wisdom has my best always in mind. So please remind me never to settle for less than what You intend for me and help me be wise enough to heed life's warnings. In Jesus' name, amen.

He Did the Unthinkable

When they reached the place God had told him about, Abraham built an altar there and arranged the wood on it. He bound his son Isaac and laid him on the altar, on top of the wood (Genesis 22:9).

Scripture: Genesis 22:1-14
Song: "O How Happy Are They Who the Savior Obey"

As winter settles in, an unthinkable process transpires: the wood frog (*Rana sylvatica*) becomes . . . a frogsicle! Yes, wood frogs can tolerate freezing. In fact, they freeze and defrost with their surroundings. When water in the environment becomes frozen, up to two-thirds of the frog's bodily fluids freeze. Normally, ice in body tissues is lethal. So what enables a wood frog to "die" and come back to life without experiencing these problems?

Its liver produces glucose, a form of sugar, which acts as an antifreeze. This thick syrup protects vital organs while the frog is frozen. When the frogsicle thaws, it does the unthinkable. It immediately begins breathing, its heart beats again, and it returns to normal living.

Abraham could have headed in the opposite direction from where God directed. He might have chosen to sacrifice an animal. He could have refused to submit to God at all. However, Abraham's love for God, complete trust in Him, and unwavering obedience enabled him to do the unthinkable: prepare to sacrifice his son on the altar.

Lord, help me obey You, led by Your Word and the good guidance of others in Your church. Give me a deep passion for submission to Your will. In Jesus' name, amen.

I Am His!

He anointed us, set his seal of ownership on us, and put his Spirit in our hearts as a deposit, guaranteeing what is to come (2 Corinthians 1:21, 22).

Scripture: 2 Corinthians 1:18-22
Song: "O Love That Wilt Not Let Me Go"

My husband and I looked at many houses when we were downsizing. After awhile, they all began to look the same. We waffled in our decision making. By the time we expressed interest in making an offer, the homes we considered were sold. Someone else saw the value in the home before we did.

Then one day our realtor gave us a peek at a home that had just hit the market. "It's a fixer-upper that might meet your needs." And indeed it did. Many projects lay ahead for us with this home, but we could also see its wonderful potential. With labor and love, this house could truly become our home. We didn't want to let this one go.

So we made an offer on the spot. When the realtor told us she would need a deposit, we didn't hesitate to write a check. We wanted this house. That deposit guaranteed our good faith with the mortgage company, and in due time, the house became ours.

Similarly, Jesus will not let us go. He paid for us with His precious blood. The Spirit He placed within us, His deposit toward our final redemption, will help us to find His purpose in our lives.

O Great King, thank You for Your sacrifice on the cross. You paid the ultimate price for me, and I want so much to become the person that you see, hidden within. Thank You for valuing me so highly. In Your precious name I pray. Amen.

Here He Comes!

You saw the suffering of our forefathers in Egypt; you heard their cry at the Red Sea (Nehemiah 9:9).

Scripture: Nehemiah 9:6-10
Song: "Leaning On the Everlasting Arms"

Jamie looked out the window and dabbed at stinging tears. Since learning of her son's terminal diagnosis, her life abruptly changed. Now she needed to learn nursing skills in order to care for him in their home. And ultimately, she had to prepare for the day her child would go to Heaven. Overwhelmed, the young woman cried out to God for help. Did He even hear her?

The Israelites felt overwhelmed and frightened as they faced the Red Sea with Pharaoh's angry army hot on their heels. Imagine their terror, looking out at a billowing sea, hearing the clatter of horse's hooves approaching. They had nowhere to turn.

So they turned to God and cried out to Him, "Help us!" The Lord heard and delivered them in a miraculous way. With a wave of His hand, God parted the waters of the Red Sea and led them across dry land. Then He shut the waters back up, so that the Egyptians could not chase them any further.

Are you in distress? God surely hears your cries. He attended to Jamie's needs and helped her, day by day, to face great difficulty. He hears and remains present with His children through all things.

Heavenly Father, I need Your guidance! Help me to walk faithfully with You and to turn to You in my distress, as my forefathers did. Through Christ, amen.

December 20–25. **Barbara Tuttle** is a freelance writer who contributes to several Christian publications. She and her husband enjoy hiking and cross-country skiing throughout Michigan.

Our Song of Faith

Clearly no one is justified before God by the law, because "The righteous will live by faith" (Galatians 3:11).

Scripture: Galatians 3:6-12
Song: "Falter Not"

"No Admittance." To the small boy who could not yet read, the words on a sign that hung above the concert hall door meant nothing. While his mother chatted away with friends and waited for the concert to begin, the bored child simply wandered off. Now he stood alone in the private section reserved for musicians. Upon opening the door, he saw a magnificent piano. Enthralled, the boy sat down and studiously began to plunk out a little tune.

Imagine his mother's surprise when the curtains suddenly opened, and there sat her son—at the master's piano! Suddenly, Paderewski walked onto the stage. Stretching his arms around the boy, he composed a harmonious accompaniment for the child as he plinked away.

The unsuspecting child in this popular story could not read or follow, the "No Admittance" sign. But the audience delighted to see how the accomplished musician affectionately embraced the child and his song. We too are surrounded by many, many instructions and admonitions in the Scriptures. No one could follow all that it requires of us. But with childlike wonder, we can play our song of faith for Jesus, and He will accept us.

Dear God, I cannot begin to keep the requirements of your holy law. It seems the more I try to do everything right, the more I fail. You are a just and Holy God, and I thank You for sending Jesus to accomplish salvation for me. In His name, amen.

A Sure Foundation

Brothers, let me take an example from everyday life. Just as no one can set aside or add to a human covenant that has been duly established, so it is in this case (Galatians 3:15).

Scripture: Galatians 3:13-18
Song: "Father, Whose Everlasting Love"

"I do." Many a jittery bride and groom can attest to a case of nerves when speaking their wedding vows. Marriage is an honorable, sacred covenant, and it's natural to tremble at the altar.

Yet in many cultures, the marriage union begins the moment promises are conferred, before the actual ceremony to seal the vows. When a man proposes to his beloved, he makes a promise, and she eagerly accepts.

Sometimes, families of the prospective bride and groom arrange the marriage. They may barely know each other, but the promise is conferred. These individual and collective promises are generally recognized by a period of engagement, or betrothal, before the ceremony. The promises made in our hearts and affirmed in community then enable us to live out our marriage vows. We rest in the promise of loyalty to one another, no matter what trials may come.

Many years ago, God promised blessings to Abraham and his seed. It was an honorable, sacred covenant. And down through time, the promise has not been set aside. Through faith in Jesus Christ, it continues now to all who believe!

Gracious Father, thank You for the covenant You have made with me through Your Son, Jesus. Teach me to have respect for promises. I don't want to make promises to others carelessly; I need Your help to keep them. In Jesus' name, amen.

One Heart, One Will

"I am the Lord's servant," Mary answered. "May it be to me as you have said." Then the angel left her (Luke 1:38).

Scripture: Luke 1:26-38
Song: "Ye Servants of God"

"I knew what I was getting into when my husband enlisted in the army. I anticipated long deployments overseas. But I love my husband, and I'm committed to our marriage, so I simply adjust to his absence in our home."

The young woman bravely faced interviewers recently on a television show depicting the lives of military families. Surely she carried a heavy load, managing the countless details of running a household and parenting alone. But she willingly learned new skills and embraced self-reliance.

Her young soldier in the field must have felt blessed to have a faithful wife taking good care of his family. He knew that she understood his job and respected his duty to their country. For his sake, she put her fears aside and tackled each new challenge with a can-do spirit.

Because she aligned her heart with her husband's, this military wife possessed the grace of acceptance. Military families endure unique hardships willingly. They faithfully follow their commander-in-chief.

Am I following my commander-in-chief? Are my heart and will aligned with God's?

Dear Lord, cultivate in me a willing heart and spirit to do Your will. Sometimes I resist doing the hard things, and often I fear the unknown. But I do want to wholeheartedly embrace the adventure of serving You. Through Christ I pray. Amen.

Leap, O Spirit!

When Elizabeth heard Mary's greeting, the baby leaped in her womb, and Elizabeth was filled with the Holy Spirit (Luke 1:41).

Scripture: Luke 1:39-45
Song: "Mary's Boy Child"

John the Baptist, the child Elizabeth carried in her womb, would grow up to preach a baptism of repentance for the forgiveness of sins. But John had no authority to forgive. He preached and baptized to point people to Jesus, the Messiah, who alone could forgive sins.

Even as a baby in his mother's womb, John's spirit recognized the Holy One inside Mary's womb. No wonder he leapt with joy! John would spend his life preparing the people's hearts for Jesus and His righteous message.

The authority of Jesus continues to bring people under conviction for their sins. Many worshipers "grip the pew" in front of them when God's Word pricks their heart and conscience. I've been there. And I am thankful when Jesus convicts me of sin. After all, I know that I can confess my sins and be forgiven.

Oh, that our spirits too would leap within us when we sense the presence of our Lord!

Almighty and most merciful God, teach me to worship You with great joy. Help me to recognize greatness each time that I hear Your name. May I honor You in all I do, and may my spirit leap within me each time I hear of the great things You have done. Give me the courage to speak of Your greatness to others. In the name of Jesus I pray. Amen.

Make Room for Jesus

She gave birth to her firstborn, a son. She wrapped him in cloths and placed him in a manger, because there was no room for them in the inn (Luke 2:7).

Scripture: Luke 1:46-55; 2:1-7
Song: "My Heart, Your Home"

We recently downsized into a smaller home. Of course, this meant we had to part with many of our belongings. Everything in the old household received a questioning look: *Do we really need that?* We scrutinized our closets, kitchen cabinets, and furnishings. We hauled numerous dusty things from the basement and attacked the clutter in our garage. We even repeated this process several times, constantly confronting our emotional attachments to familiar things around us.

As we whittled away at our belongings, finding things to donate, locating people with needs, the process grew easier. One thought guided our choices: What do we want to make room for in our new, smaller house? We wanted our home to be a peaceful place and a soft place to land at the end of a long working day. We also wanted it to be a welcoming place for family and friends.

Because there was no room for Him in the inn, Jesus was born in a manger. Perhaps the cluttered state of our home in some way reflects our heart. As I look around today, I am asking, have I made room for Jesus in my home and in my heart?

O Lord, I want my heart to be a welcoming place for You. I pray that You will show me anything there that blocks communion with You. Please prick my conscience when I allow any manner of ungodliness to creep in. I love You. Through Christ, amen.

God Is Already There

He called down famine on the land and destroyed all their supplies of food; and He sent a man before them—Joseph, sold as a slave (Psalm 105:16, 17).

Scripture: Psalm 105:16-22
Song: "Do I Trust You?"

"How could this be part of God's plan for my life?" my 16-year-old daughter, Sarah, asked. My recent cancer diagnosis had shaken her faith.

I wondered about this too but I said, "God has a plan for our good and His glory. He knows the future. He is already there."

Sarah could not see past her concern. Fears of the future loomed with menace. What if her mother died? How could God allow this?

Sarah didn't yet know that her experience could serve to comfort others or that it would draw her nearer to the heart of God in ways that nothing else would. Five years later, God called Sarah to minister to orphans in Kenya.

Similarly, Joseph must have wondered how being sold into slavery by his brothers could possibly be God's plan. With a broken heart and his feet in fetters, could Joseph even imagine that he would one day rule over the king's house? Yet God sent Joseph ahead to prepare for the future during a time of famine. Whatever the future holds, God is already there.

Eternal God, You hem me in with Your love. All the days ordained for me were planned before one of them came to be. Thank You! In Christ's holy name, amen.

December 26–31. **Julie Kloster** is a freelance writer, speaker, and teacher living in Sycamore, Illinois, with her husband and three daughters.

God Is with Me

Because the patriarchs were jealous of Joseph, they sold him as a slave into Egypt. But God was with him and rescued him from all his troubles (Acts 7:9, 10).

Scripture: Acts 7:9-16
Song: "God Is with Me"

"This will probably be the most difficult classroom you will ever experience," the administrator told me during the interview. Her message left me with some fears. But she couldn't dissuade me from the task at hand. After being a stay-at-home mom for 20 years, God was leading me back to teach in the public schools.

The first few months were a daily battle for the hearts and souls of these scarred and hurting children. Autism, bipolar disorder, emotional disturbance, and oppositional-defiance disorder accounted for their struggles. God reminded me that His mercies were new every morning, and in the evenings He reminded me that He had been faithful and ever-present. And eventually I gained the goodwill of my students and faculty.

This same God was also with Joseph thousands of years before I was born. Though Joseph was sold into slavery, God was with him and gave him wisdom. This young man eventually gained the goodwill of Pharaoh who made him ruler of Egypt. In that position Joseph provided for the very ones who had sold him into slavery. God rescued Joseph from his troubles and gave him the grace to forgive.

God, even on days when I feel I can't go on, Your compassion sustains me. Though I walk in the midst of trouble, You are with me. Thank You, in Jesus' name. Amen.

Not My Will

Father, if you are willing, take this cup from me; yet not my will, but yours be done (Luke 22:42).

Scripture: Luke 22:39-46
Song: "I Surrender All"

"Your baby may not live." The doctor's voice was just above a whisper. "Because she's 15 weeks premature, she needs a full respirator and 100% oxygen. We are doing everything we can."

I nodded numbly as my heart cried out to God. "Lord, my God, You know how I love this child. I beg You to heal her." I physically opened my clenched fists to signify the release of my will. Hot tears dripped on my open palms as I prayed, "Lord, You love her more than I do. She is yours. Not my will, but Yours be done."

I learned these words from Jesus, who prayed them fervently in the Garden of Gethsemane. Facing the cross, Jesus struggled in prayer. Praying in the garden with His disciples was Jesus' usual custom, yet this time Jesus told His disciples to pray to fight temptation. Was this the temptation that wants our own will more than God's?

Through fervent prayer God gives us the grace and strength to trust Him. My premature daughter is a musically gifted 16-year-old today. Yet if God had called her home, His character would have stayed the same. He is a God of mercy and kindness who does all things for His glory and our good.

Father, You know how many hairs are on my head, and You are intimately acquainted with all my ways. Please give me the strength and courage to trust Your will, even when I do not understand Your ways. In the precious name of Jesus I pray. Amen.

Warning Examples

These things happened to them as examples and were written down as warnings for us, on whom the fulfillment of the ages has come (1 Corinthians 10:11).

Scripture: 1 Corinthians 10:1-13
Song: "Come, Thou Fount of Every Blessing"

"She doesn't have any food in her house," Sheila said, expressing heartfelt concern. "The minute she gets paid she finds a bar, and then she asks me for money to pay her bills." Sheila had grown up in a single-parent home with her alcoholic mother, and she still dealt with the emotional turmoil.

"I don't know how to help my mom," Sheila explained. "But this I do know—by God's grace, I will *not* continue the typical generational cycle of alcoholism."

Sheila had learned a life lesson from her mother's negative example. In a sense, God used Sheila's childhood pain to warn her, and she allowed God to provide a way through the years ahead. She would not fall into the same temptations with alcohol that had enslaved her mother.

Today's Scripture tells us that the Israelites' choices and behaviors are recorded to warn us. God wants us to understand important lessons from the failings of those who have gone before us. We are all human and easily capable of giving in to temptation. However, thankfully, God is there to help us through every potential hazard.

God, You know my thoughts and motives. Though I love You, I know I am prone to wander. Please forgive me for the many times I have sinned against You, and keep me from temptation in the days ahead. I pray in the name of Jesus. Amen.

Wonder of Wonders

Let me understand the teaching of your precepts; then I will mediate on your wonders (Psalm 119:27).

Scripture: Psalm 119:25-32
Song: "God of Wonders"

In 1943 Dionisio Pulido, a Mexican farmer, began his spring planting. Suddenly, a 150-foot fissure opened in the ground. "I felt a thundering," Pulido explained. "The trees trembled . . . there was a hiss or whistle, loud and continuous; and there was a smell of sulphur." In the middle of Pulido's field, a volcano was born. Over the next few days, the volcano hurled flaming rock bombs more than a thousand feet into the air. Lava buried his cornfields. Pulido and the world watched in wonder.

God reveals himself in the wonders of nature, in the Grand Canyon, Mount Everest, the Northern Lights, and so many other awe-inspiring sites worldwide. Everyday beauties of nature, like the pink, azure, and frosty white sky at sunrise on an icy morning are often just as breathtaking.

Nature causes us to stand in awe of God, yet the psalmist in today's passage speaks of a different kind of wonder—the wonder of meditating on God's Word. Weary and full of sorrow, the psalmist pours out his heart to the Lord. And the Lord listens, answers, strengthens, and sets the psalmist's heart free. Is there any greater wonder than knowing that God speaks to us with the love letter of His Word?

God of Wonders, You are holy. Maker of the universe, please reveal Your heart to me anew every morning. I stand in awe of You, God. The world was formed when You spoke, and You speak to me daily through Your Word. In Jesus' name, amen.

Seeking True Success

The LORD was with Joseph and he prospered, and he lived in the house of his Egyptian master (Genesis 39:2).

Scripture: Genesis 39:1-6
Song: "I'd Rather Have Jesus"

"A kind heart and a good attitude can take you to new heights of success in your personal and professional lives," says Victor Parachin in an article for *Advisor Today*. Parachin suggests that to be successful in business we need to learn from criticism, maintain an upbeat attitude, help our coworkers, and show appreciation.

Finding grains of truth in criticism demonstrates the humility that God calls us to have. And by showing kindness and appreciation, we glorify God, enjoying a success that is eternal not simply temporal.

It is likely that Joseph lived by these principles too, as they flow from the Scriptures. The Bible makes it clear that Joseph was successful in everything he did because God was with him. Sold into servanthood, Joseph quickly became successful and was put in charge of Potiphar's house. (Even Potiphar was blessed by God's faithfulness to Joseph.)

We tend to view success in terms of dollars and cents, don't we? Yet true success can't be measured that way. Even as a servant, we can be successful if we walk with God.

Lord, I'd rather have You in my life than all the riches of the world. Eternal success is found in You alone—in walking close by Your side. When You are with me, I can do all things for You strengthen me. Your ever-present help comforts, consoles, and guides. Please help me to express my gratitude each day. In the name Christ, amen.